SEA·KAYAKER's
Deep Trouble

True Stories and Their Lessons

from *Sea Kayaker* Magazine

Matt Broze and George Gronseth

Edited by Christopher Cunningham,
Sea Kayaker Magazine

R·M·P

Ragged Mountain Press
Camden, Maine

International Marine/
Ragged Mountain Press

A Division of The McGraw·Hill Companies

10 9 8 7 6 5 4 3 2 1

Library of Congress Cataloging-in-Publication Data
Broze, Matt C.
    Sea kayaker's deep trouble : true stories and their lessons from Sea kayaker magazine / Matt Broze and George Gonseth ; edited by Christopher Cunningham.
        p.   cm.
    Includes index.
        1. Sea Kayaking—Northwest, Pacific—Safety measures.   2. Sea kayaking—Accidents—Northwest, Pacific.   I. Gronseth, George.   II. Cunningham, Christopher.   III. Title.
GV788.5.B76   1997
797.1'224'09795—dc21   *97–15179*
                                                              CIP

Questions regarding the content of this book should be addressed to:
Ragged Mountain Press
P.O. Box 220
Camden, ME 04843

Questions regarding the ordering of this
    book should be addressed to:
The McGraw-Hill Companies
Customer Service Department
P.O. Box 547
Blacklick, OH 43004
Retail customers: 1-800-262-4729
Bookstores: 1-800-233-4726

A portion of the profits from the sale of each Ragged Mountain Press book is donated to an environmental cause.

Sea Kayaker's Deep Trouble is printed on 55-pound Sebago, an acid-free paper; it is set in 10-point Adobe Garamond.

Printed by R.R. Donnelley & Sons,
    Crawfordsville, IN
Design by Dan Kirchoff
Production by Mary Ann Hensel
Edited by Jonathan Eaton;
    Kathryn Mallien

Warning

Sea kayaking can take paddlers into harm's way, exposing them to risks of injury, cold-water exposure and hypothermia, drowning, and other hazards that can lead to serious injury or death.

This book is not intended to replace instruction by a qualified instructor nor to substitute for good personal judgment. In using this book, the reader releases the author, publisher, and distributor from liability for any injury, including death, that might result. It is understood that you paddle at your own risk.

Contents

| Preface | by Christopher Cunningham .... v |

| Introduction | Kayaking Safety .... 1 |
| | Index to Safety Sidebars .... 11 |

1 Drifting with the Current 12

2 Another Lesson from the School 18
of Hard Knocks

3 Of Risk, Knowledge, ... 27
Choice . . . and Special Vulnerability

4 A Tale of Two Rescues 31

5 The Open Coast, ... 40
or, All Your Eggs in One Kayak

6 Risks Compounded 50

7 Sea Caves, Arches, and Narrow Passages 59

8 Long Swims 70

9 Rough Passages 83

10 The Phantom Barge 94

11 Run-in with a Great White 101

12 Double Fatality in Prince William Sound 106

13 Happy Endings 117

14 Surf Zone Accidents 124

15 Saved by a Drysuit 133

16 Vanished 141

17 Ferry Rescue in the San Juans 146

18 Rosario Strait Rescue 155

19 Nighttime Accident on Willapa Bay 166

20 Lessons in Judgment 169

21 Ice Fall in Blackstone Bay 172

22 Carried to Safety 178

Index 183

About the Authors and Contributors 186

location of accident

Glacier
X

Preface

By Christopher Cunningham

A kayak puts you in touch with the elements. You feel the water on your hands, the wind on your face, and the sights, scents, and sounds of the coast surrounding you. The kayak feels like an extension of your body: It responds to your every move, and through it you can feel the water moving beneath you. For many of us a kayak is the means by which we can take in the full measure of the rich coastal environment. But the environment where air, water, and land meet is notoriously variable, and the intimate connection a kayak provides with that environment leaves us exposed and vulnerable to forces that can easily overpower us.

A kayak has limited speed and power and is only as seaworthy as its paddler makes it. These limitations require that we pay attention to our senses and learn to interpret the signs that the environment provides. A change in the color of the water, a sudden drop in air temperature, a new smell on the wind—all these signs have meaning beyond the play they may give our senses. To interpret signs like these we need to educate ourselves about the workings of the weather and the tides. Kayaking is as much an exercise of the mind as it is of the body. While paddling may provide relief from the strains of the working world, it is not a time to zone out.

Many sea kayaking accidents begin with a lack of observation and knowledge. When paddlers overlook or misinterpret the clues around them, they often find themselves in conditions they had not anticipated and are ill-prepared to face. Suddenly that intimate connection with the kayak becomes a liability. Every passing wave requires an immediate response from the paddler. Skilled paddlers can survive appalling conditions in a kayak, as long as they can paddle, brace, and roll. Wise paddlers understand the waters they paddle on and avoid overstepping the limits of their skills.

The circumstances of the accidents reported here vary greatly. But so often, the lessons to be learned are the same: Have complete information, including weather reports and an understanding of the local environment, before setting out. Wear proper attire, including a PFD and wet- or drysuit. Bring safety equipment and signaling devices, including a VHF radio, and keep these things where you can reach them if you capsize. Above all, plan ahead and practice,

practice, practice—in rough conditions (but in a safe place), in the kayak and clothing you'll actually be using, and, if possible, in the environment where you'll be paddling.

The Pacific Northwest figures prominently in the accident reports included in this book. This is not because the region is kayaking's Bermuda Triangle. Recreational kayaking has a long history in this region. Paddlers of folding kayaks, then the only type available, were enjoying the San Juan Islands of Washington and the Gulf Islands of British Columbia as far back as the mid- to late 1940s. With the advent of molded fiberglass kayaks in the 1960s, a number of manufacturers set up shop in the areas around Seattle and Vancouver. Between those two large population centers lie the San Juan Islands, a popular destination for vacationers and an attractive cruising ground for kayakers. But the San Juans lie at the mouth of the Strait of Georgia, a body of water roughly 130 miles long and 15 miles wide. With each change of the tide, a lot of cold water moves from the Pacific Ocean via Juan de Fuca Strait, through the San Juans, and into the Strait of Georgia. Strong currents surround the San Juans. In some areas, the currents exceed four knots, pulling paddlers into rough water over shoals and around points. The same topography that funnels the water intensifies the wind and creates very difficult conditions.

Many of the kayaking accidents in the San Juan Islands could happen anywhere. The lessons learned there can be applied to other areas. Paddlers who invest time and effort and fully engage their senses not only have a greater degree of safety—they discover more of the subtle textures of the waterways they travel.

Kayaking Safety

Matt Broze

Since its beginnings, sea kayaking has been a relatively safe sport, with few injuries or fatalities. However, the large influx each year of paddlers new to the sport is worrisome. Sea kayaking is so easy to learn that anyone with a few minutes' practice can unknowingly paddle into a hazardous predicament. In fact, in the roughly 50° Fahrenheit (10°C) water of the Pacific Northwest, capsizing less than one-half mile from shore could easily be fatal to a lone kayaker unable to get back in the kayak, get his or her body out of the water, or attract the attention of rescuers.

I worry about the impact of those macho kayakers who relay tales—or tall tales—of high adventure in remote and dangerous circumstances, where they relied only on strength and skill to save themselves from disaster. While we all should be free to choose our own risks, novice or intermediate kayakers who listen to those stories and want similar tales to tell may challenge conditions for which they are totally unprepared and in an environment where there is little room for error.

No less worrisome are the novices who believe that someone else will take care of them. Some of the reports included here make it clear that conditions can get so rough that even experts with whitewater skills may be hard-pressed to save their own lives.

The purpose of *Sea Kayaker*'s accident reports is to convey important safety information to new and experienced sea kayakers. For many years we have reported on accidents and near accidents so that, whenever possible, we all might learn from the experiences of others rather than having to learn the hard way. This book gathers some of the most compelling of those reports, outlining the circumstances of each accident and providing detailed analyses: What did the paddlers do wrong? What did they do right? Most importantly, how might the accident have been prevented?

Safety is a personal issue. Each of us must decide what level of risk we are

1

willing to accept, what compromises we are willing to make, and what dangers we most want to guard against. I prefer to make these decisions from a clear understanding of the hazards involved instead of relying on fixed rules and regulations.

I see concern for safety not as a response to fear, but as a way to maximize freedom within the level of risk one chooses to accept. Reasonable people often trade a little safety for a lot more comfort, convenience, or excitement. Our goal in this book is to provide information that can serve as a sound basis for making your own choices.

In skilled hands, kayaks are extraordinarily seaworthy craft. Sea kayaking has proven to be a safe form of recreation for those who have taken the time to learn basic skills and understand potential hazards. What follows is a summary of the skills and equipment necessary for safe paddling. Learn, and practice, these rules of paddling safety—they'll help you to be a safer participant in this great sport.

Be Prepared

- You must have the skills, knowledge, and equipment to match whatever conditions you might encounter.

- Practice skills—including rescues—in advance, with the gear and safety equipment you'll actually be using.

- Know when to swim and when not to swim.

- Have a plan of action (and a backup plan) worked out in advance for any emergency, including capsize, separation from your kayak, or separation from your group. A plan will help prevent panic and a feeling of helplessness that can be immobilizing.

- Beware of goals that may cloud your judgment. Getting to work on time or avoiding the embarrassment of having your friends call the Coast Guard is not worth the risk to life.

- Get a comfortable life jacket (also called personal flotation device, or PFD) and wear it whenever you paddle.

- Always have plenty of secure flotation in both ends of your kayak. This means enclosing most of the space not taken up by your body.

Paddling in Groups

- The paddling ability and judgment of the group members is more important than the size of the group. When you are no longer dependent on others, you can be an asset to the group rather than a liability. But this doesn't mean it's safest to paddle alone. Solo paddling is far more dangerous than paddling with a partner. Paddling in a group of three is safer yet, because there are more options for coping with a crisis. With four paddlers, one could stay with a disabled paddler (on shore) and two could go for help. That way, even when the group is divided, each member has a partner.

- Having said that, there is not necessarily safety in numbers. An expert is probably safer alone than with two or three novices who are likely to run into trouble. With each additional member comes an increased chance of risk. Ultimately, *you* are responsible for your own safety.

- Groups of more than three should pick a leader to keep the group together, select a safe route, and assess the physical and psychological states of the other group members. When inexperienced paddlers are on the trip, the leader should make sure they have the necessary gear and proper flotation in their kayaks. Before the group embarks, the leader should inform everyone of his or her role should a capsize or other emergency occur and a rescue be required. Knowing what to do in advance will help novices avoid the panic that could cause an emergency, delay rescue, or endanger others. It will also make all group members aware of the possibility of trouble and encourage them to question whether they have the skills and equipment necessary to handle an emergency.

- Never leave a novice or group of novices alone. This includes kayakers who have paddled for years but only in calm conditions.

- Be prepared to voice your strong objections to any plan you think would be risky for you or some other member of the group. Insist on a safe course of action.

- Group paddlers should follow the lead kayak and not go off on their own without notifying the leader of their intentions. The lead kayaker must be careful not to leave anyone behind, and everyone should stay within range of easy communication. It is easy to become separated, so agree in advance on a meeting place.

Know Your Equipment
- Regularly check your equipment for damage and wear.

- Your kayak must have flotation—secured both in the bow and stern—adequate to float a swamped kayak level with the paddler aboard and minimize the amount of water that must be removed. Flotation in only one end will allow the other end to sink, making reentry difficult for a group and virtually impossible for solo paddlers.

- Your spray deck (or spray skirt) should be tight enough on the cockpit rim to prevent it from popping off when a wave dumps into your lap. Its shock cord will lose elasticity with time and use, so it may need occasional tightening.

- Practice capsizing and wet exits so you'll know how to remove your spray deck and climb out without losing your grip on your kayak or paddle. Be careful not to create a trap with your ropes, loose gear, spray deck, or foot braces that could hold you or your feet and prevent a wet exit. Practice several spray deck removal techniques: use one or two hands; release the spray deck from the inside and from the outside, and so on.

- Carry repair kits for your kayak and paddle, and one for yourself—a first-aid kit.

Improve Your Skills

- Learn the high and low braces—the most important physical skills in kayaking. The high brace is a bracing forward stroke, and the low brace is a bracing reverse stroke. Practice them first in warm, shallow water where you won't be afraid to capsize.

- Practice paddling in progressively stronger winds and rougher waves, in safe locations where the wind will push you to a safe landing on a beach if you capsize. Dress for a capsize and have sources of help, shelter, and warmth at hand. Practice in rough conditions with your kayak both empty and loaded with gear.

- Master crossing eddy lines. Find a safe place on a river or tidal stream where an obstruction in the current forms an eddy, and practice crossing the eddy line both ways. To counteract the force of the water sliding under your kayak, lean your kayak away from the current you are moving into by using a paddle brace downstream for stability. Expect to capsize! Practice with experts so you'll have a source of instruction and rescue. Have a source of warmth ready, or wear a wetsuit.

The Case for Safety

On November 26, 1983, Jeff Spears died as the result of a paddling accident. He was a new paddler in a stable single kayak. With him were one expert kayaker in a narrow single and two couples, each in a double. Each of the men except Jeff had over five years of whitewater kayaking experience.

The group left camp at Cabbage Island (just north of Tumbo Island) in the Canadian Gulf Islands. Weather permitting, they planned to cross three miles from Tumbo Island to Patos Island during slack current. The single paddler was not quite ready, so the rest of the group departed to make it to the crossing point by 10:00 A.M. Because he was the strongest paddler in the group, in the fastest kayak, the others expected him to catch up quickly.

Upon reaching Tumbo Point, the group found the conditions calm. The wind was blowing from the south, with the flood current, creating long, smooth seas. The current was also near slack and, though the group's charts showed "very heavy tide rips" to the north, they showed no problems in the area of the crossing. It looked to be the ideal time to make the crossing, so they decided to set out, again assuming the fast paddler would soon join them.

The paddlers were not aware of the current moving them southeast (caused by a rotating eddy several miles across). Twenty minutes later, the wind shifted to

- Learn to Eskimo roll your kayak. Contact a club or kayak shop to find expert instruction.

- Practice other rescues to back up your ability to Eskimo roll. Even the best rescues are marginal if they haven't been practiced in difficult conditions.

- Practicing rescues and rolls in a pool can be very valuable, but wind, waves, cold water, and 100 pounds of gear create a far more realistic rescue situation. The best rescues require little or no help and do not require lifting and dumping the kayak. They get you out of the water quickly to minimize your risk of hypothermia and allow you to aid in the pumping or bailing of your kayak. They should also be easy to execute with a minimum of extra gear, if any.

- Rolling and rescues are only safety backups. Whenever possible, avoid the need to use them by exercising sound judgment.

Use Safety Equipment

- **PFD/Spray Deck.** Always wear a life jacket and a spray deck. The Coast Guard requires an approved personal flotation device (PFD) for each person in a boat. Wear it! If the wind and waves come up while you're paddling, you may find it impossible to put it on.

- **Flotation.** Maximum flotation at both ends of your kayak is a must. This could consist of large float bags, waterproof gear bags, truly watertight

blow directly opposite this current, creating steep waves. The tide rip off the point, caused by the rotating current colliding with the tail end of the incoming tide, created confused seas. The group turned back only to find the steep following seas unmanageable. Their kayaks surfed down the waves, submerging the bows so deeply in the troughs that the paddlers feared pitchpoling. This plus uncontrollable broaches (sideways skidding) convinced them to take the only course they could maintain, toward Patos Island.

The wind strengthened, and breakers swept over their kayaks, stripping loose gear off one and filling both doubles with water at an alarming rate. The group was becoming separated as each member paddled for all he was worth toward Patos. They hoped to make it there before their kayaks sank or capsized. Ultimately, the two doubles made it to Patos Island, but Jeff did not.

When the trailing paddler arrived at Tumbo Point, about twenty minutes behind the rest of the group, he saw the rough conditions toward Patos. He assumed his friends would not have tried the crossing. Unable to find them near the point, he landed and climbed a tree to scan the area with binoculars. Not sighting them, he figured they must have paddled on around Tumbo Point. The paddler then circled the island and then started off toward Patos Island but was forced back by the conditions.

(continued on page 6)

hatches and bulkheads, a waterproof cockpit sock, or better yet a combination of these.

- **Bailing Device.** A means of removing water is a must. A high-capacity hand-held or deck-mounted pump is best, because it can be used with the spray deck closed to prevent further water entry. Slip the hand pump through the top of your spray deck at your chest. Your pump should be readily available but stored securely so it won't float (or sink) away.

- **Towline.** You can buy a ready-made towing system or make your own towline. Braided nylon line (³⁄₁₆" diameter and about 50 feet long) is strong and stretches to absorb shocks, but nylon towlines will sink, so they require an attached float. A piece of closed-cell foam can serve both as the float and as a place to wrap the line to keep it from tangling.

- **Equipment for Staying Warm.** For cold-water paddling, wear a drysuit or a wetsuit and—if you're likely to get splashed or rained on—a waterproof paddling jacket. Spare dry clothing and fire-making materials should be kept in an easily accessible drybag. For keeping warm and dry ashore, wear only quick-drying pile or wool clothing and, if necessary, rain gear.

- **First-Aid Kit.** A first-aid kit adequate to your situation should be readily available from the cockpit.

- **Repair Kit.** A roll of duct tape (stored in a safe, dry place in the kayak) can temporarily repair almost any damage to a kayak, paddle (with a splint), or

(continued from page 5)
The next morning, the paddler crossed to Patos, found the group, and learned that Jeff was missing. He paddled on to Sucia Island, found a boat with a VHF radio, and notified the Coast Guard. The Coast Guard had already found the kayak about fourteen miles away and a little later found Jeff's body near Waldron Island. Jeff had been wearing a life jacket.

As much as we plan to avoid them, bad conditions can develop quickly and catch us when we are the most exposed and vulnerable. Conditions can quickly get so bad that even the expert paddlers—whom novices may be relying on—may be hard-pressed to save their own lives.

This group followed many of the "safety rules" of sea kayaking, including wearing PFDs, paddling in a group, having a high ratio of experienced paddlers in the group, and crossing areas of strong current during slack. Unfortunately, on the sea just obeying the "rules" is not always enough. You also need to thoroughly understand the potential hazards and what creates them.

Learn all you can about the hazards of sea kayaking and don't let others make decisions for you. We hope the stories in this will help improve your knowledge and judgment.

even flotation and gear bags. A more extensive repair kit would include spare fittings and other more permanent materials to repair a hull and float bags.

- **Locating Devices.** Equipment for signaling an emergency and your location should be kept handy, or, better yet, carried on your person. Locating devices have saved many kayakers. Consider flares (hand-held and aerial), smoke canisters (day only), dye marker (day only), orange distress flag, foghorn or air horn, whistle, signal mirror, and strobe light (night only).

  Many of these items are small, inexpensive, and readily available at marine supply stores. If you paddle at night, the U.S. Coast Guard requires you to carry a white light. It must be visible for one mile and be shown in time to avoid a collision. They also require three flares or an emergency distress beacon that automatically flashes SOS for use on international waters. On inland waters, a high-intensity white light that flashes fifty to seventy times per minute can replace the SOS signal.

- A device called the **406 MHz EPIRB** (Emergency Position Indicating Radio Beacon) transmits an emergency signal that SARSAT satellites can home in on to locate your position within a one-mile radius. The Category II version is appropriate for kayakers as it is manually deployed. This type of EPIRB costs about $800. Commercial tour guides and solo paddlers, especially, should consider using them. (Class B EPIRBs have a slow response time and are not recommended.)

- **Radio.** Weather radios, which receive VHF weather channels, are inexpensive and very useful. Tour guides and group leaders might consider a hand-held VHF marine band radio; these allow you to contact potential rescuers on the emergency channel (channel 16) and then give a description of your situation. VHF radios also receive weather stations and make it possible to communicate with boats or ships in the area. A flexible, waterproof case is now available for some hand-held VHF radios, allowing them to be used even after exposure to salt water. Some models of VHF radios are now being advertised as waterproof; I recommend even these be kept inside a waterproof bag.

- **Spares of Critical Items.** Bring extra paddles, charts, tide and current tables, timepieces, and compasses. Many of these spares could be shared among a group, but you would be wise to be the person who brings them.

Beware of Hypothermia

- Hypothermia is the greatest danger sea kayakers face. Be aware that most paddling fatalities result from hypothermia following a capsize and subsequent failure to execute a rescue.

- Reduce heat loss by wearing a wetsuit or drysuit.

- Eat sufficient carbohydrates before paddling.

- In the event of a capsize in cold water, get out of the water as quickly as possible, and then get the water out of the kayak. By lying across the kayak you will reduce cooling and may be able to paddle to shore. Don't abandon the kayak and swim for shore unless it is very close or you have no other hope for rescue.

- It is imperative to get a capsize victim out of the water as soon as possible. Watch the victim closely for signs of hypothermia—he may not recognize the symptoms in himself. In order of severity, the signs of hypothermia are shivering, slurred speech, memory lapse, lack of coordination, indifference, blurred vision, drowsiness, ashen skin, muscle rigidity (replaces shivering), exhaustion, incoherence, collapse, and unconsciousness.

- Once back in the kayak, a victim who shows any symptoms beyond shivering should be dressed as warmly as possible and then carried as a passenger or towed in his kayak to shore, where he can be placed in a sleeping bag. Additional heat can be provided by another person in the sleeping bag.

- In cases of severe hypothermia, heart failure is a risk; refrain from stimulation such as shaking or rubbing the limbs. Don't try to rewarm the victim too quickly or give him alcohol or hot drinks, which might speed the return of chilled blood from the extremities to the core, dropping the core temperature even further.

- Get help, prevent further heat loss with insulation, and transfer the hypothermia victim (even if rewarmed) to a hospital as soon as possible.

Know the Weather

- **Wind.** Wind can be a big adversary for sea kayakers. It can increase quickly in velocity and make controlling a kayak and paddle difficult, if not impossible. Making headway against very strong winds is a struggle. You could be blown offshore, or blown onshore into dangerous regions such as big surf or a rocky coast. In mountainous areas, the terrain can deflect and funnel the wind, creating strong gusts, down-drafts, and twisters.

  When the wind approaches gale force, it can snatch a paddle out of your hands or catch a paddle blade squarely from the side and cause a capsize. Unexpected gusts can be much more "upsetting" than a steady wind of equal velocity. Keep your paddle blades low while paddling and point the paddle into the wind with the upwind blade held low.

- **Waves.** When the wind picks up, the waves soon follow. Waves make a capsize more likely and create difficult control problems and broaching if they are approaching from the side or from the stern quadrants. When waves are reflected from a cliff or wall, or are arriving from different directions for any reason, they can create a very steep and confused sea. Take care that your paddle reaches the water. A surprise "air" stroke or brace can throw you off balance.

- **Fog.** There are no landmarks in thick fog. Without a compass or some means of judging direction, such as wave angle or a distant, repeating sound, you will paddle in circles. Even those potential navigation aids can be misleading: Wave direction can be altered close to shore or behind an island due to refraction or, if the waves are small, by a change in the wind; a distant, repeating sound could be a moving ship. In fog you need a compass. In fact, you can become so disoriented that you may need two compasses pointing in the same direction just to assure you that one is not broken. Group members should stay very close together since separation is a constant possibility in thick fog.

  Paddling in thick fog can be dangerous because it's much more difficult to see or even hear hazards until they are very near. Don't cross even seldom-used shipping lanes in fog, mist, or rain that limits your vision. Even if you have a radar reflector held high above the kayak, the "noise" caused by the mist or rain will probably blot out your echo. If possible, avoid paddling out of sight of the shore in a fog.

Avoid Surf

- The size of surf is difficult to judge from seaward, but you can easily differentiate the less-violent spilling surf from the abrupt, dumping surf, which is much more likely to damage you or your kayak. A dumping surf on a steep beach can be extremely violent. You can often find a much smaller surf and a place to land in an area protected by a point of land or an island.

Kayaker's Checklist

Review this checklist before *every* trip—whether it's your first or your fifty-first!

- clothing such as wetsuits or drysuits designed to keep you warm in the event of a capsize
- life jacket (or personal flotation device [PFD])
- spray deck
- maximum flotation in both ends of the kayak
- paddle float or other self-rescue devices
- pump or other bailing device
- towline
- warm, dry clothes in a waterproof container
- food and water
- waterproof matches and lighter
- spare paddle
- compass and chart
- tide and current tables
- timepiece
- first-aid kit
- repair kit
- whistle
- signaling devices
- other items that may be appropriate for the particular time and place

- Stay well outside the surf line while paddling; larger wave sets will break farther out from shore. This can occur quite intermittently and come as a real surprise. Waves can break in any shallow place, not just near shore. Underwater rocks, plateaus, or shallows well offshore can cause intermittent breakers (called boomers), which you might not notice unless you've been watching far ahead. Clues include a steepening of the waves, an area of foam, a change in water color, a patch of kelp, or underwater rocks and shallows marked on your chart.

- If you capsize and wet exit in the surf near shore, your kayak could be a great danger to you. If the surf is big, swim to one side to get well clear of your kayak and then swim for shore. The breakers should deliver your kayak to the beach if you have proper flotation. If you can't make progress swimming for shore, you may be in a rip current (also called beach rip), formed by water that builds up behind a sandbar and flows back out to sea in a narrow channel through the bar. Swim to one side before again making for the shore. Currents running parallel to shore can pull you back into the rip, so keep angling away from the rip.

Understand Tides and Tidal Hazards

- Get the best current tables and current charts you can find and learn how to use them. Some small-craft charts provide the direction and average maximum speed in mid-channel, but with headlands and underwater topography affecting the flow and direction of the currents, these charts still can be woefully inadequate. With good current tables and some knowledge of what causes rough water, you can spot hazardous areas and avoid them when they are most dangerous.

- Some areas affected by tidal currents can become treacherous. Even mild currents can take you well off course. Currents can slow or stop your progress, so plan your paddling times to take best advantage of them.

- If you must paddle against a current, take advantage of eddies and the usual slowing of the current in shallows near shore.

- Currents can create rough and confused waters where they meet. This is called a tide rip.

- When a current is moving opposite of the wave motion, the wave length is shortened, steepening the waves and often causing breaking waves.

- Underwater obstructions, headlands, narrows, and shallows can combine with a current to cause waves, eddies, boils, whirlpools, overfalls, and water so agitated that it hisses or gives off a steady roar. Headlands, narrows, and shallows also can increase the speed of the current locally. On charts these areas are sometimes labeled "tide rips" or "overfalls" and are shown as wavy lines.

- On an outgoing tide, you could become stranded in tidal basins or on tide flats (shown as olive drab areas on charts) with wide areas of muddy shallows such as often occur where a river enters a bay.

- A long, shallow beach could mean a long carry to a resting or camping place at low tide. The tide also comes in very rapidly on this type of beach, so on shore you must be especially careful not to leave your kayak unsecured for even a few minutes. Carry your equipment well above the high-tide line, and then tie it to a fixed object in case you misjudged the tide.

Watch for Other Craft

- Ships are deceptively fast. They only appear slow because they are large. Never try to paddle across the path of a ship. If you must cross a busy shipping lane, cross at a right angle to minimize your time in it. Group members should stay close together to make it easier for any craft to notice and avoid them.

- While assuming that ships, speedboats, and sailboats won't see you, give them every chance. Make yourself visible: Bright colors on the kayak, spray deck, life jacket, and hat help, but the most visible thing from speedboat eye level probably will be your paddle blades waving up and down. Paddle blades that are a light, bright color, such as yellow, orange, or white, will be your best warning. Reflective tape on your kayak and paddle blades will increase your visibility at night.

Safety Sidebars

This has been a brief overview of sea kayaking safety concerns and procedures. You'll find more detail on these topics in the various sidebar discussions throughout this book. Here's a listing of them, with page numbers:

The Case for Safety 4
Kayaker's Checklist 9
How Important is Equipment? 14
Improve Your Skills 15
Wide Kayaks vs. Narrow Kayaks 17
Reckoning with Fear 22
Sudden Drowning Syndrome 28
Turns and Spins 32
Paddles and Wind 35
Powerboater in Distress 36
Paddling the Open Coast 42
The Coast Guard Behind the Scenes . 52
Buoyancy 55
Rescuing a Sunken Kayak 60
Leaky Hatches and Flotation 62
More Lessons in Arches 64

The Sirens 68
Twice to the Rescue 74
A Personal Statement 84
Pumping out a Kayak 88
Self Rescues 91
Paddling in Wind 108
Survival Rafts 112
When the Tide Steals Your Kayak .. 120
Reenter and Roll Problems 122
A Kayak Surfing Accident 126
A Broken Paddle 128
Hazards of Rip Currents
    and Breaking Waves 129
Seasickness 139
Working toward a New Wildlife
    Ethic for Kayakers 143
Doubles and Sea Socks 148
Paddling in the Lee 151
Releasing a Spray Skirt 162
Wind and Shallows 166
Cold-Weather Paddling 171
Survival Sense for Sea Kayakers .. 173
A Ride to Shore 180

Drifting with the Current

Matt Broze

Some of the most compelling of *Sea Kayaker*'s accident reports are those submitted by the survivors themselves. Here, K. Anderson shares his experience of May 16, 1984.

"Our trip had been a perfect one. Under a full moon on Lummi Rocks, we felt pleased that such beauty was easily accessible. By just hopping into my 19-foot Beachcomber fiberglass double kayak, affectionately called the *Wonder Barge,* this could become our own beach-front property. I'd actually come to seek out freedom on Puget Sound's tidal currents, using the tidal current tables like a train schedule to reach my island paradises. So, on a whim, on Tuesday, May 15, my friend Martha and I had hopped the Full Moon Express out of Anacortes. In four hours it had carried us ten miles north to Lummi Rocks; we'd barely lifted a paddle. Next morning at 5:00 A.M. the Ebb Tide Limited departed on Track 2 for points south—fastest ride of the month. Martha had a 2:00 P.M. work shift in Bellingham. The fastest way there was to go the opposite direction, with the southward-flowing ebb tide, back to Anacortes. That is, it would've been had we not derailed in what we came to learn is called Hell's Half Acre, off the easternmost point of Cypress Island.

"I, like many others, had been seduced into a sense of complacency on the lakelike conditions of the Sound, thinking the lack of oceanic waves meant immunity from danger. Yet the very islands that protect the Sound from those waves also create bottom and shore configurations which, combined with tidal currents, can emulate whitewater river conditions. Sure, I'd seen the whirlpools and tide rips from a distance: In the decade I'd been boating around out there in the *Wonder Barge* I'd developed a healthy respect for their power. Surely an old whitewater rafter like me could always steer clear of such nastiness out there

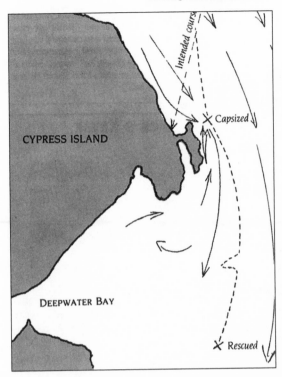

in the wide open Sound, I thought.

Yet here we come, confidently flowing down the coast of Cypress, with no sign of danger but those white-capped standing waves way off on our left bow toward the center of the channel. Too far away to be concerned about. The next minute our cooperative current is rushing us directly toward that mess with amazing strength and deftness, instead of toward the point we'd wanted to disembark on. Even paddling hard, we couldn't intercept the last point of shore. By then we just wanted out of that ill-fated current. It looked calm across the eddy line around the point. Not until we were committed to crossing did we notice that, far from being calm, the water was a counter-current subtending the main current in almost reverse direction, and where the currents met, hungry whirlpools danced. The moment the bow crossed currents, our attempts to keep control became next to useless. In one shocked gasp we were forced broadside between the dueling currents; a second later our hull was torqued over with a force only an expert whitewater brace could've withstood.

"Almost before we even saw danger, we were looking upside down at cold, green water. With alarm we bobbed up to see life jackets, paddles, bailer, anything loose quickly split the scene in the confused waters. I'd always figured I could put my life jacket on when need be. Now where was it? Strike one! It was all we could do to not get plucked off the capsized kayak by the whirlpools. The kayak was still afloat. Although I'd never tested it, I trusted the sealed air chambers in the bow and stern. Strike two! Within minutes of our righting the kayak and climbing back into the cockpit, the stern had sunk, and to our infinite dismay all that remained to hang on to was a couple feet of bow.

"We hadn't seen a boat all morning. If only another kayak had been along. Strike three, you're out! Almost. Must've been a foul tip. We spent half an hour in the water. Once, in desperation, we tried to swim into the counter-current that headed back toward shore. Don't plan on covering much distance swimming when you're that cold and tired. We couldn't even make it back to the kayak by then.

"We were saying our last farewells. I thought of all who'd miss me and wondered how they'd take it. I felt a sickly grief for getting Martha into this. It got harder to keep our heads above water. I wondered how many minutes longer we could struggle and what those last few moments of consciousness beneath the surface would be like. I took one last look around. A boat! A good mile away but moving up the coast of Deepwater Bay in our general direction. I took what strength I had and somehow made it back to the kayak and waved my arm like my life depended on it. It did.

"The boat was a quarter of a mile away and nearly parallel to us. Ben Nelson thought he saw a bird flapping its wings. He got curious and investigated. If he'd gone fishing at Cattle Point instead, as he'd originally planned, we wouldn't be here to pass on these warnings. With amazing dispatch we were whisked to Anacortes, plucked from Ben's hoisted boat into a waiting ambulance, and wrapped in blissfully warm blankets. In the hospital we shivered violently for ninety minutes as our bodies climbed from perilously close to the 86-degree cut-off point of consciousness back up to good ol' 98.6.

"Our deepest thanks to all involved, especially Ben Nelson. May others profit from our hard-learned lesson. Check out your flotation and rescue techniques before emergency time. Don't spend more on hospital bills than you'd spend on a kayak with adequate flotation. Avoid going out alone; and don't use your life-jacket for a seat! Above all, enjoy our "tranquil" Sound as you would a sleeping tiger: It's beautiful but potentially lethal. Respect the force of moving water meeting unmoving land."

How Important is Equipment?

Accident prevention starts with planning for your needs and purchasing or constructing your kayak and equipment. Arguments rage between proponents and detractors of various types of kayaks and safety features. Unfortunately, these well-publicized arguments (or are they advertisements?) tend to overemphasize the importance of the kayaks while ignoring the abilities and preparedness of the paddlers.

While there are differences in the quality and capabilities of kayaks and equipment, your safety depends far more on your knowledge and abilities. In fact, I believe that safety is 5 percent equipment and 95 percent paddler. A new kayak may be better in many respects than your old familiar one but, until you become familiar with the new one in a variety of conditions, you probably will be safer in the old one. For instance, the spray skirt may be more secure in a new kayak, but if you haven't practiced taking it off in a capsize, your usual removal method may not work.

I guarantee (from personal experience as a novice river kayaker) that after a surprise tipover you are not going to analyze how the new spray deck is released while you are upside down and underwater, unless you practiced beforehand.

LESSONS LEARNED

Plan ahead for the effects of winds or currents. Try to err in the direction that will be easiest to correct. In other words, aim for a point farther upwind or upcurrent of your goal than you think is necessary, so you won't have to fight that wind or current if you underestimate its power. The more you learn about the effects of terrain on winds and currents, the better you can estimate their effect on you and your kayak.

At 36 inches wide, the Beachcomber must be among the most stable of kayaks—yet it quickly overturned in an area of colliding currents. Paddlers of stable craft must make a special effort to become expert at handling current turbulence (confluence, boils, eddy lines, etc.). Prepare for strong currents by developing the ability to lean the kayak with a downstream brace (away from the current you are entering). This is a situation where anything but an instantaneous slap support upcurrent will result in a sudden capsize as the undercutting current carries your intended support paddle beneath the boat.

If conditions become difficult to handle, don't stop paddling: Instead, quicken and shorten your stroke. Each stroke serves as a mini-brace to adjust your balance. If you start to capsize, a sharp, quick brace is much more effective

Improve Your Skills

Bracing

Those who come to sea kayaking by way of river kayaking have an advantage: Whitewater conditions have forced them to develop several reflexive paddle braces. As a result, these paddlers are less dependent on the inherent stability of the kayak to keep upright.

Even if you have no plan to paddle rivers, I recommend you develop good high and low braces. The high brace is a bracing forward stroke; the low brace is a bracing reverse stroke. Practice bracing in warm, shallow water where you won't be afraid to capsize. Throw yourself progressively further and further off balance and use your paddle to recover.

To test yourself further, have a friend or two stand at the ends of your kayak and purposely try to capsize you. You should be able to remain upright no matter how hard they try. Also practice a sculling high brace and alternating between a high and low brace to support you while you lean over to one side. Expert bracers can lie right over into the water and recover by sculling back up.

You'll learn more about bracing, in a shorter period, paddling in small surf than you will paddling anywhere else—even whitewater rivers. Paddle in progressively stronger winds and rougher waves, but in safe locations such as near an easy landing beach toward which the wind will push you if you capsize. Dress for a capsize, wear a helmet, and have sources of help, shelter, and warmth at hand. Try paddling in rough conditions with your kayak loaded with gear as well as empty. This practice will not only improve your paddling skills, but also will give you experience that will improve your judgment.

Crossing Eddy Lines

Learn to lean your kayak away from the *(continued on page 16)*

than one held so long that the paddle sinks under the surface.

I have very limited experience with double kayaks. However, *Sea Kayaker* founding editor John Dowd suggests two other techniques for double paddlers who find themselves beyond their ability in extreme situations, as K. Anderson and his companion did. 1) When entering a confluence of currents or a zone of unpredictable boils, use the wing-on-wing approach: The bow paddler braces on one side and the stern paddler holds his or her paddle out to the other, each ready to fend off a capsize toward their side. 2) Lower the center of gravity: Slouching or lying down in the kayak increases stability immensely.

The paddlers in this incident did not know that their built-in bow flotation compartment was too small to support their weight if they had to climb back into the swamped kayak. Given the bow-up position of K. Anderson's kayak even after the paddlers were back on board, it seems the small bulkheaded flotation chamber in the kayak's stern may also have had a leak that they were unaware of. Do not put your faith in equipment you haven't tested personally—practicing rescues with the kayak you'll be using is the only way to get to know the peculiarities and quirks of your craft.

Clothing that could dramatically increase survival time in the near-50°F

(continued from page 15)
current you are moving into by using a paddle brace downstream for stability. This will counteract the force of the water sliding under your kayak, which often causes a capsize to the upstream side.

Find a safe place on a river or tidal stream where an obstruction in the current forms an eddy going both directions. Expect to be capsized. Practice with a group that includes some experts. Have a source of warmth at hand or wear a wetsuit.

Eskimo Rolls

Rolling skills are potentially more valuable to sea kayakers than river kayakers, because the distance to shore when sea kayaking can be much greater. Unfortunately, since capsizes are so rare on still water, sea kayakers may not realize the importance of learning to roll.

The best way to learn Eskimo rolls is from an expert; contact a club or kayak shop to find out about classes. I prefer teaching Eskimo rolls using a float attached to one paddle blade. (A flat piece of foam does not retard the paddle as much as an inflatable float does during the fast sweep stage.) Attach the foam with cord or, better yet, cut a pocket in the foam and slide the paddle blade into it. Practice paddle rolling using a float until you can execute the roll quickly and correctly; then remove the float and practice without it. The float allows you to practice a successful roll even in the early stages of practice.

Contrary to popular opinion, it usually is easier to roll a gear-laden sea kayak (if you have adequate thigh or knee braces and a seat with side support) than it is to roll an empty kayak. Be sure that your gear load is secure so gravity can't shift it to one side and hold the kayak on edge. And be sure to learn to roll the kayak you will actually be using, both with and without a gear load (you may need to add good foot, thigh, and hip bracing).

Wide Kayaks versus Narrow Kayaks

One dispute over equipment concerns the safety of narrow kayaks versus wide kayaks. Given novice paddlers of equal abilities, the wider, more stable kayak probably is safer, as it will be far less likely to capsize. An expert may have slightly less chance of capsizing using a more stable kayak, but the chances of an expert capsizing either kayak are remote.

Strangely, paddlers of narrow, tippy kayaks are safer on the average than paddlers in wide stable kayaks, for two reasons. Those paddlers most likely to choose a narrow kayak tend to be more experienced; and paddlers who use narrow, tippy kayaks are forced to learn effective bracing skills very quickly— a paddler in a wide kayak might paddle for years without ever learning those skills.

Is one style of kayak better, or safer, than the other? No. No matter how stable the kayak you paddle, one of your first priorities should be developing effective braces. You want the ability to keep that kayak upright whenever you might find yourself in conditions that could capsize your craft. A kayak is only as safe as the person paddling it!

(12°C) waters of Washington and British Columbia may be too hot and uncomfortable to wear while paddling, especially on a hot summer day. But in the case of a quick self rescue (or group rescue), a coat will be a great help as you try to warm up. Attempting to swim for shore in 50°F (12°C) water, unless it is less than a quarter-mile away (and other means of rescue appear unlikely) or you are wearing good hypothermia protection, is a mistake.

Safety gear and clothes won't be any help, however, if they've floated away after a capsize as K. Anderson's did. Make sure emergency equipment will still be with you when you need it. Life jackets and small items such as flares, signal smoke, and waterproofed matches should be fastened to you. Larger safety items and equipment used in conjunction with the kayak (spare paddles, bailing buckets, pumps, and floats) should be securely fastened to the kayak. If the wind is blowing or there are significant currents, consider fastening your paddle—or yourself— to the kayak with a tether (I prefer shock cord) that has enough slack that it won't interfere with exiting or reentering the kayak. (Remember: "It was all we could do to not get plucked off the capsized kayak by the whirlpools.") However, do *not* fasten yourself to the kayak if you will soon be paddling in surf.

Carry signaling devices and deploy them as soon as there is any indication that you may be unable to rescue yourself quickly. Give rescuers time to respond before you are overcome by hypothermia. If you think you're in danger, don't hesitate to signal for help—the Coast Guard and other rescuers would much rather respond and find out they weren't needed than arrive too late.

Paddling in a group is safer than paddling alone, especially if you are with paddlers more skilled and experienced than yourself. In the case of K. Anderson, another kayak could have been used to ferry victims to shore.

2

Another Lesson from the School of Hard Knocks

Matt Broze

I once attended a very special reunion: A group of paddlers had gathered to discuss their memorable July 1984 kayak trip and to produce an accurate account of their experiences with the hope that it would help other paddlers planning an open coastal trip. The camaraderie of this group of paddlers was only one indication of how much they had shared.

The trip had been conceived as a small, private, week-long kayak foray from Hotsprings Cove to Tofino on the west coast of Vancouver Island. By departure day, however, it had grown in size until sixteen paddlers in fifteen kayaks were taking part. The group and its leader were safety conscious: All had life jackets; waterproof gear bags assured adequate flotation in both ends of each kayak; group members carried weather radios, compasses, spare paddles, charts, tide and current tables, tow ropes, pumps, whistles, and flares.

Most of the paddlers had experience on whitewater rivers. Although they all were paddling stable and forgiving sea kayaks, only a few had experienced open, exposed coastlines. The trip leader had years of experience paddling the West Coast and had made numerous trips in the area.

The group arranged to be ferried along with their gear to Hotsprings Cove (getting a ride to Hotsprings Cove didn't commit them to paddling the outer coast, because there was a protected inside route available from there back to their cars). They spent three days near Hotsprings Cove. The weather was perfect. On the evening of the third day, the group made plans for a three-hour paddle south, along the outside of Flores Island, to a camp beyond Rafael Point. Weather permitting, they would leave in the morning.

The group leader was well aware of the strong on-shore winds that blow up every afternoon on a hot summer day: The heating of the land causes the air over it to rise, drawing in cool ocean air to replace it. Winds thus created often exceed twenty knots. He also knew from experience that the waters around Rafael Point can be very rough and insisted that the group get an early start the next day in order to be off the water before noon.

Breaking camp the next morning took a little longer than planned, but they were on the water by 8:30 A.M. The day was already warm and sunny and the water calm. Most of the paddlers dressed as they had for the previous days' paddles in hot weather—a few wore bathing suits; several others had on little more than T-shirts and shorts. On such a hot day, the one paddler wearing his parka and sou'wester seemed slightly comical to some of the rest.

As the kayakers started down the coast, a small swell coming from behind helped them on their way. The swell continued to build and later became uneven and at times confused due to reflections from some distant cliffs. By 10:00 A.M., the seas had built to such an extent that several of the paddlers, unused to these conditions, became nervous. (They all commented later that they were reassured by seeing how well the other paddlers seemed to be doing.)

Throughout the morning the wind steadily increased. The leader kept up a fast pace, hoping to be off the water before the wind really became strong. Several of the paddlers later said they felt they were having to push near their limits to keep up. Although no one was falling behind, the wind and waves, and the resultant risk of collisions between kayaks, kept everyone far enough apart to make communication difficult.

Ahead of the group, a fog bank became visible. Many expected the hot sun to burn off the fog before they reached it, but it did not. Some mistakenly believed the fog bank would provide relief from the wind and calm the seas. But to most of the group members the fog seemed ominous. A fishing boat heading in came near, and someone on it hollered " —— on the other side!" to a couple of the paddlers. The paddlers didn't catch the full message; later they were sure that the missing words must have been "it's rougher." Some of the paddlers felt that if the fishing boats were heading in, they should as well.

As they entered the fog, one paddler suggested turning back, but the leader disagreed. Well acquainted with navigating in fog, he figured they were more than halfway to their goal and they would have to paddle much longer—into waves and along an ever-increasing on-shore wind—to return to the old camp. What's more, there was no reliable landing area between their current position and the old camp.

The paddlers continued along in the fog. The wind speed did not decrease, and the waves grew bigger and steeper. Spray was blowing off the breaking crests, soaking the paddlers. It was too rough for those with spare dry clothes to put them on; likewise, those paddlers who hadn't worn life jackets had no chance of donning them now. With the fog blocking the sun, most had gotten chilled. The kayakers could not open their spray skirts, and even putting down their paddles was out of the question because they were needed for bracing. The paddler who had started the day in a parka and sou'wester no longer seemed at all silly.

A compass course was increasingly difficult to follow, due to swells coming from at least two directions. The crossing swells turned the kayaks first one way and then another in a zigzag course. Progress slowed even more as many of the paddlers spent more time bracing than paddling. The waves sweeping through the group seemed mountainous. At one point, a capsize whistle sounded; on hearing the signal, another member of the group quickly turned to help and almost capsized himself as a wave broke over him from the side. The capsize signal turned out to have been a false alarm, the paddler apparently having just disappeared from view behind waves.

After a time, the paddlers felt they should be well past Rafael Point. They altered their course 90 degrees to a heading that would take them to the safe landing beaches beyond it. They soon found themselves in an area of even bigger, steep, pyramid-shaped waves rolling in from the ocean; occasionally a larger wave swept through with a breaker steaming along on its crest. Several paddlers heard a hissing noise made by their kayaks as they were involuntarily surfed down the faces of these big, steep waves.

They struggled to keep in visual contact with one another while staying far enough apart to avoid a collision. One biggie caught two of the paddlers from behind as it started to break at the crest. The more experienced paddler was surfed off to one side in what she later described as the wildest ride of her life. The other (and the least experienced of the group) broached on the wave and was caught sideways by the breaker. She leaned away from, instead of into, the breaker and instantly capsized down the wave.

One paddler heard a whistle and looked over his shoulder to see the bottom of a kayak being pulled along by a breaker. He turned around to help, but by the time he reached the victim he was amazed to see her already back in her kayak. Luckily, just behind her had been one of the few paddlers in the group with previous rescue practice. He had pulled alongside, righted her kayak, stabilized both of their kayaks by bridging them with his paddle, and helped the victim climb back in. Following his instructions, she lifted her chest up onto the back deck, put her feet into the cockpit, and then twisted down into the seat (all the while keeping her center of gravity low and keeping one hand on the rescuer's kayak for stability).

A third paddler arrived to help stabilize the rescuer. Another group member gave the capsize victim a hand pump, and, as she started to pump, someone suggested that she reattach her spray deck to prevent further water entry. She slipped the pump down through the waist of the spray deck and continued pumping while another kayaker stabilized her swamped kayak.

There was a small break in the fog, and the paddlers saw that they were in a different location than they had expected. They were being pushed toward an area of huge surf crashing over and against big rocks. It was a frightening sight, and the thought of being lost at sea became a real possibility. They realized that if another breaker hit while they were close together, they would collide and be injured or be swept into the rocks. They had to get out of the area in a hurry.

Using the bow line of the capsize victim's kayak, the original rescuer attempted to tow the small group away from the area while the others worked to pump out the swamped kayak. He had no place on his kayak to attach the line, and he nearly dislocated his thumb trying to hold the line as he paddled, but he held on. He tried holding the rope in his teeth, but it was immediately yanked loose; he returned the line to one hand and continued to paddle with the other.

The group headed even farther out into a wild sea. The water actually appeared less threatening than the shoreline of giant surf and rocks behind them. A few paddlers watched a huge wave break well out beyond them: It looked and sounded like an explosion followed by a tremendous roar. They felt lucky not to be in front of it and terrified that the next one might get them.

Within a few minutes, the group leader joined them. He had a long, light-weight towing rope. He looped it over his shoulder and across his chest and began towing the capsize victim. This longer towline worked much better for about twenty minutes, until it broke. But by this time the capsize victim had finished pumping our her kayak and could paddle on her own.

The capsize frightened many of the group members. Most were already cold, and the prospect of capsizing into the cold water seemed painfully real. Some had serious doubts that they would make it to shore alive. (One man said later, "I just wanted to get to shore. The worst that could happen, I thought, was that I'd lose my boat and maybe break a leg, but I didn't want to die on the water.") As the group entered an area of less violent seas, several paddlers went in close to shore to look for a landing place. They weren't going to be too picky.

Two of the paddlers found a thin strip of cobble beach in a narrow slot through the ten-foot-high plateau of tide-washed basalt. The slot was just wide enough for one kayak. Using paddling skills honed on river rapids, each managed to maneuver into the slot and get to land. They quickly set about looking for a better landing spot, found one, and shot off flares to get the others' attention. But it wasn't clear to them that the flares were meant to designate a landing spot.

A cluster of paddlers saw the flares and went in closer to investigate. They found their two companions signaling them to come in through an area that looked to be rock walls behind some surf—nothing that looked remotely like a landing. One paddler, desperate to get to shore and trusting those on shore, decided that if he went in successfully the rest would follow. Fortunately, he understood the river paddling signals the two on shore used to guide him in: They held a paddle straight upright, so he paddled straight in through small surf; then they leaned the paddle to his right, and he turned in that direction, finding himself behind some barely exposed rocks that protected the area from surf and led down an eroded passage in the rock.

Six other kayakers followed and made it to the protected landing area without incident. The paddlers had to unload their kayaks in the water before lifting them out; then they had to carry the boats about one hundred yards across slippery rock, channels, and tide pools to an exposed camping place on the sand above the high tide line.

The seven paddlers still at sea had several reasons to look for a better landing: The capsize victim didn't think she would make it through the surf without capsizing; those in the group's only double weren't sure they could turn quickly enough to make it into the channel; another paddler felt sure they must have just rounded Rafael Point and that Siwash Cove was just around the next point of land. The group leader thought they were a few miles farther than that along the coast, but he knew that safe landings would greet them around the next bend in that case as well. They landed at Siwash Cove just before 2:00 P.M.

The first group spent the next two hours ferrying kayaks and gear over slippery rocks. Two from that group bushwhacked along the shore for forty to

Reckoning with Fear

Deborah Davis

"Fear—before it gets to the stage of panic—is healthy. Like pain, fear signals that something may be wrong. It tells you that you're getting into something that may be beyond your abilities. Fear has evolved as a mental characteristic to help us survive."
        —Bill Farthing, University of Maine psychology professor and kayaker

I had thought fear was getting in the way of my enjoying kayaking. Could I not simply eliminate fear from my kayaking experiences? Fear is a provider of information. I stopped judging my own fears as unnecessary and unfair. I began to understand when Farthing said, "Moving through fear is what helps us grow. I think sea kayaking is appealing to people because it makes them afraid. I wouldn't like kayaking if the sea was always calm."

Still, it seemed to me that some fears are more helpful than others. "Fear can drive you into a negative cycle or jar you into taking action, into escape," concurs Eric Carlson, a kayaker who teaches psychology at the University of Massachusetts. His behaviorist orientation teaches that most of our fears are learned and can be unlearned: "We want to reduce our fears only if they're debilitating, if they prevent us from taking care of ourselves."

How does one define fear in the first place? Farthing describes it in two ways: It's a subjective feeling, and it's a set of fifty minutes and found the other group. Everyone was exhausted, relieved, and feeling lucky to be alive. The paddle that should have taken less than three hours in better conditions had taken them over five hours. The leader—who sometimes jokingly convinces wide-eyed innocents that the relatively mild waves they're paddling in are the largest he has ever seen—admitted that, this time, these really were the biggest waves he had ever seen from a kayak.

LESSONS LEARNED

Better preparation for their surroundings could have saved these paddlers from a serious scare. Two members of this group had weather radios, but with the clear weather and the rush to get an early start, they didn't listen in. Had they done so, they would have heard broadcasts of gale warnings. Before setting out, always listen to the weather report.

Plan your routes using tide and current tables. Several of the paddlers in this incident now think that a one- to one-and-a-half-knot current was running against them, causing their misjudgment of when to turn in the fog. From a look at tables and charts of the area, I don't think this current would be easy to

physiological, "fight or flight" responses. In behavioral terms, the responses to fear are physiological and emotional adaptations to fear-provoking stimuli. They cue us to take action or escape such stimuli.

What are these stimuli that provoke us to quiver, shake, gulp, flutter, chatter, grow silent, or paddle in a wild frenzy? The list is a long one.

There are rational and irrational fears, beginner's fears and those of more advanced kayakers, and some common to us all, regardless of our kayaking experience. Some are so obvious that it almost seems trite to mention them. Others are more abstract and undefinable.

Beginners, lacking experience and skills, usually fear capsizing, entrapment in their boats, and immersion in cold water. They are also prone to performance anxiety: Will they look foolish? Have they chosen the right boat? Will they be strong enough to keep up with the more experienced paddlers? Beginners face the uncertainty of having to rely on those who instruct or accompany them. Can they trust their companions to navigate safely through the fog? To determine their position accurately? To stay close by if conditions turn rough? Above all, beginners fear the unknown. Novices' fears tend to diminish as they practice wet exits, simulate rescues, master navigation skills, and increase their physical endurance. Even for more experienced paddlers, weather conditions evoke our greatest fears: getting lost or run down in dense fog; being blown out to sea by an offshore wind or driven

(continued on page 24)

predict. It might have been a product of the general northward ocean current in that area speeding around the obstacle of Rafael Point. (I have heard of groups encountering strong southerly currents reaching Rafael Point and beyond from an ebbing tide out of Sidney Inlet.) It seems unlikely that the ebbing current from Clayoquot Sound would have much effect on the ocean side of Flores Island, especially north of Rafael Point. It is more likely that the waves they encountered, their difficulty staying on course, and the large size of the group all contributed to the slower-than-estimated progress made through the fog.

Clearly, navigating in fog is tricky. Even with a compass, finding your location in fog depends on your ability to accurately estimate your speed. The variables of wind, current, waves, and the pace of new paddling companions can all work to confuse you.

Inland paddlers who have grown up in areas where radiation fog that forms over land in the morning is common associate fog with lack of wind. Sea fog, which is found over water in coastal areas during the summer, is different. It forms when winds up to twenty-five mph bring warm air over colder sea water; once formed it can persist even during much higher winds.

Mount a compass on deck and provide for a secure way to read your chart without having to open your spray deck. One paddler in this group said he was confident that if he'd had his own chart and compass, he could have figured out his location once they had reached the slightly calmer area. He then would have

(Reckoning with Fear, from page 23)
against a rocky coast by an onshore gale.

Other fears arise from previous frightening experiences. These are conditioned responses to fear. According to Carlson, we could retrain ourselves to experience these anxieties differently.

If the fear is superstitious, its source may be difficult to trace. There are experienced paddlers who have been stricken with the idea that they have used up all their luck. Others have reported having omens or feelings of foreboding about an outing. The source of such an anxiety might be traced to an unconscious awareness the person had regarding weather patterns, a group member's lack of preparedness, or other potentially dangerous conditions. Whether or not they have a basis in reality, such omens can affect our experiences by making us psychologically vulnerable.

The human body can't distinguish between real, imaginary, or exaggerated dangers. The paradox of fear is that it limits us when no real danger is present, but it helps us move beyond self-prescribed limitations when we face real danger. "It's strange [that] we call these responses by the same name. One heightens our perceptions and gives added energy to perform beyond our normal capacities, whereas the other distorts our perceptions, tending to paralyze us and decreasing the competence. We need to work at decreasing the second fear; the first is welcome." (Gallway and Kriegel, *Inner Skiing*, New York: Bantam, 1977)

In Carlson's behavioral terms, kayakers develop more respect for the range and had the option to forgo the difficult landing in favor of Siwash Cove. Another paddler, who had his own compass and chart, did exactly that.

Limit the size of your group. As conditions worsened, it became increasingly difficult for the group members to stay together or keep track of each other. I consider six paddlers to be the maximum number a leader can keep track of in ocean swells. When more than six paddlers want to go on the same trip, they should break into entirely self-sufficient, equally matched groups of three to six, each with its own leader.

If your group intends to paddle in an area where a safe landing is not immediately available (cliffy shore, big surf, or open crossing), try to maintain a ratio of one experienced ocean paddler (capable of handling emergencies) for each less-experienced paddler. This buddy system can focus responsibility in a large group, preventing the usual formation of experts way out in front and novices struggling to keep up. Most members of the group discussed here lacked experience with open coastal conditions. Luckily for them, they had sufficient bracing abilities to keep upright in the face of breaking waves and violent seas. If a significant number of the paddlers on this trip had been without bracing skills, the trip could have been a major disaster.

Beware of points. A point of land with an area of shallows beyond it can focus the wave energy on the point, creating extremely rough waters from a much milder swell. A point protruding into a current increases the speed of the

variety of situations they can get into. We come to acquire more effective anticipatory skills and a wider range of avoidance behaviors. We become more sensitive to the weather, spend more time planning, considering routes, currents, tides, and so forth—yet the processing of this information occurs increasingly within the subconscious. We use our awareness with greater selectivity.

Reducing fears, then, must also be done selectively. Reality checks—a kind of counter-conditioning—are a simple way to reduce fears, especially those of beginners. "Anything that reduces the apparent adversiveness of the stimuli, especially pairing them with positive events, reduces fears," says Carlson. "Kayakers' fears can be reduced through carefully graded skills sessions, moving to more challenging conditions." At the same time kayakers will develop the skills to make accurate assessments of risk under "real world" circumstances.

Sometimes, despite our best planning and hazard-avoidance measures, true panic does occur: We get caught offshore in high winds; we capsize and our rescue options appear limited. Ironically, it is at the same moment when the realization of hopelessness hits that amazing solutions can occur—if we don't succumb to panic. The key is to relax, to accept the unalterable circumstances and stop fighting them.

Fear is not a sign of weakness; it is a sign of vitality. Diminishing my kayaking-related fears has become an adventuresome, even fun, process. While it used to diminish my enjoyment of sea kayaking, fear now enhances that experience.

current and can cause rough water, eddies, and whirlpools.

Keep warm clothing easily available and put it on at the first sign you might need it. Several paddlers in this group were very cold, and the severe conditions prevented them from doing anything about it. Had they capsized, hypothermia would quickly have posed a further complication to the group's already precarious position.

Carry your own emergency and rescue equipment and store it where you can get to it under the severe conditions that are most likely to make it necessary. Some members of this group had towlines and pumps but would not have been able to get them had they been needed because they were not stowed readily at hand.

Towlines should be at least as strong as parachute cord and at least fifty feet in length to be effective in big sea conditions. Too-short towlines put both paddlers in danger of colliding. You'll need a way to release or cut a towline quickly without having to bring the kayaks together to disengage. If the kayak being towed has a line running between a bow fitting and the cockpit, the kayaks won't even have to come together for the tow to begin. The person being towed can retrieve a thrown or trailed line, clip it into his bow line, and then release the bow line, if necessary, to disconnect quickly. A throw line can double as a towline and is indispensable when you need to get a line to someone in a location too dangerous to approach.

Few members of this group had ever practiced deep-water rescues. If three or four paddlers had been in the water at one time, the rescue would have been far more than three or four times as difficult. They would have needed many more pumps and towlines than they had. In a rescue situation in cold water or near a hostile shoreline, speed of rescue can make all the difference; two pumps emptying one kayak are faster than one. Imagine several paddlers who have reentered their cockpits: They are now in their (very unstable) swamped kayaks, trying to keep their balance while sitting waist deep in cold water, moving closer to waves crashing into the cliffs, waiting their turn for the pump and towline. On the trip described here, one more big wave could easily have created just such a situation.

Nervous paddlers should speak up, and others should pay attention. Even if the fears are groundless, one frightened paddler can have a big effect on the capabilities of the group, and this must be considered when courses of action are planned.

Beware of funneling yourself into a trap. Gather all the information you can and then periodically review your options. Try to foresee what options might ensue from each of the choices you are considering. If you see your options becoming more limited or riskier, you may at some point find that you are forced to take the only course left—one that will require a do-or-die commitment just to get to where conditions *might* be a little better. This group lacked the most significant information they could have had: the gale warning from their weather radios and, later, the fisherman's shouted warning. Once the following sea had become big enough, this group was literally pushed into going around Rafael Point in the fog for lack of a place to land. Based on the information they did have, returning did not appear easy, especially in the face of increasing winds. Furthermore, they did not suspect how rough Rafael Point would be.

3

Of Risk, Knowledge, Choice . . . and Special Vulnerability

Matt Broze

Some novices have a way of biting off more than they can chew. In the accident report that follows, an inexperienced paddler found himself in conditions beyond his capabilities. The lessons learned apply in Chapter 4 as well. Sadly, we will be the only ones to learn from these paddlers' mistakes.

Between 3:30 and 4:00 P.M. on November 13, 1984, Carsten Gursche was seen at the Jericho parking lot preparing his Seafarer single (16'8" by 24") for launch into English Bay, on Vancouver's outer harbor. The waves were unusually large and steep for the area and there was a westerly blowing at twenty knots.

Sudden Drowning Syndrome

In sudden drowning syndrome, the victim is thought to gasp involuntarily when immersed suddenly in cold water. The gasp sucks water into the lungs, and the victim dies quickly from suffocation by submersion, or drowning. Non-swimmers would be far less likely than experienced swimmers to control or delay this gasp reflex during a surprise cold-water capsize.

Since people's reactions to cold water will vary, if you're a good swimmer you might consider jumping neck deep into cold water, keeping your head out (and with help standing by) and seeing if you can control the gasp. If you can't, you should invest in a comfortable wetsuit or drysuit—even if its only advantage is to prevent the sudden shock of cold water in a capsize. A lightly dressed paddler feels the cold more suddenly and is therefore more likely to gasp before getting his or her head out of the water.

A word of caution here: Sudden immersion into cold water has been known to trigger ventricular fibrillation—a type of heart failure—in susceptible individuals. This is one possible result of an abrupt increase in heart rate and blood pressure, which are also among the body's first responses to sudden immersion in cold water. This type of heart failure has been determined to be the cause of death in some cases of sudden drowning.

If you stay in cold water more than a few seconds, you will experience another notable feature of cold-water immersion: pain. This pain is intense if the water is below 45ºF (7.2ºC). If you are like me, you probably won't want to stick around in cold water long enough to discover that this stinging pain subsides somewhat after a few more minutes.

If the cold-water capsize victim survives the initial threats of aspirating water or heart attack (as most do), there are a few other dangers that can cause drowning in those first few minutes. If rapid breathing (gasping) lasts for several minutes, it can lead to respiratory alkalosis and reduced blood flow to the brain. The reduced blood flow can result in confusion, and the alkalosis can reduce the calcium in the blood, resulting in muscle cramping. If the victim is without a life jacket, drowning can easily result. Panic increases the breathing rate and can therefore bring on or aggravate these problems. Again, practice is the key: If you are prepared for a capsize and understand that no matter how cold the water is, hypothermia will not kill you within minutes, you'll reduce the panic and feeling of hopelessness that are so dangerous in this situation.

Another early response to immersion in cold water is a drastically reduced blood flow to the skin and muscles for the purpose of conserving heat and insulating the body's core. This, combined with the cooling of the muscles of a capsize victim not dressed for immersion, results in significant weakening of the arms and legs. Without a life jacket or some other source of flotation, a capsize victim of thin or normal build may drown when he or she becomes too weak to swim or tread water, even though he or she may not yet be seriously hypothermic. This loss of dexterity and strength can make rescue more difficult if too much time is spent in the water preparing the rescue, as can be the case when pumping out a kayak before reentry instead of after it. Hanging on to flotation

Windsurfers who had just left the water were loading their car and noticed Carsten's upturned kayak about one hundred yards offshore. Seeing no sign of the paddler, they quickly called the authorities. Within a few minutes, two Coast Guard vessels and a helicopter were searching for the maroon kayak; they located the empty boat at around 5:00 P.M. By 6:30, five Search and Rescue (SAR)–trained surface vessels with searchlights were covering the area; within an hour, the helicopter had been replaced by a Buffalo aircraft with flares and a searchlight-equipped Labrador helicopter from Comox Air Base. By 8:30 two more surface vessels had joined the search, but it had to be called off when, at 9:00, all illuminating flares had been expended over an area extending a full two miles out to sea.

Carsten's body was found washed up on shore on November 14, about twelve hours after the capsize. Some who knew Carsten later said he had a history of doing things beyond his ability. He had been a weak swimmer and, in spite of the conditions, he wore neither a PFD nor a wetsuit. According to the coroner's report, he had been wearing hiking boots, blue jean pants and jacket, a shirt, two pairs of socks, a t-shirt, a sweater, a rain jacket, nylon overpants, and a spray skirt. The report listed his death as accidental drowning and showed no evidence of alcohol or drugs. His rapid disappearance points to sudden drowning syndrome as the cause of death.

Although this may not have been related to his death, Carsten's kayak had no bow flotation and was therefore floating bow down. When he bought his used kayak, it contained float bags in both ends; he later installed his own bulkhead and hatch in the stern from purchased parts. He probably was convinced that this was a safer system than float bags, and may have been unaware of the need to maintain secure flotation in both ends of the kayak. If so, this could be another instance of the hype surrounding a potential improvement in safety (bulkheads over float bags) overshadowing the basic safety principle (maximum flotation secure in both ends of the kayak).

instead of wearing it—or being attached to it—becomes difficult as the arms and fingers get weak and numb.

Note: Inhaled freshwater is absorbed through the lungs into the body, but salt water in the lungs causes water *from the body* to enter the lungs. As a result, drowning is a little more likely in saltwater. This pulmonary edema, triggered by salt, compounds the situation even for a victim who is breathing, as he or she may suffer pulmonary edema later. Since the water in question comes out of the body, the resultant dehydration and decreased blood volume create problems that can lead to heart failure in much the same way as will the dehydration accompanying hypothermia. Anyone who has inhaled saltwater or gone through a stage of severe hypothermia should be taken to a hospital as soon as possible.

LESSONS LEARNED

Carsten Gursche was a weak swimmer, yet he chose not to wear a life jacket. Wearing a PFD is imperative, even for good swimmers. If yours is uncomfortable to wear in the kayak, get a comfortable one, even if it isn't Coast Guard approved, or modify a Coast Guard–approved PFD for greater comfort. Wear it and keep an approved, unmodified PFD readily available to satisfy the Coast Guard requirement (a type II kapok "horse-collar" accomplishes this and could also serve as the float for an outrigger paddle-float rescue or a float roll).

Good swimmers can consider wearing inflatable life vests or buoyancy compensators that can be inflated or deflated as needed. Most approved PFDs slow swimming speed drastically. An inflatable could offer real advantages in the few situations where swimming or diving is the best option. *Any* PFD you are actually wearing is better than even the *best* PFD stowed on deck or in the cockpit.

Learn about the dangers of sudden drowning syndrome and hypothermia associated with cold water. A wetsuit, or insulation inside a drysuit, provides a much wider margin of safety if you capsize.

Unless you are traveling with responsible experts who can more than make up for your lack of skill, do not make open-water crossings before you have expert skills at preventing and recovering from capsize. Even experts are taking a serious risk when paddling alone on open crossings, in areas swept by currents, along ocean coastlines, or in bad weather. Two people in one double basically are paddling "alone." Learn capsize recovery techniques and test them in cold, rough water with the equipment you will be using. Do this with expert paddlers in a safe area near shore.

4

A Tale of Two Rescues

Matt Broze

Even the most skillful kayakers can find themselves in trouble when conditions
deteriorate beyond their range of expertise.

On November 9, 1985, Dan Corrigall made plans to paddle in Howe
Sound, just north of Vancouver, British Columbia. Dan planned to make
the three-mile crossing from Eagle Harbor, across Queen Charlotte Channel, to
the ferry dock on Bowen Island. Dan planned to go alone, but his friend, Andy
Bennett, arrived in town in time to go along. Both men were experienced
kayakers, and both could reliably Eskimo roll. They each paddled an empty
Nordkapp HM kayak (the expedition version with the long fin keel).

The water temperature was a chilly 41°F (5°C), and a ten-knot breeze was
blowing from the north, creating a small chop when they began paddling at
2:20 P.M. Both men wore ¼-inch-thick farmer-john wetsuits, wool sweaters,
paddling jackets, and type III life jackets. Andy had four Skyblazer flares and
a towline, as well as an inflatable paddle float for self rescue.

In *Sea Kayaking Canada's West Coast* (The Mountaineers, 1996), John Ince and
Hedi Köttner wrote this about Howe Sound: "Avoid Queen Charlotte Channel,
as boat and ferry traffic is heavy. Occasionally a strong wind, called a *Squamish,*
which blows south out of the mountains, can whip up dangerous seas."

Howe Sound is a steep-sided, glacier-carved fjord that extends back into
the mountains about twenty miles. *Squamish* is the local term for the
Sound's katabatic (gravity-powered) winds, which reach high velocity and
hit suddenly. Dan and Andy were not aware of the katabatic winds, nor
had they heard a weather forecast for the day. If they had, they would have

Turns and Spins

Sea kayaks can be difficult to turn when the wind is strong enough to produce whitecaps. At some point as the wind increases, it will be impossible to spin the kayak through a full 360 degrees. However, if you have practiced the following technique, you should be able to turn a sea kayak into even stronger winds.

Make sure you have plenty of room in the direction in which you start paddling, because your turn will be far wider than it would be in calm conditions. If you have to slow your speed or stop because of an obstacle, this technique won't work. First, get up to full speed across the wind. The weathercocking effect of all hulls helps turn the bow into the wind (or the stern into the wind if you paddle backward—a good way to turn downwind). Use powerful, wide sweep strokes to one side that finish by strongly pulling the stern over. Avoid any reverse or braking strokes on the other side, as these will only hinder you. For the same reason, take care not to angle a rudder too much, or the braking effect that results will hinder your ability to turn by slowing your speed, thus reducing the weathercocking effect. This is nearly always more effective than turning to spin the kayak around in one place with alternating forward and reverse strokes. Note: If you can spin your kayak in place considerably faster than you can turn it in a circle while moving forward, your kayak may be an exception to the above-mentioned generality. You probably need to practice quick turns. I have found short kayaks with rocker at the bow and a deep fin keel near the stern to be the only kayaks that I can spin in place much faster than I can turn them in a circle. Obviously, the skill of the paddler at

fast turns and spins will make a big difference in strong winds. If you have a good brace and are capable of tilting the kayak toward the sweep stroke with your knee (and using a skimming low brace on the return for support), you will significantly improve your turning speed and, therefore, your ability to turn into a strong wind. A turn made by spinning in place will also be quicker if you tilt the kayak, because kayaks are more curved on their sides than their bottom. Tilting the kayak shortens the waterline and increases the rocker, both of which aid maneuverability.

It may not be fair, but strength and weight are big advantages to paddlers maneuvering in strong winds. These factors, as well as differences in skill, kayaks, and gear load, explain why some paddlers tend to have far more difficulty in winds than others. If necessary, one kayaker can help another turn or stay on course in a strong wind by placing his or her kayak and torso ten to twenty feet upwind to shield the bow or stern half of the other kayak. If the problem is severe, a stern-to-bow towline can help both kayaks turn into the wind and hold that course.

Sea kayaks, like any long, narrow, floating object, are difficult to turn in strong winds. Lightly loaded or empty kayaks are much more difficult to turn into a strong wind than are heavily loaded ones. Stiff-tracking kayaks are harder to turn than are maneuverable ones. Kayaks with more keel at the bow than at the stern turn upwind more easily. Kayaks with the most keel at the stern turn downwind more easily.

Unbalanced windage in front of and behind the paddler makes the end with the most windage harder to turn into a wind. Windage farther from the paddler (such as known of the small-craft warnings and expected strong winds. A large mass of cold Arctic air was moving south; the cold, heavy air built up behind the mountainous dam known as the Coast Range. As Dan and Andy started their crossing, the cold air was spilling over that dam and gaining momentum as it poured down into the Squamish River valley.

A mile into the crossing, they saw violent whitecaps and a wall of mist rapidly bearing down on them from the north. Andy wanted to head back for shore; Dan wanted to go the same distance again to Passage Island, which lay downwind. They had paddled in whitecaps before, and he wasn't that worried.

By the time they decided to go back, however, the Squamish hit them. Neither man had realized how intense this wind would be. Dan was still facing west, but Andy already had turned back to face east. Dan tried to turn around into the screaming wind to realign himself with his companion, but he couldn't fight the strong wind. The waves built up quickly. After several more attempts to turn upwind, Dan decided to turn around downwind. However, he may have leaned too far into the wind, and he capsized. (Gusts of sixty knots were measured at the nearest weather station that afternoon.)

Dan was confident in his Eskimo roll. He had practiced it in many different conditions, including ocean surf. He tried to roll up, but didn't quite make it. He tried again, but felt the wind push him back down before he could completely right himself. He started a third roll, but everything seemed wrong.

with a longer kayak) will make it more difficult to turn in strong winds. However, there are factors that are more important than windage, such as how much weight is carried near the ends of the kayak, as well as the size, shape, depth, length, and location of the keel. Slower-turning kayaks are much harder to turn into a wind because, as the bow sticks out over the crest of a wave, it will be blown back (which depends on windage at the bow—including the bow keel—and the length of the bow). If the bow is pushed back as far as it can be angled upwind between crests (which depends on turning speed), no progress will be made. Note: If the wind is strong, it will no longer be possible to turn more quickly by using the crest of a wave to free the ends of the kayak, because the wind will overpower the paddler. A gear-laden kayak has less of a problem turning into high wind because the inertia of the mass in the bow keeps it from being pushed back as quickly as a light bow.

It is a common misconception that the addition of a rudder will make a kayak more maneuverable and easier to turn in wind. It is the length, width, and shape of the hull that determines maneuverability. Note: A rudder that can't be turned through nearly 180° will actually hinder the spinning of a kayak in one place unless the rudder is lifted out of the water. Here's a test for rudder users: Time yourself turning in a full circle, with and without the rudder. If you turn faster using the rudder, you should practice with the rudder retracted until you can turn just as fast without it.

Depending on the kayak, there can be (continued on page 34)

Almost out of air, he tried to scramble out of his kayak, but the spray deck held him in. Realizing the problem, he calmly and methodically removed his mitts, released the spray deck, and slipped out of the boat. When his head broke the surface, he couldn't believe the change of scene from only a minute before. Waves were now breaking all around him. Even though immersed in cold water and acutely aware of the danger of hypothermia, he wasn't worried because of his farmer-johns. To his surprise, however, he quickly began to feel extremely cold. He climbed up on his overturned Nordkapp for relief. The tippy, slippery hull and the strong wind soon had him back in the water.

The frightening thought crossed Dan's mind that Andy wouldn't be able to turn around and get back to him, but Andy soon arrived. Dan had lost contact with his paddle, and Andy offered to stay with Dan's kayak while he swam upwind a short distance to retrieve the paddle. Dan is over 6'3", 200 pounds, and a strong swimmer. When he got to his paddle and looked back he saw that Andy and his kayak (without Dan hanging on and inadvertently acting like a sea anchor) had blown more than fifty feet away. Dan's arms were very cold and, as he chased the kayaks, they became so weak he found himself unable to swim. Fortunately, the life jacket he wore allowed him to keep his head above water without effort.

Andy, who knew Dan to be a strong swimmer, had difficulty realizing that Dan could no longer move. He felt reluctant to leave Dan's kayak to go to him.

(continued from page 33)
some advantages to using a rudder to control a kayak, especially in winds. However, these advantages have mostly to do with ease of holding a straight course—not with maneuvering. In extreme winds, a rudder also can be used as a brake to get the bow pointed downwind (the best direction to go if the wind tops forty knots—unless it is taking you out to sea). Once you are pointed downwind, the rudder may keep you on course without your having to use the paddle for anything but a low brace (a sea anchor or long towline trailed from the stern might also help but would be harder to deploy in horrendous conditions).

A paddler using a rudder can be as skilled as any other in using the paddle. However, many rudder users become rudder dependent because this is all they ever practice. Even if rudder systems were indestructible, strong winds give rudder users plenty of incentive to learn to use the paddle and tilt the kayak for control. In addition, learning to tilt teaches essential bracing skills that are often neglected by paddlers with stable kayaks. You learn what you practice.

The easiest way to ensure you will be able to turn in wind is to add weight to your kayak. More weight will also increase stability and maintain the boat's momentum if you are paddling into wind and waves. Warning: If you add small logs or rocks, make sure they are in your boat's extremities or held to the hull (wedged in by float bags or in some other way). If the weight shifts to one side during a capsize, Eskimo rolling will be far more difficult, if not impossible.

He didn't have a towline to tow him and doubted that he'd be able to paddle into the unbelievably strong wind even without towing another kayak. But none of the alternatives seemed like good choices, either. Andy launched two of his four Skyblazers about one minute apart. To Dan the flares seemed insignificant and short-lived against the background of the wild scene surrounding them.

Andy managed to fight his way upwind to Dan, and they tried to decide what to do. Should they try for shore? Dan didn't think he could hang on that long and badly wanted out of the water. Should Andy leave Dan and try to make it to shore for help? Could Dan last that long? Would searchers be able to

Paddles and Wind

If you are caught by a strong wind, especially a side wind, keep your paddle low so the gust won't catch the flat of your blade. Unfeathered paddles and small blades have the advantage here, but don't switch to unfeathered unless you know from experience that your reflexive brace will still work with the different angle on the paddle blade. When you see a gust coming, hunch down and hold your paddle to the boat; point it into the gust, keeping the upwind blade lowest. Angle it so the gust can't catch a broad surface and in such a way that it will be more likely to be pushed down into the water rather than up into the stronger winds screaming above your head. If your paddle does get caught by the wind and yanks your arm up over your head, let go of it with the upwind hand, but try to hang on to it with the downwind hand.

A lost paddle created a real problem for Dan and Andy. A spare would have been one solution—even a cheap heavy one, provided it was of sufficient strength. As one fellow said after spending a few days paddling alone in Glacier Bay in search of his paddle after a high tide, any paddle is unbelievably superior to your hands and kayak seat.

Another solution is to attach three feet of shock cord from the middle of your paddle to your kayak near the front of the cockpit. This will make it easy to retrieve the paddle should it get out of your grasp, and there will be no need to untether the paddle to perform an Eskimo roll or an outrigger self-rescue. If you capsize and wet exit with this cord securely attached, as long as you hang on to either your paddle or your kayak you will still have both. This paddle leash makes it much easier to hang onto the boat while fastening a paddle float device. I tie about a forty-inch length of $\frac{3}{16}$" shock cord to my paddle shaft and attach a strong plastic clip to the other end of the cord. I roll the cord up on the paddle and hook the clip to the same loop that fastens the cord to the paddle. When the wind comes up, I attach the clip to the kayak in front of the cockpit. Be careful to use secure knots when tying shock cord; I use a figure-eight on the clip and a bowline around the paddle.

The paddle leash can double as a paddle park. With this system in place you will no longer have to keep grabbing your paddle as it slides into the water while you try to concentrate on photography (with dry hands) or put on more clothes. As a firm believer in backing up critical systems, I suggest sea kayakers both carry a spare paddle (well secured on deck but easy to get at, so it can be in use in seconds) and make themselves a paddle leash.

Powerboater in Distress

Gord Pincock started out on a long solo kayak trip from Vancouver, B.C., to Port Hardy near the north end of Vancouver Island in July 1985. He was four or five days into the trip when, just before dark, he arrived at a campsite ten miles north of Lund. He was tired, so he had a quick dinner and crawled into his sleeping bag. As he drifted off to sleep he heard some runabouts racing around and people shouting. Two hours later a heavy tugboat chugged by—then came a faint shout: *Help, help . . . I'm drowning.* Gord thought he was dreaming. The tug sounds faded but the faint calls did not. Gord woke with a start and realized the voice was real and was calling out to the tug. He turned on his flashlight to signal his presence. He could hear the caller choking after getting out only half a word; the man obviously was in the water.

Gord gathered up his rescue equipment and tried to light a candle so he could find his way back to camp, but each time the wind blew it out. He got into his Seafarer and tried to pick out landmarks in the moonless night. He spotted the faint outline of a cliff on the horizon; this would be his landmark. He turned and paddled hard toward the distant call. Three to five minutes later, with the help of his flashlight, he spotted the victim in the water.

Realizing that a frightened swimmer could easily capsize him, Gord stayed ten feet away and told the man how vulnerable he was in his kayak and that if he didn't do exactly as he was told they would probably both die. The man, named Norm, said he understood, and Gord let him grab onto his bow loop. Gord realized later that he should have given him some flotation to hold on to instead, such as his homemade paddle float/self-rescue kit device.

Gord blew up his Sea Seat (a large square air pillow that can be used like an inner tube) and described to Norm how to climb onto it. Norm grabbed the seat but wouldn't let go of the kayak and threatened to capsize Gord by trying to climb up on his bow to hoist himself up to the floating cushion. Twice Gord had to push him off with his paddle and warn him not to do it again. Eventually the Sea Seat blew away in the light breeze; dragging Norm on the bow, Gord chased after it and just barely caught it. Gord tied the line on the Sea Seat to himself and had Norm try again. Norm was drunk, very heavy, and his legs were cramping. He couldn't get up on the seat.

Gord began to tow Norm toward shore. Norm pulled himself forward on the line, and was halfway up on the back deck before Gord realized it. He shoved Norm off with his paddle and yelled at him that he would leave him if he didn't cooperate; the threat controlled him. Gord paddled at maximum effort and twenty minutes went by. Because the shore was cliffy except at his camp, he had to struggle along just offshore for another few minutes before he found the campsite. Norm lay in the water. He couldn't get himself out because he was drunk, hypothermic, and his legs were cramped. Gord helped him ashore and up the beach.

Gord gave Norm some dry clothes, his sleeping bag, and his insulated sleeping pad. He built a big fire, and the two men talked for a long time. Norm had been in Lund drinking with his buddies. On his way back home to Squirrel Cove, he and some friends had been racing around in their aluminum outboards, jumping each other's find him floating alone? Dan decided he should try to get back into his kayak. Andy gave Dan his paddle float to inflate over the paddle blade. By this time Dan's hands and arms were so useless that he gave up and soon lost track of the boat. Andy began towing Dan and his paddle downwind among what were by now big waves.

The race was on: an empty wind-driven kayak versus Andy, who paddled furiously but barely moved as he dragged Dan through the water from his stern toggle. Dan was painfully cold. He said later that it was all he could do to keep from climbing up on Andy's back deck; but they both feared this might capsize Andy and make their situation far worse. Andy was ever so slowly gaining on the kayak—or was it just wishful thinking? He soon became exhausted with the effort. He stopped to catch his breath and decided to set off a third flare.

They started off again, helped along by the steep breaking seas which seemed to be surfing them a bit as each wave passed. The kayak they were chasing may also have slowed as the waves grew larger and shielded it somewhat from the wind. After five more minutes of exhausting struggle, the two men finally caught Dan's boat.

Should they set off the last flare or save it to help rescuers zero in on them—if they ever came? Time was running out fast for Dan. Andy set off the last flare.

Andy had a rope and, because Dan was so weak, they decided to try the loop rescue they had learned in a swimming pool. Andy was worried about staying upright in the howling wind if he shifted his hands from his paddle and shifted his attention to tying knots, so he asked Dan to tie a loop in his tow rope. Dan

---

wake. This was the noise that Gord had heard as he dozed off after dinner. Norm's friends left for home, but Norm stayed jumping his own wake, putting his boat through its paces. He was drunk and rambling, so Gord heard two stories of how he ended up in the water. In one, Norm was thrown out of his boat after too sharp a turn. In the other version, he was relieving himself over the side and fell overboard. (Pop quiz: Which is the most likely reason Norm found himself in the water? Hint: An inordinate number of drowning victims are found with their trouser flies open. Most of them had been drinking. Relevant fact: Over 60 percent of all drowning victims over the age of 11 are intoxicated [have a blood alcohol level of 0.10 percent or more].) Norm had been unable to get back in his boat but stayed with it for some time before deciding to swim for the shore, which he could see. He had been doing all right until his legs began to cramp. My guess is that he lasted as long as he did because he was large and had a lot of insulating fat to protect his core.

Norm finally warmed up and fell asleep in Gord's sleeping bag, leaving his rescuer to spend the night shivering in his tent. Gord wasn't feeling too friendly the next morning. As much as he might have liked to, he couldn't see leaving Norm to his own devices in the wilderness, so he paddled ten miles back to Lund to send one of Norm's friends after him—twenty miles out of his way, round trip. *(Hats off, Gord!)*

was becoming muddled and lethargic, and couldn't lift his arms out of the water to help tie the knot. Andy managed to tie it himself and Dan slipped the paddle through the loop hanging between the boats; however, he could not keep the paddle perpendicular under the boats because of the waves. After several minutes he gave up on the rescue and again lost his paddle.

They were back to square one, but now far weaker. Dan wanted to try to climb up on his own kayak, but Andy worried that he might himself be capsized while assisting in the attempt. Just then Andy saw a boat that seemed to be coming in their direction, and he asked Dan to stay in the water just a minute longer. While Andy looked the other way, Dan, with a surprising surge of strength, jumped up on his kayak. He straddled it (upright this time) and rafted up with Andy to wait another three or four minutes before an 80-foot powerboat came alongside.

The large craft had no way to lift Dan up over the side, so it stood off and broke the wind for them. About two minutes later a sailboat appeared and got Dan up on deck. He tried to stand up and walk but collapsed; he doesn't remember how he got down inside the sailboat and in bed. At some point volunteers in a rescue boat boarded the sailboat and helped with his rewarming. After an hour in the sailboat, Dan was transferred to a Coast Guard hovercraft, which took him to a hospital. By the time he got there (an hour and a half after the rescue), his temperature was back up to 97°F (36°C).

Shore residents had been watching Andy and Dan, wondering what they were doing out there with strong winds predicted. They saw the Squamish hit them and called rescuers at the first flare. Dan would like to thank the people living on that shore for their vigilance.

LESSONS LEARNED

Dan often paddled by himself and counted on his skill at Eskimo rolling to help him out of a capsize. He had no other self-rescue capability and now considers himself to have been irresponsible.

The list of things Dan says he plans to do differently when paddling is extensive. He will buy and use a weather radio; not paddle alone more than a few hundred yards from shore; carry a waterproofed VHF radio, EPIRB (Emergency Position Indicating Radio Beacon), and/or big parachute flares; always carry a spare paddle; not let himself get separated from his paddle or kayak; be prepared to get out of the water quickly; practice turning and bracing in strong winds; and get himself a wetsuit or drysuit top to go with his farmer-johns.

You might think Andy should have used his towline to tie onto Dan's kayak so it wouldn't float or blow away. This might have prevented an exhausting chase, but keeping a kayak pointed into a forty-knot wind is difficult, and, even for a strong paddler, paddling against it is extremely slow. Would you tow a kayak that is being tossed around by the waves into stronger winds if you had never tried it before and weren't sure you would manage to paddle into the waves even without the added drag? Just getting out your tow rope might be dangerous unless you have it set up in advance. To be effective in rough conditions, a towline must be easy to hook up with one hand during a quick pass, and should be at least fifty feet long to keep the kayaks far enough apart to prevent collisions.

Like Andy and Dan, you'll have no idea how difficult it is to paddle in extreme winds until you experience it. Get this experience by seeking out a safe beach where the wind is blowing onshore, and practice in conditions you think are beyond your ability. Go with others and dress appropriately: Plan to spend some time in the water. Practice near a source of shelter and warmth, such as your car. What you could learn about the conditions and your equipment will be invaluable later.

The rapid loss of strength in the extremities caused by cold-water immersion became a life-threatening problem for Dan. Get out of the water quickly. Even without a spare paddle, Dan should have gotten back in his kayak by rafting up with Andy for support. They may not have been able to get his paddle later, but at least they would have slowed Dan's cooling. Rafted correctly, a pair of paddlers can ride out just about anything aside from large breakers and dumping surf. To raft together, each person bridges both kayaks with his or her paddle and then leans across the paddle and hangs on to the other person's kayak. By using the paddles as bridges, it is impossible to fall between the kayaks as can happen when you just hang onto the other kayak's cockpit rim.

I was amazed by the sudden burst of strength that enabled Dan to leap up on his kayak after his arms and hands had become useless. Because Dan wore a wetsuit, it's possible his legs were still strong enough for a powerful swimming kick. His pectoral muscles would have been somewhat protected by his farmer-johns, and warmed by his core; this would have allowed him to hunch his shoulders up and pull down his elbows as he scissor-kicked and slid up the low afterdeck.

Its low, flat afterdeck makes the Nordkapp easily able to carry a prone passenger. If Andy had practiced this type of rescue, he probably would not have hesitated to have Dan slowly slide up onto the kayak's back deck and straddle it. Even with Dan's legs dragging in the water for stability, he would have been far easier to transport than to tow, and would not have lost heat so rapidly. Practice carrying someone on your kayak. Because of the higher center of gravity of the passenger, this will be more difficult with high V'ed or rounded-back decks. (To avoid buckling a thin, arched deck, support it from underneath with a full gear load.)

5

The Open Coast, or, All Your Eggs in One Kayak

Matt Broze

Experienced kayakers know the importance of keeping their options open—
especially when negotiating the hazards of an unprotected coastline.

On Sunday, January 12, 1986, at 10:30 A.M., David Zibell prepared to launch
his kayak into the Quillayute River near the Coast Guard dock in La Push,
Washington. La Push is at the mouth of the river; farther west there is nothing but
open ocean. One of his objectives for the day was to scout out the conditions
around James Island, because he had learned of the kayak race to be held there the
following Saturday as part of the Second Annual Winter Surf Frolic. Dave and his
wife had agreed that if he wasn't home by 3:00 P.M., she would alert the Coast
Guard. Dave left his pick-up truck near the Coast Guard dock so that the Coast
Guard could easily find it and determine whether he was still out on the ocean.

Dave knew no other sea kayakers in the La Push area, so he usually paddled
alone. He had been paddling this area for three years; for two years in a home-

made double and, since the previous winter, in his Seahawk. He often launched from this same spot by the Coast Guard dock.

Dave bought the Seahawk (17' by 25") partly because it was one of the most stable fiberglass kayaks he had tried. His was equipped with a rear hatch and foam bulkhead. He had one float bag secured in the bow and another backing up the hatch and bulkhead in the rear. He kept a hand pump, bailing bucket, and paddle float made from a one-gallon Wesson Oil jug in the cockpit area; the jug was hooked to the kayak.

Although it was about 45°F (7°C), mild for January, Dave was dressed for winter paddling. He wore full-length woollies, a heavy, long-sleeved polypropylene top, a ³⁄₁₆" farmer-john wetsuit, wetsuit booties, a windbreaker with elastic at the sleeves and waist, and wool, fingerless gloves. He also wore a Helmsman type III life jacket, with panels of flotation at front and back held together by webbing straps under the armpits. He kept pogies—large hand mitts designed to attach around the paddle shaft—in the bailing bucket in case his hands needed further protection. He had a whistle and a compass on one string around his neck, and sunglasses on another.

The single, orange triangular flag on the tower at the base of the jetty indicated small-craft warnings. Dave had paddled under small-craft warnings in the area several times before and foresaw no weather problems. Although it was not yet high tide, the water level was already as high as he'd seen.

The swell was fairly large, but the river mouth, protected by the jetty and James Island, was free of surf. Dave paddled out of the river mouth and out past James Island. It was quite rough west of the island but no worse than he had experienced before. Dave saw extreme whitewater to the north along the shore of the island and decided to stay well offshore, outside the foam line.

Dave had been out about half an hour when the swell became much larger. From his low angle it looked as if the spray from the waves breaking on the cliffs to the north was exploding as high as James Island itself. This was exciting to watch and, in the deep water outside the island, the big waves weren't causing him any serious problems.

However, as the waves got bigger, he began to worry that he might have difficulty getting back into the river mouth. This could close off his only reasonable route back to shore. Once Dave could see up river he realized that the waves were already steep and close to breaking. The swell had increased from seven feet earlier that morning to over fifteen feet. A fifteen-foot swell creates even higher breakers as it steepens in the shallows and its crest peaks up before it breaks. Some friends later told Dave that the waves had been breaking over the berm with the high tide and pouring into the parking lot at Rialto Beach, just north of the river mouth. If it hadn't been for the offshore wind holding the tops back and the deep water (a result of the highest tide there until the following November), the huge waves probably would already have been breaking across the river channel.

In previous solo excursions, Dave had never seen the river mouth blocked by surf, but it seemed possible now. He decided to start in immediately. The waves

Paddling the Open Coast

An unprotected coastline is an area exposed to the full force of ocean swell over much of the shoreline, so that easy landing sites are few and far between with even a moderate swell. An open coast is full of hazards, many of which are unpredictable. Most paddlers find the risks of paddling the open coast unacceptably high. If you really want to paddle unprotected coastlines and are willing to undergo the considerable training it requires, you will need both expert skills and a good understanding of the coastal environment.

One great thing about sea kayaking is that you don't have to go to the ends of the earth (that is, you don't have to paddle ocean coasts) to find adventure and the excitement of discovery. Almost anywhere you explore on the water is interesting—the boundary between water, land, and air always teeming with abundance. Like the advertisement says: "You never know how pretty the shore is until you stop standing on it." While I have a good time whenever I paddle, one of my favorite pastimes since childhood has been camping at the ocean.

There is always so much to see and do. When conditions are good, my kayak adds to the things I can do. But when the paddling gets rough, my options may become severely limited, just as Dave Zibell's did. Learn the rules of open-coast paddling so you'll have more options when you need them.

The Rules of the Game

Enter the open-coast environment during good weather, in a safe area. Overnight trips are far riskier because of a greater likelihood that changes in weather or waves could tie you to one spot without an easy retreat. Practice and take your first few trips in the company of skilled paddlers who are familiar with the area.

Most of the boating hazards on inland or protected water are likely to be present or intensified on the outer coast. These include cold water, wind, wind waves, fog, and hazards from tides and currents. Add to this the effects of ocean swell; surf on beaches; large confused seas caused by the swell reflecting off cliffs or coming from several directions as a result of two or more distant storms. Compound with this the focusing of swell onto cliffs because of the shape of the shallows off points; mix in an automatic wind generator that often causes strong onshore winds by the afternoon of a hot summer day; throw in an area of underwater rocks playing peek-a-boo in the swell and areas of shallows where the swell breaks only with the biggest waves or where waves break for the first time in hours due to a falling tide. In such conditions, the safest place may be nowhere near shore. Now cloak all this in a blanket of fog or even darkness (if you're still out after dark because you have been unable to reach or land at your intended stop). It is no secret that the weather and the height of the swell can change drastically in a few hours; conditions can worsen (did I mention the squalls and thunderstorms?) as easily as they might improve.

The most confident among us can become anxious long before things get nearly as bad as I described. When you perceive danger on the sea, it doesn't hit you like the quick adrenaline rush of an exciting river rapid. Anxiety at sea builds and gnaws at you, wearing you down, were big and steep as he began paddling up the river, but he couldn't look back often to see them coming because he had to pay attention to waves reflecting off the cliffs on the south side of James Island, which were creating a confused sea and bouncy ride. Suddenly he was hit by a wave he hadn't anticipated, and he capsized. After a first unsuccessful attempt to struggle out of the cockpit, he told himself to "get logical" and calmly pulled off his spray deck and tried to slip out. He found himself held in by the plastic jug between his knees. He unfastened the jug with one hand as it had been designed to do, and got out of the kayak, keeping a firm hold on both kayak and paddle. He quickly righted the kayak, gathered up the other items floating around him, and returned them to the cockpit.

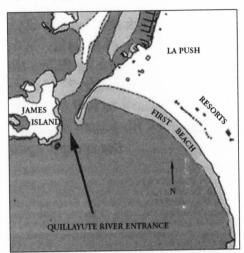

As Dave drifted back out with the river current he began to bail his kayak with his one-

draining away your reserves, making you more vulnerable—and you have plenty of time to worry about that, as well.

I am a firm believer in learning to understand the forces at work instead of operating from a set of fixed rules. Obeying rules without an understanding of the reasons behind them creates an approximation of competence which leaves one vulnerable to the exceptions. If you want to paddle the coast, do so—but remember to make your first trips training trips. Learn how to handle difficult conditions while you still have a wide margin of safety.

Wind. For open-coast paddlers, wind is one of the most dangerous variables; it can increase in velocity quickly and make control of a kayak and paddle extremely difficult. It has the potential to blow a kayaker offshore or onshore into dangerous regions, such as big surf or a rocky coast. Making headway into strong winds is a struggle at best.

In mountainous areas, the terrain can deflect and funnel the wind, creating strong gusts, downdrafts, and twisters. Cold air can build up high in the mountains over vast snowfields on a calm day, and then suddenly be triggered into an avalanche that spills down a valley and out a fjord, creating extremely high winds where a few seconds before conditions had been flat calm. In temperate or even tropical regions, cold fronts can pour over mountains into the warmer air on the other side, creating the same effect. Strong winds and gusts are often associated with rain squalls. But they are also associated with sunny summer days when the land (continued on page 44) gallon bucket. He removed most of the water and then proceeded to try the outrigger paddle-float rescue, which he had read about but never tried. The Seahawk has three one-inch nylon webbing straps securing the rear hatch; as Dave bobbed up and down in the big waves he slid his paddle under the middle strap. This held his paddle well enough. Using one hand, he attached his float to the throat of the paddle, thankful that he had devised an easy shock cord attachment that left his other hand free to hold on to the kayak. His heavy clothes and woolen mitts appeared to be keeping him warm; he was having no problem with dexterity.

Dave tried to climb up on the afterdeck, but failed. He made several more attempts but each time the float simply sank. The afterdeck seemed too high. There had to be a solution. Then he had a flash of insight: Why not lower the deck by filling the kayak up with water? After working so hard to bail out the kayak, he now tipped it and filled the cockpit again.

With the kayak swamped, Dave was able to pull himself up on the afterdeck and get one foot into the cockpit on the first try. By this time he was exhausted, and he spent three or four minutes draped over the stern for a much-needed breather. Then he put his other foot into the cockpit, but something was in the way. After a short struggle to move his bailing bucket, Dave easily twisted around into the seat. He bailed until there was only about an inch of water left in the kayak.

By now it had been twenty or twenty-five minutes since the capsize. Dave

(continued from page 43)
surface heats up and warms the air; the faster-moving molecules of warm air take up more space, making the warm air lighter than the air cooled by the ocean. The heavier cold ocean air flows in over the land, displacing the lighter air upward and resulting in a strong afternoon onshore wind. Many kayakers limit their paddling to the morning hours to avoid this wind.

Waves. When the wind picks up, the waves soon follow. Waves make a capsize more likely, and they can get you wet from splash or spray. Waves can create the difficult control problem of broaching (turning quickly and skidding at the stern on the face of a wave) if they are from the stern quadrants. Waves from any direction can knock a kayak off course. They are most difficult when they are steep and have a wavelength roughly the same as the length of your craft. When waves are reflected from a cliff or wall, or when they arrive from different directions for any reason (such as wind waves superimposed on a swell or swells from two or more distant storms arriving from several directions), they can create a steep and confused sea. Large waves meeting from opposite directions can throw water upward (clapotis) with enough force to lift a kayak into the air. Clapotis is most likely near a wall or cliff reflecting waves directly back on themselves. An interesting high-speed zipper clapotis occurs when direct seas and refracted seas meet at a very slight angle to each other. In a confused sea, be careful that your paddle reaches the water; a surprise "air" stroke or brace can throw you off balance. Large or huge waves created slipped the paddle out of the hatch strap and moved the stabilizing float to the middle of the shaft; he wanted the float handy in case he capsized again. He started up the river, moving close to James Island because it looked calmer there, and he thought it might offer some protection from the swell. (In retrospect, he thinks this may have been a mistake because the waves reflecting off the cliffs were angling back across themselves in steep peaks with the next big wave cycle moving up the river.) Suddenly, a big wave appeared out of nowhere and broke right on top of him. It may have been an especially large wave or one that broke where it crossed itself; either way, the next thing Dave knew he had capsized again.

When his head broke the surface, his kayak was twenty or thirty feet away. Halfway between him and the boat was the rear hatch cover, floating right-side up in the foam. It must have been one violent breaker to pull the hatch cover loose from the three straps holding it down. Dave's paddle was nowhere in sight. It seemed as if his best bet was to swim for the nearby island, but it soon became obvious that the river's current was taking him away from the island faster than he could swim. It was time to formulate plan B; maybe he could make it to the jetty. He tried, but it was too late for that; Dave's legs were starting to cramp and his face-down position and the rough water often left him with a face—and airway—full of water.

Dave's options were by now drastically reduced. Maybe if he drifted south with the current, he could regain the beach without using up too much more

by distant storms (known as swell) will likely have such long wavelengths that they will only carry you up and down slowly, causing no real problems unless you are in water shallow enough to cause them to become breakers.

Surf. The size of surf is difficult to judge from seaward, but you can easily differentiate a less violent, spilling surf from the abrupt, dumping surf that is much more likely to damage you or your kayak. A dumping surf on a steep beach can be extremely violent, with the dumper crashing directly down on the beach gravel. When on a kayak trip, avoid surf as much as possible. You can often find much smaller surf and a better landing place in areas protected by a point of land or an island. But if you intend to paddle open coasts, you must practice paddling in surf; be sure to

start with small, easy surf. Always wear a helmet in surf, get plenty of support from experts, and make sure you have long throw lines available to aid in rescues.

Surf can be hard on kayaks, especially if they happen to be full of water when they hit something, such as when the bow or stern rams the beach. Maximum flotation helps prevent damage and maintains better control when water starts getting in the kayak—which it always does in surf. I use a sea sock to ensure maximum flotation. But remember that a sea sock can make knee braces more slippery; you may need to work on your own knee braces so they are not dependent on friction to be effective. Good knee or thigh bracing is essential in dealing with surf.

Stay well outside the surf line when *(continued on page 46)* energy. He switched to a back float to rest and went with the current. He now had his hands free, and he started blowing his whistle, hoping that it might be heard above the roar of surf. He looked up at the sky and shouted "I want to live!" a couple times, so there could be no misunderstandings.

The current turned as he had expected and began to take him south amidst huge steep rollers. After about ten minutes, a bigger set of waves arrived off First Beach and began breaking farther out. As the first one hit, he felt as if six fire hoses had been turned on him at once. After about thirty seconds of being tumbled over and over, he surfaced, choking, coughing, and barely able to breathe. He managed a couple lungfuls of air before the next wave crashed over him. Much wiser for his experience with the last wave, he held his nose with one hand and his life jacket with the other to prevent it from being torn off when the wave hit. He felt that the life jacket was about all he had left, and he didn't want to lose it. The wave hit, and Dave spent another thirty seconds or so tumbling below the surface before he surfaced again, coughing, choking, and gasping for breath. The big waves pushed him into an area of relatively small breakers of six feet or smaller. By now Dave was quite cold and was having trouble getting enough air. He drifted on his back head-first into the waves, which slowly pushed him toward the shore.

As Dave neared the shore, he was spotted by La Push Ocean Park Resort manager Jerry Manley and some of his guests. Dave saw one of the people on the

(continued from page 45)
paddling, because larger waves will break farther out. This can occur intermittently and come as a real surprise. Waves can break in any shallow place, not just near shore. Most rivers and many bays have a sandbar well offshore where breakers form. Be especially careful of a falling tide, since the outgoing current will steepen the waves in water that is getting progressively shallower, making them more likely to break. Underwater rocks, plateaus, or shallows well offshore can cause intermittent breakers (called boomers) that you might not notice unless you have been watching from afar. Other clues to the possibility of boomers include steepening of waves; an area of foam; a change in water color; a patch of kelp; or underwater rocks and shallows marked on your chart.

If you capsize and wet exit in the surf near shore, your kayak could become a great danger to you. In small surf, swim toward shore, pushing the kayak in front of you or holding on to an end toggle. If the surf is big enough that it would be difficult to hold the kayak away from you, it is probably best to get well off to one side of your kayak and then swim for shore. The breakers usually will deliver your kayak to the beach if the boat has proper flotation. If you can't make progress swimming for shore, you may be in a rip current (sometimes called *undertow*), which is formed by the water that builds up behind a sand bar flowing back out to sea in a channel through the bar. If this happens, swim parallel to shore for thirty or more yards before again making for the shore. Keep angling away from the rip, because an alongshore beach, and also noticed that he was near some very large beach logs that had been floated by the unusually high tide. Although he could easily have been crushed by the logs as they rattled around in the shore surge and small breakers, by now he was hypothermic and was unaware of the danger. He was just glad he had been spotted.

As two resort guests waded in, pushing small logs aside to clear a channel to Dave, Jerry Manley ran to call the Tribal Police and the Coast Guard. He alerted them about the man barely alive in the floating logs, and resort guests, trying to save the man, all in danger of being trapped and crushed by the logs. A guest rescued Dave and dragged him to shore.

The Quillayute Tribal Police arrived in less than two minutes; Dave, now semi-conscious, was rushed to the hospital in Forks, Washington, where he arrived fourteen minutes later. Dave was coughing up salt water; according to blood oxygen tests, his lungs were operating at 50 percent of normal capacity. This condition is referred to as aspiration pneumonia. Dave's core temperature was 88°F (31°C) after having spent a total of about an hour in the water. He was given oxygen, a heating pad was placed under his torso, and hot water bottles and chemical heat packs were placed on and around him. Within an hour his temperature was up to 93°F (34°C).

A week after his ordeal, Dave still had painfully bruised ribs, either from the logs or from being thrown against the edge of his cockpit during capsize. The "six fire hoses" in the breakers might also have been a factor.

---

current feeding the rip could sweep you back into it and take you out to sea.

Currents. Some areas affected by tidal currents can become treacherous. A calm place can become rough within a few minutes. In some locales the effects of tidal currents can amount to an awesome display of whitewater. Currents on an exposed coast are usually caused by the mouth of a river or a bay having a narrow entrance relative to its size. When a current is moving in a direction opposite to wave motion, the wave length is shortened; this has a steepening effect on the waves. A current changing with the tides to run against the wave direction can turn a mild sea into a rough one. This combined with shallow water makes the bar off a river or harbor a dangerous place. Underwater obstructions, headlands, narrows, and shallows can combine with a current to cause waves, eddies, boils, whirlpools, overfalls, and water so agitated that it hisses or gives off a steady roar. Headlands, narrows, and shallows also can increase the speed of the local current. Charts will label these areas "tide rips." River kayaking experience and bracing skills can be a great help in dealing with some of the effects of tidal currents.

An ebb current, or outflowing current, is the most dangerous—and don't expect the current direction to change with the change of the tide. Depending on the constriction and volume of flow in the river or bay, maximum current speed will occur when the difference in water levels to either side of the constriction is greatest, and this could be delayed until nearly low tide if the channel is very constricted, damming up a large

(continued on page 48)

Dave never saw his kayak again after the second capsize, although the Coast Guard reports finding some small pieces of fiberglass of the color he described. Both halves of his old but strong fiberglass-shaft paddle were found; the paddle had broken at the joint. Dave now feels that an oval-shafted paddle would have been useful to him because when the paddling was most difficult, he had trouble being sure that his paddle was correctly oriented. This had nearly caused him to capsize when he first started up the river. Dave has gained a healthy respect for the coast; he plans to continue kayaking and become better at Eskimo rolling.

LESSONS LEARNED

Familiarity breeds contempt. Dave had never heard of surf closing off the river and had never experienced anything close to that in the more than twenty times he had paddled out that way. (The mouth of the Quillayute is generally the only surf-free landing between Juan de Fuca Strait and Gray's Harbor.) In the end, of course, David's assumption that the route back to shore would remain open left him with two very poor options: coming in through huge surf, or staying outside and waiting for help, which probably would not have come until after dark. He took what

(continued from page 47)
volume of water. There will always be some delay between the tide change and the current change. The current will not change until the rising tide goes above the level of the impounded waters. If there are no current tables available for your area (there probably won't be for any but the major rivers and harbors), you'll have to practice in the area and learn from experience what kind of delay you should expect. There have been many sea kayaking accidents in which the paddlers assumed that slack tide also meant slack current.

Tides. On an outgoing tide, you could become stranded in tidal basins with wide areas of muddy shallows; these often occur where a river enters a bay. At low tide, a long shallow beach could mean a long carry to a resting or camping place. But when the tide comes in at this type of beach it will come in rapidly, so you'll have to be especially careful not to leave your kayak unsecured for even a few minutes. The beach where you landed at a favorable time could be completely different at another tide level. Recently I was at a beach that had a landing through small surf at high tide; at low tide, however, it was protected by a plateau of barnacled and kelp-covered rocks that extended out over one quarter of a mile.

Fog. Fog can interfere with your senses. What you don't see can hurt you on the open coast, where knowledge of and alertness for danger are of paramount importance. Don't start a trip along an ocean coastline in fog; however, if there is a chance that you might be caught offshore in fog but persist in traveling, then at least know at all times exactly where you are and seemed to be the best option: to get to shore before things got rougher. If Dave had been better prepared, he might have known before setting out that the swell, and therefore the surf, might cause him problems—the VHF marine weather channel had predicted a seven-foot swell increasing to fifteen feet by the afternoon.

Paddling with others would also have given Dave more options when things turned dangerous. While the river could have cut off access to a group of paddlers almost as easily as it did for Dave, members of a group would have had the option to stand by while their companions paddled in one by one. Group members could have helped each other in the event of capsize. Furthermore, paddling in a group would provide a better chance that one person would make it through and notify the Coast Guard that the party needed help.

Aside from this, a VHF radio or EPIRB could have brought Dave help from the Coast Guard well before dark. A VHF radio, with its two-way capabilities, would at least have made it possible for him to have the Coast Guard watching as he attempted to enter the river. Flares may well have been seen from the resorts on First Beach or from parts of La Push.

Dave is not the first kayaker to come to grief in this area. Several years ago, a kayaker also found the route back up the river blocked by big surf; he paddled to just outside the surf line and swam to shore.

Dave expended a lot of energy bailing out his kayak, partly because he stayed in the water. If you have a pump or bailing bucket, it is almost always best to get back in the kayak before you start removing the water, assuming of course that you have adequate flotation in the bow and stern to support your weight. If you don't have enough flotation to support your weight in a swamped kayak, with some kayaks you can spill out most of the water quickly by pushing the stern under, twisting the kayak to break the suction at the cockpit, and drain it. As a last resort, you can try bailing the kayak while you're in the water. Even after he had bailed the kayak, Dave had trouble climbing on; his one-gallon float kept sinking. Two gallons is the practical minimum for this type of float, a little less if it can be fixed on the blade or held in position below the blade.

where the safe landings will be. That way, if the fog rolls in, you'll be able to use your map and compass or GPS skills to find a safe route.

Keep in mind that some coastal areas are safer to paddle than others. In many areas the coast is penetrated by bays and inlets from which you can approach the outside coast safely. In some areas, such as Vancouver Island's Barkley Sound, you can paddle to the outside islands in calmer waters because the swell is broken up by numerous islands and the tidal current is practically nil. In fact, this coastal environment is safer than many popular inside areas, such as the San Juan and Gulf Islands, San Francisco Bay, the Inside Passage to Alaska, Maine's Kennebec River entrance, or New Brunswick's Passamaquoddy Bay, which are well protected from ocean swell but where strong currents flow much of the time.

6

Risks Compounded

Matt Broze

On November 9, 1985, two couples left Terrill Beach on the north side of Orcas Island in Washington's San Juans. They paddled the two miles to Sucia Island in a northeast wind of about ten to fifteen miles per hour, planning to spend Sunday there and return on Monday. One of the attractions of paddling to Sucia Island in November is that, although fall and winter weather in the Pacific Northwest is often quite mild, hardly anyone visits the island during the off season. Storms in this region are accompanied by southwest winds, so the day's northeast wind was taken as a sign of clear weather to come.

Bob Bresnahan and Emily Zopf had been paddling their double kayak, a Pacific Water Sports Sisiutl, for about two years. This was their seventh or eighth trip to Sucia Island. Their companions, Robert McIntosh and Marion Bennet, were getting their first taste of kayaking. Emily and Marion shared the double, and Bob and Robert used two older Sea Otters borrowed from a friend.

During the crossing to Sucia Island, Bob had some trouble staying on course. They were quartering into the wind, and Bob's bow was being blown more off the wind than the others; he was being drifted off to the left. Once in the wind shadow of Sucia Island he altered course directly into the wind, and they arrived at the island together. Although Robert was a novice and was paddling an identical Sea Otter, he was not having trouble staying on course. Once on shore they diagnosed the problem: Bob's kayak was loaded too heavily in the stern, lifting the bow higher and making it more easily pushed aside by the quartering wind.

For the rest of the day, the cold northeast wind increased steadily. By Sunday it was blowing a steady thirty miles per hour and gusting to over forty. Robert later said he had never seen a northerly wind that strong. The air was extremely clear and the views were tremendous. The Strait of Georgia, to the north, was a mass of whitecaps.

On Monday the icy wind was still coming from the northeast, but its speed had dropped to about twenty miles per hour; the temperature was still below freezing. Looking south toward Terrill Beach where they had left their vehicle, the group could see that the waves were small near the shore of Sucia Island (due to its wind shadow), although there were whitecaps in the distance. Conditions looked only a little worse than what they had encountered on the way over, but the trip back would be all downwind. The wind speed was dropping steadily—a favorable sign. They thought perhaps they should wait for it to diminish further, but the next slack current would be just before dark. They decided to start out toward Terrill Beach, check out the sea conditions, and return if it began to seem too rough.

The group paddled for quite a while in small waves. When they left the protection of Sucia Island, however, the seas, coming from the Strait of Georgia, had become much larger rollers. The kayaks had moved apart; when the waves were about four feet high, Bob decided to paddle over to the double to see how Emily and Marion were doing. As he neared the double, it became especially hard to control his direction; he was continually turning off course to the left, probably broaching on the waves. Emily and Marion turned directly downwind as Bob approached. He tried to follow, but he could not seem to get his kayak to point downwind and continued off to the left.

Throughout the trip, Robert had been concerned that, as a novice, he didn't know the limits of the sport (something that had always been important to him as a rock climber). As he entered the bigger waves, Robert worried because he didn't know what it would take to capsize a kayak. However, things seemed to be going well, his kayak was doing fine considering the conditions, and he didn't feel insecure. In fact, this kayak trip was one of the few times he had been out in the waves on a boat and not gotten seasick. He was enjoying himself.

As he approached Parker Reef, Bob noticed an area of very rough water ahead and to his left and attempted to avoid it. Although this was the time of slack water, the eddies never stop moving there, and the water seemed to be carrying him into the turbulent area. He estimated later that the steep, peaked waves to his left were eight feet high from trough to crest. Try as he might, he couldn't turn his kayak around and move away from the turbulence. As the paddlers did all they could to handle the big waves, they lost track of one another.

Emily and Marion were being hit from the side by broken waves and didn't seem to be making any progress toward Terrill Beach and the car. Emily decided they should paddle straight downwind, keeping the waves at their stern. The waves were much larger than they had been only minutes before, but now at least they weren't being hit from the side by breakers. They were still getting wet (especially Marion, as the waves washed over the bow), and they were going to miss their car by a half-mile, but they were making good progress toward shore. Farther east, Bob had made it through the first few huge waves of the turbulent area he had been unable to avoid. The fact that he had easily stayed upright bolstered his confidence. Unfortunately, he ended up in an area of crossing seas (probably a tide rip at Parker Reef), and his kayak was soon broached by a wave. The next wave crested just as it hit him from the side. He was caught by surprise, and capsized.

Bob exited his kayak easily. He was wearing heavyweight polypropylene underwear (tops and bottoms), flannel shirt, bunting sweater, pile sweater, wool socks, and Gore-Tex rain pants. He had also been wearing a wool hat that came off in the capsize. When he came up and looked around, he saw his life jacket, which had been stored behind his seat, floating away. His paddle and hat were going off in other directions. Realizing he could not recover them all, he decided to go for the paddle. He hoped to get back in the kayak and would need the paddle then.

The thought crossed his mind that he was going to die, but he countered the thought by getting busy collecting his paddle and attempting to climb back into the kayak. He was in an area of huge cross-chop. As he tried to climb in over the bow, water poured into the cockpit, dislodging a loosely filled gear bag, which floated up and out. He had no sooner grabbed it when the bow flotation bag came out as well and blew away in the wind. Knowing the bow would sink without flotation, Bob stuffed the gear bag back in as far as he could. A bulkhead and hatch were providing flotation at the stern. He reentered the kayak from the stern so he wouldn't tip the bow down and lose the gear bag that was now the only flotation in the bow.

Bob climbed up onto the rear deck from the stern and tried to maintain his balance as he pulled himself forward toward the cockpit. A big wave knocked him off the deck, and as he fell he accidentally popped the hooks on the hatch

The Coast Guard Behind the Scenes

After speaking to the Coast Guard, Marion Bennet felt they sounded awfully blasé about the incident. She saw no evidence that they did anything about the situation. I suspected that the trawler *Horizon* might have been summoned by the Coast Guard, so I called to find out. I talked to Quarter-master Robert Helle, from the Coast Guard control group in Seattle. He gave me the report, which I have abbreviated here:

10:55 a.m.   San Juan Sheriff called the Coast Guard about two kayakers reported missing near Terrill Beach on Orcas Island.

10:56 a.m.   Urgent marine information broadcast sent to all boats in the area. Port Angeles helicopter activated, and U.S. Coast Guard rescue center in Seattle notified.

10:58 a.m.   Bellingham Coast Guard station received a phone call about the incident [Note: probably Marion's].

11:00 a.m.   San Juan County Sheriff reported one person on shore and one still missing.

11:06 a.m.   Helicopter airborne.

11:07 a.m.   Vessel *Misty George* answered the broadcast to announce they were thirty minutes to the scene.

11:20 a.m.   Orcas Island Fire Department reported all rescued; no further assistance required.

bungie cords loose from their eyelets. At the same time the snap-down rear hatch cover came loose. Bob managed to hang on to the hatch cover and get it back in place. Again he tried to climb up over the stern, but a large wave crested and broke down on top of him, knocking the hatch free again. With only a five-gallon bucket for flotation to back up the hatch, the rear compartment began to take on water. The bow gear bag again floated out of the cockpit and the bucket floated out of the rear hatch opening. Within seconds the bow had sunk, and Bob's confidence sank with it. The thought of dying again surfaced. Bob managed to grab the gear bag and put an arm through its handle loop for flotation. Since there was now only eighteen inches of kayak stern sticking out of the water, he put his other arm through the big grab loop at the stern. The waves jostled the kayak around and repeatedly banged it into him. But without a PFD, the kayak and gear bag were all he had to keep him afloat

During this time, Robert had been losing sight of the others for increasing periods of time. He could only see them when he and one of the others were on a wave crest at the same time. Although the waves had gotten much larger, he wasn't having too much trouble controlling his kayak. He stayed on course toward the car, until quite suddenly he found himself upside down in the water. (As is usually the case in a sudden capsize by a novice, he had no idea why he tipped over.)

Robert struggled, his neoprene spray deck popped loose, and he tumbled out of the cockpit. When his head broke the surface he saw several items from inside his cockpit floating around him: the seat, his paddle, two gear bags from the bow, and an empty plastic jug. He righted the kayak and began putting these

11:25 a.m. Helicopter directed to stand down. Pilot landed at Orcas Island Airport to talk with the Sheriff.

This report doesn't confirm that the trawler *Horizon* received the urgent marine broadcast, but it seems likely. As for the Coast Guard, their role in the events is now clear.

Quartermaster Helle has been involved in several searches for kayakers. His three main gripes about sea kayakers are: 1) They don't hear or pay enough attention to the weather reports (and therefore paddle when they should wait it out on shore); 2) they don't carry flares or other locating devices, and are therefore hard to locate from the air if in need of aid; and 3) they don't leave good float plans with their friends and relatives that would enable the Coast Guard to find them easily should they be reported overdue. According to Quartermaster Helle, the Coast Guard would rather check up on several instances of overdue paddlers than respond to one emergency caused by paddlers trying to return so as not to worry their relatives or have anyone come to check up on them. A good float plan includes the types and colors of the kayaks as well as the planned itinerary and expected time of return. Remember to check in with the person holding the float plan at the end of the trip.

items back into the cockpit, but they kept floating back out again and he had trouble retrieving them all. Like Bob, Robert realized he had to make a choice; he let the seat and jug go, but managed to save the paddle and gear bags. He shoved the gear bags as far into the bow as he could and tried getting the water out with a plastic bailer that had been tied to the kayak by a cord. As waves broke over the kayak, he soon realized that bailing was futile.

Robert was wearing two sets of tight-fitting polypropylene underwear, Gore-Tex coat and rain pants, gloves, and a life jacket. He climbed back into the swamped kayak, surprised at how easy it was compared to what he had heard. He later recalled thinking that perhaps this was because the swamped kayak was so low in the water. (As a rock climber, he probably had the benefits of strength and excellent balance.)

Once back in the kayak, he discovered what many before him have learned: A swamped kayak has no inherent stability. He immediately capsized again and climbed back in, this time sitting with his legs hanging over the sides. Outrigger legs gave him a little more stability, but he had more trouble keeping the gear bags from slipping out. He capsized again—and again, and again—but each time he got back in and found himself able to keep the swamped kayak upright a little longer as his technique improved. He learned to avoid being broadside to the waves. Facing straight downwind, he tried paddling toward the beach, but he soon broached and capsized again. No problem—he was getting a lot of practice at reentering the kayak and could now do it quickly. He tried turning to face into the waves. This worked much better and, although he was facing in a direction opposite to where he wanted to go, he could paddle backwards and no longer had any problem with broaching. The bow was so low in the water that each wave washed over it, hitting him in the chest. But he was making progress toward shore. Robert assumed that everyone in the group was in the water as well, and he felt that he needed to get to shore to get help for the others.

Meanwhile, farther southwest, Emily and Marion reached the breakers on the shore. A person on shore helped them with the landing, and they started back up the beach on foot, looking for Robert and Bob. They assumed the two men had made it to shore before them, since the last time they had seen them the guys had been a little ahead of them, and headed directly toward the cars. As Emily and Marion went east along the beach, they spotted Robert bobbing around on the waves several hundred yards offshore. Things didn't look right: He was turned in the wrong direction and seemed too low in the water. He was, however, progressing toward shore. Marion waited for him and Emily continued along the beach looking for Bob.

After Robert arrived and got out of his kayak, a man with binoculars spotted Bob and his kayak's stern floating offshore to the northeast. When they heard, Marion and Robert ran over to some cabins for help; one occupant offered to call the San Juan County Sheriff. Marion called the Coast Guard; after she described the situation, she was calmly told that, yes, they would look into it.

By this time Robert was feeling very cold. He was shivering but was certain that he was in no real danger, because he had felt colder on a previous occasion—at the finish of a marathon in bad weather. He took a hot shower at the cabin where he had gone for help. He was still cold after the hot water ran out, so the cabin occupants put him in bed and gave him warm drinks. By the time the medics took Robert's temperature, it was back to normal.

We left Bob hanging onto the upturned end of his kayak (and gear bag) being jostled around in the rough waves. At one point, when this had been going on for about fifteen minutes, he was hit so hard on the head by the kayak that he felt he had almost been knocked out. He again thought he was going to die. He also began to think that staying with the kayak in these conditions was a mistake. He assumed that everyone in the group was in the water and thus would not be looking for him, so he decided to swim for shore.

He slid the handle of the extra-large gear bag, containing a tent and sleeping bag, up to his shoulder and held it under his chest and belly for flotation. After fifteen minutes of breast-stroking, he had only made it about halfway to shore. By this time he had been in the chilly water for over thirty minutes. Bob was fading fast, and he knew it. He struggled to maintain consciousness.

Earl Trivett and his family, staying at Smuggler's Villa, noticed people running around by the beach. Earl went down to investigate, thinking help might be needed, and was told there was a drowning man in the water. Earl spotted the end of the kayak sticking out of the water. He and his son Dan jumped aboard their 25-foot powerboat and got it started.

Emily had also gotten to a phone and called the fire department. Meanwhile, the trawler *Horizon* arrived on the scene and threw Bob a life ring. Unable to lift a helpless man over the side, however, the crew tried to launch a 12-foot dingy to help in the rescue. Then Earl and Dan Trivett arrived, and the *Horizon* stood off to block the wind and calm the seas. The Trivetts made three passes before they were able to reach Bob with their boat hook. Dan stood on the swim platform

Buoyancy

Most of us *know* the rules of buoyancy: It is needed at bow and stern, it must be secure, and it must be backed up in as many ways as possible. But just how much buoyancy does a kayak need? It requires as much as will be required to keep the cockpit well clear of the surface with the boat fully swamped and your weight on the afterdeck or across the cockpit. A heavy paddler will need a boat large enough to contain sufficient buoyancy to float his or her weight.

To see how this works in practice, swamp your boat with a full gear load in it. See how quickly you can pump out your boat in the best circumstances, and try to imagine how this might be affected by waves sweeping over the cockpit. Experiment thoroughly in controlled conditions and take no piece of equipment for granted: Even the simplest hand pump can fail you. (Without a wrap of closed-cell foam around the shaft, most hand pumps will actually sink. Without a tether of some sort, a pump that floats might well float away.)

with one arm locked on the rail, and with the other hand got a good grip on Bob.

Although they are strong, it was all Dan and Earl could do to lift Bob over the side and into their boat. Bob was incoherent as the Trivetts took him into the boat's warm cabin for the trip back to shore. Within five minutes a fire department aid car arrived, and Bob was loaded onto a stretcher for the trip to the hospital. Bob remembers passing out and waking up several times as he was being rescued. In the hospital he had hypothermic convulsions for forty-five minutes, and his core temperature was 88°F (31°C).

LESSONS LEARNED

Bob's list of things he learned from this incident is long. He wishes he'd had charts, current tables, a wetsuit, a sea sock, more secure bow flotation, a more secure rear hatch cover, flares, and a Sea Seat. He feels he should have worn his life jacket, and learned how to Eskimo roll and perform a self rescue in rough seas. He thinks a rudder, which he was accustomed to using with his double, would have helped him to avoid the most turbulent area near Parker Reef, where he capsized.

Paddlers must have the latest marine weather report, the best tide and current information, and knowledge of their location. If this group had used a VHF weather radio and heard the marine forecast, they may well have canceled the trip or changed it to a shore paddle. They encountered an Arctic Outbreak pouring cold air over the mountains and producing northeast winds over thirty knots. Most Arctic Outbreaks happen from December through February, and in this region there are up to four of them each winter. Typically, they last about three days, but they have been known to last up to three weeks. It was a very cold November in the area that year, with temperatures in the low teens compared to the average mid-winter temperature of 40°F (4.5°C).

Considering the inexperience of this group with single kayaks and rescues and their lack of safety equipment, a two-mile crossing over any body of cold water, especially without wetsuits or drysuits and signalling devices, would seem to carry an unacceptable level of risk. Adding to that the time of year, the wind, and the currents, this group was in fact well out on a limb. In describing this route (which was also *his* first kayak trip ever), Randel Washburne, in his book *Kayaking Puget Sound, the San Juans & Gulf Islands* (Mountaineers, 1990), states: ". . . this route attracts large numbers of paddlers during the summer months, novices included, to the point that I hesitated in giving it the exposed rating. However, the potential for risk remains (as the record unfortunately shows), and so does my rating."

Turning around and going back if waves are too big may seem like a good idea. But this group probably would not have been able to make much progress against wind and waves severe enough to make them turn back. A better plan might be to paddle to one side out of the protected area and then see how much progress can be made into the more exposed conditions. Then, if the group decides to start the crossing, everyone would realize the degree of commitment involved.

This group realized that the farther you are from shore as you paddle downwind, the bigger the waves will be. (This is true only up to a point, until the seas become "fully developed," but generally it is true for winds over fifteen knots.) This situation often can be deceptive: A paddler doesn't see anything but small waves nearby and can't see how rough the waves really are in the distance.

The change in the tide is unlikely to be the time of slack current. Therefore, tide tables cannot be used to predict current direction or strength unless you are very familiar with the area. Even though Bob was using only tide tables, the group did in fact make the crossing at what would be considered slack current. However, in this area it is impossible to predict the speed or even the direction of the current, even when using the best information available. Because of the fast currents to the east and west of Orcas Island and the topography of the area, to the north of the island is an area of huge swirling eddies and changing patterns of currents that often run in the opposite direction to that predicted in the *Current Atlas*. What's more, there never is a true slack current because of the momentum of these rotating eddies. (Currents up to two knots have been encountered at slack.) The more you study the area where you'll be making paddling trips, the better equipped you'll be to handle surprises in current speed and direction.

As this group discovered, when paddling conditions are bad, communications and keeping track of each other at sea becomes difficult. Staying together is the rule; however, when all group members are in very difficult conditions, it's probably best if at least one kayak makes it to shore, especially if help is close at hand. Since this group was already separated, they didn't have to risk an unpracticed rescue that might have put everyone in the water. In fact, in this particular situation, staying together might have resulted in tragedy. The trailing double would have been much more vulnerable if it had stayed sideways to the wind and not turned away from the agreed-upon on course. Furthermore, if they had stayed together, they might have attempted to raft up but may all have been swept into that dangerous area of turbulence. They could easily have become scattered anyway, each doing his or her best to paddle out of imminent danger. For a group with a repertoire of well-practiced rescues, staying together would have been better; avoiding paddling in these conditions in the first place would have been the ideal.

In rough conditions it's all the more important that you know your equipment. Practicing all possible situations with the equipment you'll be using is more important than having the best, most expensive equipment. Different models of kayaks traveling in wind often settle at different angles to the wind; as Robert and Bob discovered, this can happen even with kayaks of the same model if they are trimmed differently. This tends to separate paddlers, as each finds it more of an effort to maintain the course favored by the other's kayak. A rudder—or skill at handling a kayak without one—usually can compensate for differences in kayaks, even if it means taking a slightly zigzag course to avoid having to hold a difficult angle to the wind and waves.

Both Robert and Bob were novices at handling single kayaks and should not have paddled an exposed location in conditions beyond their expertise. Bob had the added disadvantage of being without a rudder, which he was accustomed to using; his automatic responses no longer applied. He may have been having more trouble than Robert because of his previous learning getting in the way of new learning. (Note: From his description, I would guess that Bob was being broached by the quartering seas. Given short, steep wind waves, this can be a difficult control situation even for an expert paddler using a rudder.)

Had Robert and Bob been more familiar with their equipment, they may have realized that a kayak with a relatively small bow storage area compared to the space between the foot braces may need a way to secure float bags and gear bags so they can't float out. If these had been their own kayaks, Bob might also have been familiar with the potential vulnerability of the rear hatch and backed it up with secure flotation inside and cords, rather than simple bungies, over the outside. Robert may have fastened his seat more securely or secured it with a short cord as Bob's was. (Later models of the Sea Otter have a more secure hatch and seat.)

They probably were correct in assuming that too much weight in the stern was one of the factors making it difficult for Bob to stay on course on the way to Sucia Island. Unfortunately, they "corrected" the trim on Bob's Sea Otter before the return trip to Orcas Island. With a following or quartering sea, the original stern-heavy trim would have made course-keeping far easier. (For the same reason, Robert found he could easily move backward in the direction of the waves without being broached, but he could not do the same when paddling forward. The bow of his kayak was nearly sunk and therefore was difficult to move to the side, but the stern was floating high and was easily pushed around by the wind and waves, tending to point the "anchored" bow into the wind and waves.) Packing the kayak bow-heavy for upwind travel and stern-heavy for downwind travel will help you stay on course. However, if you have to turn around and paddle in the opposite direction without being able to shift the trim, control will become more difficult.

Everyone in the group had worn life jackets except Bob; he had put his behind his seat. This meets Coast Guard requirements; unfortunately, however, many kayakers have found that once conditions start to get rough it seems more risky to stop and try to put on the life jacket than it is to keep your hands on the paddle ready to brace. A loose life jacket usually will float away in a capsize, but it is against Coast Guard regulations to fasten a life jacket to a boat. There is *no* regulation against fastening the PFD to your person. Most PFDs come with armholes and zippers or clips to make this easy (a good thing, since a modified PFD no longer meets Coast Guard requirements).

7

Sea Caves, Arches, and Narrow Passages

Matt Broze

Only a small percentage of kayakers paddle rocky coastlines regularly, but I've found that a rather high percentage of those who do have had at least one close call. Anyone who may someday paddle a rocky coast should find the following of interest. I'm sure there are hundreds more incidents among coastal paddlers that remain untold.

Joel Rogers is a freelance outdoor photographer whose pictures and articles on photography have graced the pages of *Sea Kayaker*. At the time of this incident, he had been sea kayaking for six years without so much as one unexpected capsize, although capsizes while playing in the surf are expected. Joel can Eskimo roll.

In May, 1986, Joel and Glen Sims, an even more experienced paddler, led one intermediate and two novice paddlers on a trip through Vancouver Island's popular Barkley Sound. On the second day out they battled strong headwinds during the crossing to the outer islands of the Broken Group. Ross Anderson's wrist became swollen from tendonitis, probably as a result of the tendency among novices to grip the paddle shaft too tightly when the situation gets tense. Ross also was having trouble maintaining a course with his Sea Horse kayak (he said later he thought a rudder would have helped). As is often the case, the experienced paddlers had no problem with control even without rudders and felt the winds were moderate.

The next day Ross decided to stay behind at the Clarke Island camp to nurse his swollen wrist. Carol Ostrom, Sarah Shannon, and Glen and Joel planned to make a day paddle around some of the outer islands and then return to their camp on Clarke.

Having had hundreds of miles pass under his Polaris II without a capsize, often in waters far rougher than these, Joel had become lax about safety. The possibility of a capsize on a nice day in old familiar Barkley Sound appeared extremely remote. Being an excellent swimmer, Joel had even decided to make this trip without a life jacket; his had been unavailable just prior to departure and, since he knew he would be getting it back, he couldn't justify buying a new one just for this trip.

As he prepared for the short day paddle that morning, the thought never crossed his mind that his kayak would be without flotation with most of his gear bags left at camp. He did have a sea sock (a fabric cockpit liner that reduces the amount of water that can get into the kayak) and decided to take it in case the wind came up later in the day and made the seas rougher. Still not considering his kayak's temporary lack of flotation, he stuffed the rolled-up sea sock back behind his seat.

The group paddled to the sea lion rocks just west of Wouwer Island but found no sea lions there. A narrow slot between the rocks caught Joel and Glen's interest. It was fifteen to twenty feet wide; about seventy-five feet back it

Rescuing a Sunken Kayak

A kayak that has sunk at one or both ends can be rescued. Derek Hutchinson describes this curl rescue in his books *The Complete Book of Sea Kayaking* (Globe Pequot, 1995) and *Derek C. Hutchinson's Guide to Sea Kayaking* (Globe Pequot, 1990). To perform the curl rescue, raise the sunken kayak level and parallel to the rescuer's kayak. Keep the victim's kayak upside down if possible to avoid losing any air that is trapped inside the kayak and having to crawl completely over the rescuer's deck to reach the coaming of your kayak.

The capsize victim reaches over the deck of the rescuer's kayak and finds a point on the kayak that is strong and comfortable to press his forearms against. He then grasps the coaming rim of his kayak with both hands, palms up. He pulls the kayak toward him until the coaming is against the rescuing kayak and his forearms and wrists (not elbows) are pressing against the rescuer's deck. The rescuer slowly tilts her kayak while the victim holds tightly to this position. The rescuer should be prepared to brace if the victim's position shifts or he releases the kayak from his grip. Much of the water can now be drained from the cockpit as the kayak is slowly lifted. The kayak is then flipped back upright and a side rescue is carefully executed to minimize the taking on of any additional water. The remaining water is then pumped, bailed, or sponged from the kayak.

widened out into an open area that was partially protected from the six- to eight-foot ocean swell by a rock garden. Small breaking waves were coming down the narrow channel toward them. Joel and Glen discussed going through the passage; Joel decided to do just that. Seeing the potential for problems in the channel, however, he handed his large camera bag to Sarah. The sea sock, which he could easily have installed at that time, remained behind his seat.

Joel paddled into the passage, timing things carefully in order to paddle over the shallow spots just after a breaker had passed, when the water was sufficiently deep. Upon arriving at the wider, tennis court–sized open area at the end of the channel, he found it was rougher than he had anticipated. He had a hard time holding his position in the two- to three-foot breakers, which came at him from several angles because the swell had been reflected and refracted on its way through the rocks to the west. He paddled directly into each breaker—letting it drag him back again as it passed—to maintain his position. Because the breakers kept Joel busy and limited his vision, finding the best route to take from that point was difficult. He had three possible courses: Go forward into either of two more open routes through the rocks in front of him that went out into the swell to the west; or turn around and go back the way he'd come.

Joel feared that if he turned around he would capsize or be dragged into the rocks behind him if one of the broken waves caught him sideways before he could completely turn around. The broken waves were frequent, and he doubted he could spin his boat around quickly enough. Of the two options remaining, the route to the left looked the most feasible. Joel concentrated on it as much as he could while fighting to hold his position. With the waves coming at him from several directions, he was near the limits of his paddling ability. He observed what he could for the next few minutes, but when a smaller wave finally came down the passage, Joel decided to go for it while he had the chance.

Joel paddled hard into the passage, hoping to get over a shallow plateau before the wave receded from it. Unfortunately, the small breaker held him back longer than he had anticipated, and before he could clear the plateau, the water began pouring back out into the much deeper wave trough that followed. The sudden withdrawal of water into the next trough was like a very small version of the sudden low tide that precedes a tidal wave.

Joel was rushed forward over the shallow plateau with the receding water; a six-foot-deep hole opened before him at the edge of the plateau. The water rushing out created a waterfall into the hole. Joel shot over the lip and dropped between gaping jaws of rock. He braced as he landed in the trough. The next wave hit and capsized him. Joel got into position to roll up. But before he had a chance to do so the wave spat him out of the hole and washed him back to where, seconds before, he had started his dash. But this time he was upside down and hanging partway out of his kayak. His paddle was gone. He exited from his cockpit quickly in order to get some air and see where he was. When he surfaced and reoriented himself, he saw his paddle twenty feet away to the west in another part of the rock garden. His kayak was near the passage he had come through. He righted his boat; at last it dawned on him that there was no flotation in it and there was a good chance it might sink. He didn't dare leave the kayak to recover his paddle; the paddle was not terribly important because he knew another paddler in the group had a spare paddle.

Glen had lost sight of Joel and became concerned. He paddled around to the outside of the rock garden, hoping to get a better view and find Joel without having to go in himself. He could find no sign of Joel and headed back to the protected side near the entrance where Sarah and Carol waited.

Meanwhile, Joel started swimming back out the seventy-five-foot-long channel, pushing his kayak in front of him. Soon he came upon a place where he could climb out. He tried to haul his kayak up high enough to dump it out, but the wave action was such that he couldn't manage it. He swam his kayak through the channel to just outside the entrance and tried again to empty it. The others were happy to see him—even though he was out of his boat and struggling valiantly with it on near-vertical, barnacle-covered rocks.

Leaky Hatches and Flotation

Dan Ruuska, the designer/builder of the Polaris II, has long maintained that float bags are safer than hatches ("which leak") and bulkheads ("which trap the leakage inside waterproof compartments"). As a result, Dan makes no provision for the large hatches that bulkheads require. He makes sure his customers know the necessity of keeping a maximum amount of flotation in each end of a kayak. If they choose not to pay attention or become lax about safety, then in Dan's view this is their problem rather than a problem with the system.

Dan has a point. A friend of mine had his kayak's hull crack open next to a bulkhead. There have been several reports of hatches slowly leaking and sinking one end of a solo paddler's kayak; these solo paddlers had no way to empty the compartment from the cockpit. (Some recommend a small plugged hole in the bulkhead as a means to drain the leaking compartment into the cockpit area where the water can be more easily dealt with, but this may not work unless the leak is noticed early enough. Water from the sinking end will not run uphill on its own.)

I am quite comfortable with the system in which float bags or large waterproof gear bags are loaded through the open cockpit. This is a convenient and inexpensive method of flotation. If I'm going into a situation where a capsize is likely, such as playing in surf, or where a capsize could add considerable risk, as in exposed crossings, I add a sea sock to back up the float bags. Some paddlers dislike blowing up float bags: I use an air compressor or vacuum cleaner when I can. However, since I leave the float bags inflated either inside or outside of my kayak during storage, I rarely have to do more than top off the air. This way I can also be sure they aren't developing a leak (which has been rare—and repairable). For a multi-day trip I pack deflated float bags or keep them inflated and use them to hold a small gear load in place and provide additional flotation. Then I can

Joel continued to wrestle with his kayak, trying to get one end of it caught on a rock so he could slowly lift the other end to spill the water out of the cockpit. He lost the boat three or four times while trying to empty it out as waves banged the boat into him, shoved him against the mussels and rock, or dumped him back into the water.

Glen saw a big wave come down the channel and knock Joel down on jagged encrustations of mussels and barnacles and then drop him into the sea. Joel went under in the danger zone next to the rock, and Glen guessed at that point that his friend had about a fifty-fifty chance of surviving. He wondered how he and the others would rescue Joel if he was seriously injured.

Thankfully, Joel surfaced and climbed back onto the rock. His legs were bruised and scraped. The breakers coming from the mouth of the channel had carried his kayak away, and he knew he had to think of some other way to empty it—he had lost a shoe and, with a bare foot, could no longer firmly brace himself among the mussel shells and slippery seaweed. He was surprised

---

choose to paddle with just day gear and the duly inflated float bags while leaving most of my gear in dry bags at camp.

Having said this, I empathize with *Sea Kayaker's* founding editor John Dowd, who argues that moderately leaking hatches are potentially less disastrous than leaking airbags. John insists, especially with beginners, that no reasonable safety feature, such as bulkheads, be excluded from a kayak. Even the most experienced paddlers, no matter how much they've been warned of the importance of keeping buoyancy inflated in a boat, will sometimes fail to provide it; second owners or friends often do not have the benefit of a manufacturer's or retailer's warning that the boat requires additional means of buoyancy or suggestions for securing this buoyancy in the kayak. To John, the safety advantages of bulkheads outweigh their disadvantages, though he considers it important to back them up with airbags or waterproof gear bags.

A backup is the most reliable protection against a dangerous failure. A sea sock can back up float bags in the same way that airbags or waterproof gear bags can back up a bulkhead-and-hatch system. (A sea sock, however, can't back up deck hatches or a leaky hull, so it should always be used in conjunction with some other means of flotation.) Split airbags might be considered a better backup than standard ones because there are two bags in each end of the kayak instead of one. However, it has been my experience that, unless there is a wall between them or a bulkhead to hold them in, split bags are much more likely to slip out than a single larger bag is.

Many people promote one kind of system (for or against rudders; for or against bulkheads; large versus small cockpits; etc.). But what works best for someone else might not work best for you; it's up to you to study the options and make an informed choice. Understand the strong and weak points of the system you choose and then back up that system— you will be far safer than you would using *any* system that you haven't yet played with and analyzed for weaknesses.

More Lessons in Arches

Caution in Following Waves

Many years ago, Dennis and Ingrid Hansen were taking their first coastal kayak trip without their mentor; paddling with them was David Arcese, at that time a novice. Dennis elected to take a shortcut through a sea arch, but Ingrid and David chose to go around.

Dennis paddled hard toward the arch. The following waves surfed him along, and his kayak turned as the wave crest he was riding pushed his stern along faster than the bow—a broach. A broach is difficult to control and even harder to correct. The bow of Dennis's Nordkapp caught on a rock in the arch, and he was turned over and completely sideways. The next wave swept through the arch and flushed him out the other side. Dennis had not yet learned to roll; to make matters worse, he was stuck in the cockpit.

Ingrid and David could see Dennis struggling to extricate himself and get air. They had to get to him quickly. If they ran the arch and the same thing happened to them, the situation would no doubt be worse. Luckily, there was another, easier passage next to the arch. They made it through without incident and were able to twist Dennis's kayak around enough that he could get his legs out. (Don't take this to mean that small cockpits such as the Nordkapp's—15" by 19"—are hard to get out of in a capsize. Dennis was wearing a new pair of big boots that he wasn't used to, and he has an artificial leg. The lack of articulation at the ankle, new boots, rain pants, and his twisted position in the kayak combined to hold him in.) Although exit from a small cockpit can be more difficult if you are also trying to keep the kayak upright, most paddlers can slip out of a small cockpit after capsizing almost as easily as they can from a larger one.

Dennis said he learned from the experience that if the swell is coming from behind you, go through an opening slowly so you don't start surfing out of control. If you are looking at a narrow passageway, or even a rock-strewn beach, remember that by going against the waves you have better directional control than you have going with them. It is also far easier to keep an eye on oncoming waves than it is to keep track of those coming from behind. Ingrid says she and Dennis have gone through the same arch six times since the incident, without problems.

Think Ahead

Another paddler had an experience that illustrates another lesson. He and another paddler came to a small sea arch on Bartlett Island (north of Tofino on Vancouver Island). Larger swells in the set would fill the arch, but during smaller swells there was room to go through it and into a large, open room with an open top. He went in during a lull. The room was smaller than it had looked; there was barely enough room to turn his 16-foot kayak around. If the room had been any smaller, he would have had to back out. To make matters worse, the waters in the room were surging around with the swell.

Although this paddler had watched the swells going in and had timed his entrance for a lull, once inside he discovered he could no longer see the waves. He wished he had foreseen the problem before he'd gone in. To be caught in the passageway when bigger swells came through would to find his Nikonos underwater camera still around his neck; almost by reflex he snapped off a picture of his kayak's stern pointing skyward and his sea sock floating just beyond it. It was a desolate scene, in spite of beautiful surroundings.

Glen tried to get a life jacket to Joel, but the wind made this impossible to do safely without bringing his kayak dangerously close to waves crashing on that rugged shore. Instead, Joel dove in, swam out to the life jacket, and put it on. Glen also gave Joel some polypro warm-up pants. The group tried several times to hoist Joel's vertical kayak over the decks of the other boats in order to dump some of the water out, but all attempts failed.

The Polaris was now lower in the water than ever. Carol and Sarah could tell Joel was getting colder. It was hard to get his attention, and he didn't seem to be thinking clearly. At one point Glen reached his paddle out to Joel to pull him in closer; the paddle came apart at the joint, but instead of giving his half back to Glen so he could paddle, Joel absentmindedly handed it to Sarah. Glen also noticed Joel was losing strength and beginning to show signs of hypothermia—shivering and slurred speech. He knew they had to get Joel to a warm place quickly. Carol suggested that she climb into the Wind Dancer's large cockpit

mean he would be crushed between the roof of the arch and the kayak's hundreds of pounds of bouyancy. A capsize or wet exit could save him; but the arch was only three or four feet wide—not wide enough to capsize. There wasn't enough room to paddle either; he had to glide through the confined space under the arch on momentum. Although the arch was only about five feet long, clearing the distance would require considerably more glide than he could get from a few quick strokes in the small open area, unless he also timed his exit to coincide with the outflowing surge.

He couldn't stay in the room long because the rough waters were banging him around. What's more, the tide was coming in, and the longer he waited the lower the ceiling of the arch would be. The height of the arch now varied with the swell between zero and four feet.

The paddler decided to play Russian roulette with the waves on the next outgoing surge rather than later, when more cham-

bers might be loaded. Luckily for him, he exited on an empty chamber.

Beware Your Own Buoyancy

Jim Vermillion wasn't so lucky. A member of the Aleutian Kayak Expedition, which has paddled parts of the Aleutian chain for several years, Jim was on a paddling trip in 1984 with George Peck, Burrel Thorne, and Doug Van Etten. During one day's paddle they had visited many caves and arches. The following day, Burrel, Doug, and Jim spotted the first arch of the day well ahead of them. During the approach they could see that every fifth wave was reaching the roof. Jim and Burrel joked about running the arch and baited each other about whose kayak could fit through. The arch was more or less lightbulb shaped, only a few feet wide when the bigger troughs went by but about eight feet wide at the "bulb." The top was jagged, broken rock, with several large pointed "teeth" hanging down.

(continued on page 66)

with Sarah so Joel could use her Enetai. Glen and Joel didn't seem to hear her repeated suggestion while they struggled with the Polaris. They just couldn't seem to refloat the kayak.

The nearby shore of Wouwer Island was all vertical rock. Towing Joel the nearly one-half mile around the south of Wouwer would leave him in the water for far too long. Glen had carried smaller people on his afterdeck but assumed a 190-pound load on the back would make his empty Escape very unstable. They still had to go through some big, confused seas to get around to the protected side of Wouwer Island, where they could land. The thought of what another capsize would do to their situation made carrying Joel on a deck seem risky, especially since Glen was now uncertain, after seeing what had happened to Joel's kayak, that the gear-bag flotation in his own bow was adequate. Furthermore, a kayak's afterdeck would still be a relatively exposed position for somebody already showing signs of hypothermia.

Glen was very comfortable with switching kayaks on the water, since he had done it often. He wondered whether he should ask Carol and Sarah to take the risk of Carol's climbing into the large cockpit of Sarah's Wind Dancer. Just as he turned to suggest this to Carol (who perhaps had planted just that idea in his subconscious earlier), she suggested it again, more forcefully this time to make sure she was heard. They agreed, and rafted up together with Sarah in the middle. They bridged paddles across the kayaks, and Joel held the ends together from his position in the water. Carol climbed into Sarah's boat and sat in front of her on the floor; Carol would paddle and Sarah would work the rudder. Glen then helped Joel do an uneventful side rescue into the Enetai.

(continued from page 65)

When they arrived, Jim waited until after the regular fifth wave close-out and took off to shoot through the opening. Burrel was farther out and saw a much bigger wave coming from a direction that wasn't part of the normal swell. He hollered at Jim to stop but it was too late; Jim was already surfing the counter-surge down into the archway. He was committed, so he poured on the speed, trying to clear the arch before the out-of-sequence wave hit. When he started the elevator ride up he knew he wouldn't make it; he thought about capsizing but didn't want to be upside down for the ride back down into the narrow slot at the bottom. He instinctively braced off the roof with his paddle and ducked his head down into the blessedly large cockpit of his Polaris II. The fiberglass paddle shaft (one of the strongest in the industry) broke in two over his back. A rock tooth was jammed against his shoulder blade and shattered it as he was smashed down into his cockpit. He also suffered a compressed thoracic vertebra and a couple of cracked ribs. (A stainless steel cup tied to his flexible back deck was embossed to a depth of a quarter-inch.)

Burrel was sickened as he heard the crunching and grinding noises coming from his friend's kayak. Even with his injuries, Jim could still hold the two halves of his paddle; although one arm didn't work well, he was able to paddle out after the wave

In position in the Wind Dancer, Sarah and Carol both were able to get in the zippered spray deck, but they couldn't quite zipper it all the way closed. Sarah held up the chimney, but the rough confused seas splashed in a considerable amount of water. Sarah, no longer exerting herself paddling, began to feel cold. The two women had problems coordinating ruddering and paddling; this, combined with the bow-heavy trim, made staying on course difficult, especially when they went through steep following swells in the shallows off the southern tip of Wouwer.

They landed on Wouwer Island at a place where there were other kayakers and three double kayaks on shore. Joel had been able to paddle, but Sarah noticed that he staggered as he got out of the Enetai. Joel was shivering, but he also was laughing and he appeared drunk. Sarah dressed him in the dry clothes they had carried and gave him some high-calorie snacks. Joel asked for a beer, but Sarah and Carol, knowing the effects of alcohol on hypothermia, refused to let him have one. Sarah laid down with him on some warm, dry sand to warm him.

Meanwhile, Glen had been towing Joel's Polaris II by its bow painter. In the process of getting the bow end up rather than the stern (which didn't have a painter), they had lost even more of the kayak's trapped air, and it was no longer floating. Glen wasn't about to tie himself or his Escape to a sunken boat and foolishly paddle that huge anchor through the steep swells without being able to drop it quickly, so he held the line in his hand as he paddled. Remarkably, he moved it about a quarter-mile using this "paddle and tug" method.

On the beach, the others had been having little success convincing anyone to

had passed. Burrel and Doug towed him two miles back to camp in his own kayak, which had suffered only chips and gouges and remained seaworthy.

Back at camp, Jim wondered whether he could have flopped over sideways on a brace. He thought he would probably have had time to brace back up before dropping into the narrow slot. When Burrel photographed the arch later, the men could see that the kayak on edge might have wedged between two of the huge "teeth" on the top, in which case Jim could have been literally sheared off at the waist.)

The men used an ELT (Emergency Locating Transmitter—the aircraft equivalent of a Class B EPIRB) to call for help via satellite. Later that day a C130 transport plane flew by but had nowhere to land. The men were beyond helicopter range. A storm came up and, as a result, more than two days elapsed before a trawler was able to transport Jim to an airport.

Even when a kayak is fully loaded, as Jim's was, there are still hundreds of pounds of reserve buoyancy left to push you into a ceiling. That would be the equivalent of a weight equal to the buoyancy falling on you. Lacking room to roll, a quick capsize and wet exit would likely be the best move.

help Glen. Carol and Sarah offered to buy dinner for any helpers; the response was protests about it being "rough out there." Finally, Carol and Sarah said they weren't very experienced, but if they could borrow someone's double, they would go back out to help. This shamed some of the others, who grudgingly took a double out to where Glen was crossing the shallows only three hundred

The Sirens

There is a special appeal to narrow passages. Kayakers want to paddle through them even when the hazards are obvious and the risks unwarranted. The sirens hanging out at arches and sea caves must be singing even more sweetly than usual, since they often lure paddlers who think of themselves as conservative.

The attraction to these areas is no doubt real, but so are the hazards. Waves combined with rock walls have the potential to make a capsize an abrasive experience, especially if the rocks are covered with mussels or barnacles. Capsize is especially likely in the presence of big waves surging through passages or breaking over the rocks or shallows in them. Currents caused by the surge create swirling eddies that could easily spin a kayak around—that is, if there were enough room for it to spin. There also is the combination of low ceilings and occasional larger swells or rogue waves. Being between a breaking wave and a rock, with or without your kayak, is never a very good position.

Some of my more foolish moments as a kayaker include paddles through arches. I will never forget one narrow arch on the Washington coast. Although two friends had just paddled through it, it looked pretty marginal to me. It was long and narrow, and the swell was going up and down five or six feet in it. There wasn't much surging, but huge mussel shells protruded from the walls like instruments in some medieval

torture chamber. The unspoken challenge had been handed down; would I back down or follow in the wake of the more daring before me? My companions had had no problems and, as long as conditions stayed the same, I wasn't likely to either. (On the coast that's always the catch: Will the conditions stay the same?) Whether I followed or turned back, I stood a chance of losing face.

I put on the helmet that I had stored behind my seat for a later surf entry and surf practice. At least now I wouldn't be likely to lose an ear (or consciousness). The swell was small in the slot, so I paddled quickly down the roughly eight-foot-by-thirty-foot crack in the cliff. As I shot out the other side, I looked to the right for my friends but instead I saw the water sloping steeply up to a wave that was so big I had to tilt my head up to see the crest looming over me. Would it break? If so, where was I headed? I glanced left and saw the wall of a sheer cliff next to me. Luckily, the wave didn't break, and I settled for a fast elevator ride fifteen or twenty feet up and then down right next to the cliff as the wave bounced off. Joel Rogers and my brother, Cam, still waiting to follow me, watched the wave surge through that well-armored slot. They didn't really need me to wave them off; having seen what had just happened in the channel, they had wisely decided to turn back, even though that route, too, held its own challenges.

yards away. It would seem that in a double the stern paddler could hold the line of the sinking kayak, and the bow paddler could make headway. But the kayakers in the double kept their distance from Glen, presumably to offer moral support or a rescue if he capsized. At one point, the towline was yanked from between Glen's hand and the paddle as he rode up a steep swell. Sadly, Joel's kayak had lost its last link to the surface.

Joel spent the next hour warming up and mourning the loss of his boat. The group made the return trip to Clarke Island later that day. For that trip and for the next day's long paddle back to Toquart Bay, Carol sat down into the bow of Glen's Escape with her head on his belly, just high enough for her to see over the cockpit. She was more comfortable sitting higher, but then it was difficult for Glen to reach around her shoulders to paddle. Glen later said he didn't think they would have had any problem exiting the cockpit (16" by 35") had they capsized.

LESSONS LEARNED

There are some obvious errors that put these paddlers in danger: the lack of flotation and the missing life jacket. Joel knew the risks of not having plenty of flotation in the bow and stern, but his abilities had given him a false sense of security, and he no longer ran down the standard equipment checklist before setting out (see page 9).

Joel's only price for this lesson, besides the risk and inconvenience to his group, was the loss of a kayak, a paddle, and a little blood. He was lucky to be with paddlers willing to take risks to help him.

Even if it's unlikely that you'll have any problems on a paddling trip, the consequences of an accident should be your primary consideration. If you paddle often, eventually you'll run into trouble.

Many will think that if Joel's kayak had been fitted with fixed bulkheads or a pod (a molded plastic or fiberglass cockpit liner that functions like a rigid sea sock), he would still have it, because his flotation couldn't have been left behind. This may be true, but I wouldn't dismiss float bags this easily; the previous two chapters describe instances of hatch failure. Even the most watertight commercially available hatches have popped off when installed on airtight compartments. No system is foolproof. Whatever flotation system you choose, test it thoroughly to discover any weaknesses. Don't take somebody else's word for it.

Paddling groups can lose a kayak for a number of reasons. When preparing for a group paddle, practice carrying someone on the deck of a kayak; practice being both the victim and the rescuer. See if you can get both yourself and another adult into your cockpit—and back out again while upside down. Do this in shallow water with help standing alongside to right you if you fail.

8

Long Swims

Matt Broze

Some kayaking incidents I hear about are easy to track down, but this one took more effort than most. One of our Alaska readers sent us a copy of "Kayaker Rescued Friday," an Associated Press article published in the September 28, 1986, *Anchorage Daily News.* The article told of Richard Hudson, age 24, of Dawson City, Yukon Territories, who was rescued following satellite detection of an Emergency Locating Transmitter near Nome, Alaska. Hudson had swum to shore and started a fire after being swamped by two freak waves about a half-mile offshore. The article also mentioned that Hudson had suffered frostbite and hypothermia, and that he had left Dawson City three months earlier. From that I surmised he had paddled down the Yukon River. What were the details? Would there be some lessons in this for sea kayakers?

Directory Assistance had no listings for Hudsons in Dawson City or in the surrounding areas. The Seattle Coast Guard referred me to their Juneau, Alaska, office. I learned from the Coast Guard in Juneau that the Air Force had coordinated the rescue. The Elmendorf Civil Air Patrol suggested that the Alaskan State Troopers might know more, since they were actually on the scene. The State Troopers in Anchorage had no information but gave me the telephone number of their office in Nome. In Nome, Corporal Robert Yates, the officer on duty during the rescue, filled in more of the story. Better still, he had the phone number of Richard Hudson's parents in Ontario, Canada.

I reached Richard's brother and learned that, although it had been over a month since the accident, Richard was still in a local hospital being treated for third-degree frostbite of his feet. After spending all evening at the phone, I finally reached Richard himself in his hospital room. He was willing to share his story and later sent me a long letter describing the incident in detail. What appears here is an abridged version of his report.

"It was my second day out of Golovin, paddling my Sisiutl, a Pacific Water Sports double, toward Nome, and the end of a 1,700-mile trip. After an unusually stormy August and September (which slowed me down considerably), winter seemed to be coming early. I hadn't planned on encountering so much of these temperatures, but wanted to finish my trip nevertheless, since I had only about forty miles to go at this point. The air temperature was about 25°F (-4°C), and I estimate the water temperature was about 45°F (7°C). There was a ten- to fifteen-knot offshore wind blowing (from the north) and about three-foot seas coming from the south.

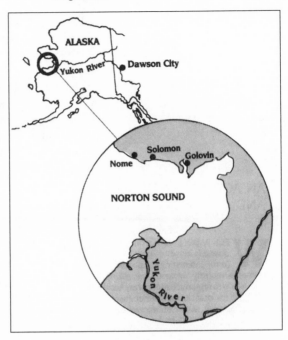

"I'd owned my double kayak for four years; had paddled along Great Slave Lake and the Mackenzie River, and now the entire Yukon River, among others, mostly alone. My kayak wasn't bombproof, but it would go fast when lightly loaded and carry enough gear to paddle all summer comfortably. It was the only kayak I'd had much experience with. I practiced paddle bracing a lot; I had great trouble rolling it when loaded. I had studied hypothermia as well, and had some experience with it. My swimming ability was not very good, but I almost always wore a life jacket. The boat was great for extensive flatwater touring, but was too big (for one man), pounded too much in waves (despite ballasting), and was too slow to maneuver (by one man) to be suitable for the ocean. [Note: Richard is six-foot, two-inches tall and two hundred pounds.] I had decided that, because of these problems with touring with it on the ocean, I would sell it at the end of my trip and get a smaller, one-man design for my next trip. I was doing this trip partly because the particular areas interested me, and partly as training and practice before I took on a bigger trip.

"I was wearing an army shirt/jacket that I wore ashore or afloat since it had so many pockets, rubber boots, pile pants with radiant barrier pants underneath, an army surplus anti-exposure suit, a warm toque, a PFD, a Gore-Tex parka, insulated gloves, and a spray skirt. Both cockpits had sea socks as well. [Note: The forward cockpit, used for storage, was fitted with a cockpit cover.] The anti-exposure suit is essentially a pair of coveralls made of rubber with canvas outside, probably not as warm as a wetsuit (I don't know for sure).

"I was heading due west along the beach, about half a mile offshore, parallel to the waves. It was about 9 P.M., sunset, and I was squinting into the sun. Perhaps I unknowingly drifted closer to the beach, or maybe it was just a shoal I was passing over. I saw a wave break in front of me, and I knew I had to turn quickly so another would not catch me broadside. I kicked the rudder hard left and paddled forward, hard on the right, trying to turn the bow into the waves. I was rising up on a wave and heard it start to break before I'd been able to turn appreciably. I leaned into the wave to brace up in case I needed it, but I don't think my paddle actually hit the water until I was bracing down on the other side, once already sideways in the water, that is, half-rolled. My buoyancy was preventing me from overturning completely. I rolled back up with a hard, sweeping brace, only to be knocked flat again immediately by another breaking wave. If I could have turned the boat perpendicular to the waves, I think I would have been able to recover, but turning was easier said than done in that position with a loaded kayak about twenty feet long at the waterline. I'd drunk enough salt water at this point that I decided to try something else.

"I pulled the spray skirt free of the coaming and slid out. Turning the boat over wasn't terribly difficult (wasn't easy, either), but I couldn't climb back in over the stern because of the rudder (last rudder I'll ever have on a kayak). The Sisiutl was too high to come in over the side, so I tried climbing in over the bow, but, as I inched my way back to the cockpit, the kayak capsized again. I thought hard about my situation. I knew that hypothermia would kill me soon if I didn't get out of the water. To be honest, I was afraid, because my chances of coming through okay were not looking good, but my strongest emotion was one of anger at myself for having gotten into such a situation. The more I thought of it, the more furious I got. Seemed like a good time for some autosuggestion, so I started shouting out, 'I will survive!' as loud as I could. This action—more, I think, than any other—saved my life. I'm not religious, but I figured I'd toss in a prayer as well, just in case. All this thinking in the water took less than five seconds, and I rolled the boat over again for another try at boarding. This failed, as did another try or two.

"I figured I had three options: 1) Keep trying to right the boat and paddle ashore; 2) swim ashore towing the boat; 3) abandon the boat and swim to shore. If I kept trying to right the boat and still failed, I figured I might be too hypothermic to make the shore by then. Swimming and towing the boat gave the advantage of having a boat full of gear to have on shore, but it would be a long swim towing a boat, and swimming cools you off very quickly. So, much as I hated to abandon it, it seemed the best choice (partly because I remembered passing the village of Solomon a few miles back). I kicked the rubber boots off and started swimming. I had gone less than twenty feet when I remembered I had left my Floater Coat in my kayak. I swam back, and grabbed it from in front of the rear cockpit. I always kept one pack of three Skyblazer flares (I have another pack in my parka, along with waterproof matches and fire-starting sticks), waterproof matches and lighters and Conglans Firesticks, and my EPIRB in pockets of my Floater Coat. My EPIRB, an ACR 21, Class B (full model #ACR/RLB-21), was a waterproof, non-floating, hand-held unit. The small fiberglass whip antenna was removable, there was an indicator light that cycled on and off when the unit was on (supposedly transmitting, also), and a fairly firm, rotation-type on-off switch. For carrying in a pocket of a jacket while wearing it, or for most other mountings, the switch would probably be sufficient safeguard against accidental operation. But mine stayed in a jacket which, when stored, was stuffed forcefully into a space in the boat; I figured it was possible to accidentally turn it on, and, not being able to see the operation light, send off a false distress signal. So I had put duct tape over the switch, which had to be removed before the switch could be turned on. I never realized that, in cold water, in a hurry, the duct tape would be too hard to take off with numb fingers. So, I put the switch in my teeth and turned, forcing it on. The indicator light went on (I later discovered that I had broken off half a tooth doing it), and I thought it was transmitting.

"I tried putting the floater coat on, to conserve heat, but couldn't get it on in the water (obviously something else I should have practiced). I probably could have figured out how to get it on, but my number-one priority was to get out of the water and build a fire before hypothermia killed me. So, I held the hood in my front teeth and started swimming for shore again. I had read in a book that a paddle could be used to swim faster, so I had a paddle leash tying the paddle to my wrist. If I'd tried swimming with a paddle before, I'd have learned earlier that it is a technique for feathered paddles only. I removed the paddle from my wrist, letting it float away, and kept swimming and shouting, 'I will survive!'

"After about half an hour in the water, I stumbled up on shore. I was very hypothermic, and couldn't think straight. I don't really remember for sure what I did. I believe I tried to start a fire by simply firing a flare into a pile of small driftwood that was just lying there. This was an idea I had thought of a long time ago, and, while never having tried it, I figured that it was a good one, but dangerous due to the possibility of the flare bouncing off something and hitting me. The wishful thought of being able to start a random pile of driftwood ablaze was, naturally, wrong, and I had wasted my first flare. What happened to the other two flares in that pack, I am not sure. I decided to get farther up the beach, onto higher ground at least, to see where to go next. I stood up, took a step, and crashed to the ground, my feet too stiff to function.

"I started crawling up the beach. The beach, all sand, with no rocks, was a peninsula, with the ocean on one side and a lagoon on the other. The next thing I knew, I was lying down on the lagoon side of the beach and it was dark. It had to have been at least two hours later for it to be this dark.

"I got up and found I was able to walk carefully on my bare feet, and I looked around for birch bark to start a fire with. Norton Sound, I should explain, has driftwood generally all around it from the Yukon River, though most of its coast is past the tree line (you will often find trees if you go far enough into the interior). So you can generally count on finding lots of birch bark on the beach, but it was too dark for me to do so. I got some small sticks and twigs and tried building a fire with them and my firesticks and my waterproof matches, but the firesticks didn't seem to work when wet.

Twice to the Rescue

In the summer of 1985, Tom Maurer, Tammy Lenz, and Jeff Kerwin, president of the North Sound Sea Kayakers' Association (NSSKA), were involved in two rescues of other boaters on successive weekends.

On the first weekend, Jeff and Rod Lafferty were paddling a double kayak along the west side of Orcas Island, one of Washington's San Juan Islands, accompanied by Tammy Lenz and Tom Maurer in another double. Nearby they saw a 17- or 18-foot, gaff-rigged wooden sailboat capsize. They paddled up and discovered two men and a boy standing on it; the sailboat was underwater, and the victims were up to their chests in water. The sailboaters' boat cushions had floated away, so the paddlers lent them their life jackets. There was no hope of righting the submerged craft, so the boy was placed on the kayak deck between Jeff and Rod, who paddled him to a nearby resort while Tammy and Tom picked up boat cushions and stood by to offer further assistance should the sailboat go down completely. At the resort, Jeff and Rod found the boy's mother, who sent a friend in a powerboat to rescue the other victims and tow in the near-sunken sailboat.

The next weekend, Jeff was paddling with his six-year-old son in his double with a group of ten other kayaks from NSSKA. The group, which included Tom and Tammy, was on a trip near Deception Pass in Washington. As the somewhat spread-out group of kayakers approached Skagit Island, Bob Pfau spotted a seal ahead and noticed some splashing well beyond it, about 100 to 150 feet offshore. Paddler Dena Peel heard strange, eerie noises that didn't sound like a seal. Trip leaders Tom and Lisa Derrer went ahead of the group, accompanied by Dena and Bob, who were paddling singles. As they got closer, they realized that the noises they had been hearing in the distance were cries for help.

They connected the yelling with the commotion in the water and paddled hard to the area. Tom and Lisa, with their two small children seated in the large center cockpit of their San Juan double, arrived first and found three men in the water hanging on to a floating snag. There was a dog in the water, circling them. One man was nearly unconscious; the other two had given up trying to swim back and were concentrating on trying to keep him from slipping away under the waves. All seemed panicky, and of the three only one still seemed coherent. Tom was hesitant; if he got too near they might all try to scramble aboard and capsize his whole family. He explained the situation, telling them they could be saved but only if they followed directions from him exactly. The most coherent swimmer said he understood and agreed to do as he was told.

Tom offered the kayak's stern for the man to grab. With his nearly unconscious friend under one arm, the man got hold of the lines on the back of the San Juan. Tom and Lisa strained with all their might (they both pulled muscles in the process) to tow all three men, and the branch supporting them, into the current toward Skagit Island.

Dena could see that the man holding the rudder lift line caused the rudder to be jammed off to one side. Aware that this would create problems, she hooked her short stern line near the back of the double and started towing, although it was difficult

"My next plan of action was to walk along the beach to where I had seen some cabins earlier in the day, and I figured I could get a fire going in one of their stoves if no one was around to help me. But the beach and all its logs proved too difficult to negotiate in the dark with bare feet, and I had to try another plan. Some time before, I had noticed a pile of logs that made a natural one-and-a-half-foot-high wind shelter, with a lot of other logs lying around it. So I went to it and built it up to a three-foot-high windbreak. I noticed some of the long grass growing on the beach was reasonably dry, so I gathered some small sticks for kindling, and, setting fire to a pile of grass first (with a flare), got a fire going, finally.

"As I huddled beside the fire, warming myself at last, I looked at my watch. It was 2 A.M.; five hours had passed since I first went in the water. I was relieved that the roughest part was over. Survival was now almost certain. I knew there was a danger of a bear attacking (a prospector had been killed by one in the area that summer), but, having no gun and nothing but two flares to defend myself with, I figured it wasn't worth worrying about.

"I slept beside the fire until morning. I began to think that it was taking the rescue people an awfully long time to find me, and I wondered if my EPIRB was working. I thought that a bad antenna connection might be causing it to malfunction, so I turned off the transmitter and checked the antenna connection. It seemed clean, so I put the unit back together. I suppose it is possible that in retightening it, I improved the connection. I then took the duct tape off

for her to stay far enough away from the double for everyone to always paddle on both sides. Tom kept talking to the victims to keep them encouraged and calm. Progress was extremely slow against the current (anyone who has ever towed just one swimmer who was doing his or her best to help can empathize). Bob Pfau hooked a towline to the double's bow and added his energy to the tow. At first Tom was sure that while hooking up the towline they lost ground to the current. However, because Bob's towline was quite long, he reached shore well ahead of the double, and the kayakers already waiting on the beach were able to pull them the rest of the way in considerably faster.

During the tow, paddler Brenda Adair caught up with the leaders. She grasped the situation and knew what needed to be done. She paddled ahead, beached her kayak, and ran to the victims' campsite. She grabbed their sleeping bags and blankets and ran back down to the beach. By the time the victims had reached shore, she was already in a sleeping bag, pre-warming it and ready to donate heat. The rescuers stripped the wet pants off the semiconscious, babbling victim and put him into a sleeping bag with Brenda. Some of the group members set about trying to get outside help, and others helped to bundle up all three men with things donated to the cause. The victim's friend begged him not to die and reminded him he had a family to live for. Brenda and others asked him about his family and children, as the victim seemed to need someone talking to him to hang on to consciousness. (Several people *(continued on page 76)* the switch, and turned it on again, to the full-stop position, and noticed it was now turned on quite a bit farther. But I still figured that it should have been transmitting all night, as the light had indicated.

"At 10 A.M. the Russian SARSAT satellite picked up my signal and told the Coast Guard in Juneau that it was coming from Solomon. Apparently the signal had bounced off the mountains, giving an inaccurate fix. They knew that a small plane had flipped over on the Solomon runway the night before in a gust of wind. First they checked out the possibility that the signal was coming from the plane. After they had determined that the plane did not have an ELT transmitting, the Civil Air Patrol (CAP) search plane in Nome got ready to go. But a scheduled Ryan Air flight picked up the signal also, and estimated the location to be one and a half miles northeast of where I was. (I was one and a half miles east of Solomon). Since there was a construction camp in that area, the Troopers drove there to find out if someone there had one. Because of this, they delayed taking off in the search plane until the ground search was complete.

"I fired off the last two flares I had at an overhead plane, probably the Ryan Air flight, but they did not spot me (flares being poor in bright sunlight). I just stayed huddled beside the fire, growing more and more dubious of my EPIRB's reliability.

"I could see the cabins of Solomon from where I was, and there were creeks and a river to cross to get there. I decided to wait until early afternoon, when it

(continued from page 75)
mentioned to me later that the attention really seemed to help him at that critical stage.) Once the victim warmed up enough to start violent shivering, he became somewhat more alert and coherent.

Among them, the paddlers had four hand-held flares, one Skyblazer flare, one orange smoke signal, and three twelve-gauge flares. There were many sailboats in the area, and the beach on Skagit Island was also directly in the line of sight of several larger powerboats that had come in through Deception Pass. These powerboats would come to within three-quarters mile from shore before turning south. Whenever it seemed they had a good chance of being seen, the paddlers set off more signals. One person had trouble ejecting the spent shells from the twelve-

gauge flare gun. Unfortunately, the group used all the signaling devices without receiving any indication that they had been seen. Since this was just before the Fourth of July, boaters who might have seen the flares could have assumed that someone on Skagit Island was playing with fireworks and sparklers.

During this time, Tom Derrer had climbed up to the highest point on the island so as to be silhouetted against the sky as he waved an orange raincoat to attract help. Still no luck.

While this was taking place, Jeff Kerwin and Tom Maurer (in a double) and John Mann (in a single) paddled furiously to nearby Kiket Island, where they had seen smoke rising from a dwelling. They knocked on the doors and windows but found nobody home. They considered breaking in—this would be low tide, and, if I had not been rescued then, to walk to the cabins. There was no firewood available except driftwood, which I felt was too clean burning to be much good for a smoke signal, especially with a fifteen-knot wind to blow it away. I had no mirror to signal aircraft.

"At 2 P.M. I decided that my EPIRB wasn't working and it was the best time to try walking out, since the next low tide would be after dark. I got up, found a decent long branch for use as a walking stick, and started walking. Some creeks I had to swim across; some I could wade. My feet, still bare, refroze quickly, eliminating any pain as I crossed the tundra. Besides the driftwood-littered tundra, which cut my feet open (not much bleeding when frostbitten), there was marsh to cross, with half an inch of ice over much of it. I crawled, and walked, and often broke through the ice to the water and ground beneath. It took well over an hour to cross the mile and a half to the bank of the Solomon River. (Solomon is built on the opposite bank).

"I stood on the bank, leaning heavily on my walking stick, surveying the river to see where to swim across. I noticed a person on the other bank, looking toward me. I tried to wave my arm, hoping to signal him over, but all I could manage was an anemic little shake of the forearm and hand. But he came down the bank and put a small, plywood dory in the water, and rowed the one hundred yards across the river. I started hobbling toward where he landed, and he walked over to me, questioningly. I told him, in a whisper (all I could

was definitely an emergency. Luckily, they found both an unlocked door and a phone. They quickly contacted the Coast Guard. A helicopter responded to the call, but a jet boat from the Swinomish Tribal Police and the La Conner Police Department picked up the Coast Guard's alarm broadcast and arrived on the scene first. The helicopter was recalled, and the jet boat transported the victim to Island County Hospital in Anacortes where he was treated for hypothermia. The other two victims needed no further treatment.

By coincidence, George Banks, one of the swimmers, later moved into the house next to my brother's. We would never have connected him with the incident except that, when he discovered that my brother and I build sea kayaks, he told me about the kayakers who had saved his best

friend's life. I had already heard much of the story from several of those involved as rescuers, but George told me how he and his friends had first gotten into their predicament.

George, Doug Nash, and Lance Mc-Farland were camping on Skagit Island. Lance had borrowed Doug's small outboard skiff, and when he returned he did not tie it to shore quite well enough. Soon afterward George spotted it drifting several yards from shore and began hollering for the others as he took off his boots. He started swimming after the skiff but was soon passed by Doug, who was swimming furiously, so George headed back to shore. The boat drifted out into the current and began moving away faster. By then Doug had almost caught it, but he began to lose *(continued on page 78)* manage after drinking nothing but salt water for eighteen hours) what had happened. He took me to his boat and rowed us across. Since the boat had a one-and-a-half-inch-diameter hole in the bottom, he hauled it out of the water as soon as we were on the other side. He helped me over to his three-wheeler and drove me up to the house he lived in.

"There, I warmed up, ate and drank, changed clothes, and generally started recovering. A pilot who was in the house at the time immediately asked me if I had an ELT. I said yes, and told him where my EPIRB was. He turned it off for me, then flew to Nome with it, and advised the Flight Service that the ELT signal belonged to me.

"Apparently the CAP search plane had been about to take off before he got there, to start an aerial search for my signal. So the CAP got a paramedic, rearranged the Beaver's cabin for a stretcher, and flew to Solomon. They picked me up and transferred me to an ambulance when we arrived in Nome. The ambulance took me to the Norton Sound Regional Hospital, where I was treated for third-degree frostbite to feet, first-degree frostbite to hands, foot lacerations, and hypothermia.

"After four days in the Nome hospital, I transferred to a Toronto hospital for a month. Now I am in a convalescent hospital in Toronto. I've kept all my toes, and will eventually heal up 100 percent."

(continued from page 77)
ground as the wind blew it faster than he could swim. When it was obvious that he couldn't catch it, he started heading back. He soon ran out of energy, could no longer swim, and began calling for help.

George knew there was risk, but Doug was his best friend and he couldn't just stand there and watch him drown. He swam out to get him. Doug's dog Two Shoes also jumped in and started swimming toward him. George saw Doug go under for a second and hoped he could get there in time. Two Shoes arrived first, and George shouted to Doug to hang on to the dog. Doug's head again went underwater, only to be pulled back up again by the dog. When George arrived, Doug grabbed him, pulling him under; George had to forcibly free himself and get hold of Doug.

George soon found he couldn't make progress back to shore while holding his friend. They drifted farther from shore. On shore, Lance found a snag to use for a float and swam it out to the other two. All three men clung to the branch; Lance and George tried to keep Doug conscious and waved and shouted for help, although they could see no one nearby. George said that when the kayaks appeared it was the most beautiful sight in the world. Two Shoes made it back with the swimmers and rescue party.

After the rescue, John Mann paddled around, found the victim's lost skiff, and tied it up securely to the distant shore. When John returned, Tom Maurer took Lance and the small outboard motor over to the skiff in a double kayak. The rescue had taken considerable time (paddler Susan Kreml estimated that two hours elapsed between the

Note: Richard's kayak was never found, and he says he's now looking for a set of plans for a very seaworthy, medium- to high-volume single seater. He's planning another trip a couple of years down the road—though this time he intends to start in a warmer spot, like Prince Rupert or Vancouver.

LESSONS LEARNED

Richard Hudson was experienced, careful, and well prepared, even for someone on a long solo expedition in the wilderness. Gear such as the EPIRB, float coat, exposure suit, and sea socks on both cockpits indicate that he had given his safety considerable thought before undertaking the journey. However, he may not have practiced enough with the equipment he had under the difficult conditions in which he might find himself. Of course, this may not always be possible if the weather doesn't cooperate or your local area has little in common with the area where you will be paddling on a trip.

If Richard had practiced self rescues in rough conditions, it's likely he would have developed a way to reenter his Sisiutl and would have been carrying whatever equipment was necessary. He probably could not have predicted the sudden appearance of breaking waves a half-mile out from shore. The course he chose may have been the most prudent, since the water is quite shallow in that area; paddling closer to shore would have increased the risk from breakers, and paddling farther out would have put shore beyond reach if he had to swim. Although the late hour affected his visibility—he mentioned having to squint into the sunset—the weather had been reasonable for paddling that day, if a little cold and windy. If he had waited, at that time of year the odds were more likely that the weather would deteriorate than improve.

Knowing the environment and your own skills, combined with good judgment, is the first line of defense for avoiding trouble. Richard rates top

time they got the victims to shore and the time the police boat arrived). The NSSKA group was now behind schedule. The wind had come up considerably, and a strong current was against them. Because of the difficult conditions and energy drain of the rescue, the group wasn't making much progress toward their take-out point; several of the group members wisely went to shore short of their destination and hitched a ride back to their cars.

The events of the day stimulated an increased interest in safety and rescues among NSSKA members. Among other changes, they now carry at least one sleeping bag on day paddles. Other NSSKA kayakers involved with this rescue were Elbert Bentley, Herb Denny, and Bill and Nancy Starkweather. A tip of the *Sea Kayaker* hat to all those who helped.

marks for knowledge and judgment; by that stage of his trip he had covered over three hundred miles along Norton Sound and had some experience in the local ocean environment. Though it's recommended that paddlers travel in groups, that probably wasn't an option for Richard once he decided to make this three-month trip.

The conditions on the ocean section of his trip did cause him to reevaluate his choice of kayak. But then again, Richard's large double kayak allowed him to carry all he needed for three months. The extra supplies he could carry might have made the difference if he had been faced with a long-term survival situation. Obviously, no kayak will be just right in all situations. As Richard mentioned, however, a more maneuverable kayak might have allowed him to turn in time to slice head-on through the breaker. A narrow kayak (such as most singles) might have allowed him to ride out the breaker sideways on a brace if he had practiced this in surf of equivalent size.

Paddling skills are the second major line of defense. With practice, Richard may have been able to lean his loaded double effectively when bracing into a wave. I have never tried surf in a double, much less a loaded one, but if it is possible I'm sure this would be considerably more difficult than with almost any single kayak.

The third line of defense is deep-water rescue, in this case, self rescue. Practice at rough-water solo reentry might have made this a minor incident, rather than a life-threatening emergency resulting in serious injury. Have you practiced rescues with loaded kayaks? In cold water? In wind and waves? You may have practiced in warm, calm water with an empty kayak, but remember that it is far more difficult to reenter a kayak in waves than in calm conditions. I often see people getting themselves back into a kayak in a swimming pool in ways that would never work in even mild waves. These people go home confident that they can rescue themselves. But in this context, a little knowledge can be a dangerous thing. A few words of advice: If the rescue requires you to maintain balance—forget it. If the rescue requires good dexterity, it is for warm water kayaking or must be done very quickly before your hands become numb and useless. (Note: If your hands aren't working you can try substituting your teeth. Richard broke his tooth doing this but did succeed in turning the duct-taped switch on his EPIRB that his hands had failed to budge.) If you do capsize in cold water, keep your hands and forearms out of the water as much as you can; the buoyancy of your life jacket and your kayak will make this possible in most situations.

To get the most out of practicing in a swimming pool, you must simulate difficult conditions. Have friends yank your kayak around or even try their best to capsize you by twisting the ends while you practice bracing or try a rescue. (For bracing practice, caution your friends to stay well out of range of your flailing paddle.) If you are in a group, your partners can have a lot of fun throwing water in your face. Two people can make waves at both ends by simultaneously pushing a nearby kayak up and down in the water while others attempt to capsize your kayak. Another helper could simulate wind by pushing the kayak away from you if you let go of it.

Once you can do specific rescues under this kind of abuse, try them for real on a stormy day, in cold water. Try the rescues with the victim's kayak both loaded and empty, and make sure you are wearing the clothes and equipment you would normally be paddling with. Warning: This could be hazardous in very cold water for someone subject to heart attack or sudden drowning syndrome, so be careful. Since water temperatures in the ocean usually vary only 5 to 10 degrees from winter to summer, dress for the water temperature rather than that of the air. Do this dress rehearsal only with plenty of experienced help at hand and a source of warmth nearby. For group rescues, make sure you get a turn both as rescuer and as victim.

Richard was well prepared for the fourth line of defense, minimizing heat loss. He was wearing a surplus exposure suit (like a drysuit, with seals at the neck, wrists, and ankles), lots of warm garments underneath, a parka, and insulated gloves, and he carried a Thermofloat coat. The UVIC Thermofloat is insulated with closed-cell foam and includes a wetsuit-style crotch panel and a bright orange reflective hood; it was developed by hypothermia researchers at the University of Victoria.

Useful as this product may be, I can empathize with Richard's problems in trying to don his floater coat in cold water: I found donning mine difficult enough in swimming pool conditions. Until you try using a piece of clothing or gear in cold water, don't consider it part of your on-the-water safety system—even as a backup measure. In practice, make sure you can reenter your kayak while wearing such clothing—even if you don't foresee problems, the possibility remains that the clothing will somehow hinder movement. Doubt the worth of any new equipment or procedure until you have personally proved it in some rigorous tests. Once you have found equipment you're confident won't disappoint you in an emergency, maintain it and test it again periodically—and have a backup. (As it turned out, the survival suit Richard had been wearing did little to keep him dry.) Often by changing and refining your technique, a procedure or piece of equipment that did not work at first can with practice become second nature. Practice may not make perfect, but when it comes to kayaking emergencies it sure beats anything else.

The fifth line of defense is letting others in a position to help know that you are in need of their assistance and then helping them to locate you. Richard was more prepared than most in this regard—and still his system came close to failing. Richard's experience with the EPIRB demonstrates several things that could go wrong even though the device did not malfunction and the batteries were charged. Richard knew how to operate his unit but wasn't familiar enough with it to know its idiosyncrasies. He now writes: "'Despite the problems I had with my EPIRB, I wouldn't go kayaking without it. I plan to ask the manufacturer if a better switch could be installed and, if not, I can think of lots of ways to build a switch protector myself, so I won't ever have to resort to duct tape again."

The eight-second burn time of Skyblazer flares seems to make them excellent (but hazardous) fire starters. However, they failed Richard in their primary purpose, signaling for help. Large parachute flares are far better signals: They fly higher and burn brighter and longer than other aerial flares. Unfortunately, parachute flares also cost considerably more than Skyblazers and are bulkier to carry. Still, a couple of parachute flares would have nicely filled the gap between the EPIRB and Skyblazers. When the plane flew over he would have had a much better chance of being spotted with parachute flares or dense, orange smoke signals for better daytime visibility. Dye marker could also be valuable during daytime in the water or on snow. Other daytime signals might include a signal mirror or a bright orange square or rescue streamer.

And none of us should forget that even in a high-tech, gadget-ridden world, the old ways can still work. A huge SOS stomped in the sand (or snow) would certainly make your presence more obvious and convey the clear message that you need help.

Wisely, Richard had carried much of his safety equipment in his coat and shirt pockets (with the notable exception of a space blanket, which he now says would have been an excellent thing to have had on shore if he had thought to retrieve it from his cockpit). Some equipment didn't operate as well as he had expected; he had problems opening his folding knife, for instance, due to the marine environment, and his commercial fire-starting sticks weren't as water-proof as he thought. Again, test equipment rigorously.

Another very real lesson from Richard Hudson's ordeal is that you must consider the usefulness of footwear for walking and swimming as well as kayak-ing. Most of us have become dependent on shoes. Once deprived of them, we suffer cuts, bruises, blisters, punctures, burns, frostbite, and in some areas poisonous bites or parasitic infections. If when paddling you must abandon your boots to swim, you'll need a satisfactory substitute for shoes upon arrival on shore. Wetsuit-style booties with a good sole are a good choice, despite the bad smell.

Like many solo expeditioners and survivors of serious emergencies, Richard had the creativity to make do with what he had and the ability to see alternate uses for what would seemingly be single-purpose items (for example, turning a flare into a fire starter). It's worthwhile to go over your kayaking and camping equipment and make up other uses for items. Imagine possible situations and then work on discovering solutions that would have you rely only on items you know would be available, either from your own equipment or from the environment. This should give you several solutions to try out when you simu-late emergencies to see which of your solutions might really work—and which were just mental exercises.

9

Rough Passages

Matt Broze

David Kelley, age 26, died on February 13, 1987, in Rosario Strait near James Island in Washington's San Juan Islands. As is often the case in kayaking deaths, he was paddling solo. Although there were no eyewitnesses to the tragedy and we will never know exactly what happened, we can piece together what might have transpired based on available information.

The day after the accident, an article appeared in a Seattle newspaper that provided a somewhat distorted picture of the accident. The headline read, "Kayaker dies five hours after helicopter rescue," making it appear David died in the hospital. However, with a core temperature of 72°F (22°C), he probably was already dead when he was picked up. Standard procedure is to *not* declare a drowning victim dead until he or she has been rewarmed, because occasionally young people who seem to have drowned in cold water and exhibit the normal signs of death (no heartbeat, no breathing, cold temperature), make remarkable and complete recoveries with treatment that includes cardio-pulmonary resuscitation and rewarming.

Dan Crookes, operator of the 28-foot work boat and private ferry *Can Do*, was monitoring the VHF and Citizens' Bands with his radios that day while picking up passengers on Blakely Island. At about 4:00 P.M., he heard the Washington State Ferry *Hyak* call Seattle Traffic on VHF channel 14 to report the sighting of the bottom of a small craft. The U.S. Coast Guard was contacted; they launched two cutters, diverted a Navy helicopter, and radioed the sighting to all craft in the area on the emergency channel, VHF 16. Dan also heard the capsized kayak discussed on VHF channel 22 and Citizens' Band channel 10. From the radio exchanges, it appeared that two pleasure boats were at the scene and that people on one had spotted a body in the water, lost sight of it in the waves, and finally relocated it four or five minutes later. Dan determined the location and headed for it.

A Personal Statement

Matt Broze

David Kelley's accident was an especially troubling one for me. My brother, Cam, and I designed and built the Mariner II David was using, and I personally developed and publicized the Mariner outrigger paddle-float self rescue, which David may have been attempting. I also developed and manufacture the version of the float he had on his paddle. My intention for the outrigger rescue was to provide a backup for the Eskimo roll for use by solo paddlers or for groups of paddlers who might become separated or caught in conditions that force an "everyone-for-themselves" situation.

In the effort to encourage the use of this rescue as a backup to rolling, perhaps we have unintentionally encouraged paddlers to rely on it like some form of talisman. But anyone who chooses to accept the extra risk of paddling solo must have not one backup, but *multiple* backups, so that every "what-if" scenario is covered. Learn, through repeated practice, the limitations of any technique or piece of equipment upon which you rely. It is hard to imagine too many backups for a solo paddler on the edge of his or her skill level. That said, the best skill of all is the judgment to back down from a situation that's likely to require the use of backups.

Few pleasure craft are equipped to lift a helpless person from the water, and as the *Can Do* approached the scene it was clear that the pleasure boaters had not picked up the body. Dan called them on the radio and asked them to stand aside. At 4:23 P.M. the *Can Do* arrived, and Dan spotted the victim, wearing a life jacket and floating face-up. The *Can Do*'s four passengers had the victim aboard in a few seconds. Although he was not breathing and showed no signs of a pulse, one of the passengers, trained in CPR, attempted to resuscitate him. As he administered CPR it was obvious to him that there was water in the victim's lungs.

Within a few minutes, a U.S. Navy helicopter arrived and dropped a diver into the water. The diver came aboard the *Can Do* and soon had David lifted into the helicopter, which then flew to St. Luke's Hospital in Bellingham (which is not the closest hospital but is one of the Northwest's best equipped for the treatment of severe hypothermia). David was admitted at 4:45 showing no signs of life. He was treated and rewarmed, and was pronounced dead at 9:00 P.M.

LESSONS LEARNED

The crucial factor in this tragedy is that David failed to recognize, or chose to ignore, the dangers inherent in a crossing of this type, especially in winter. There are times when an error in judgment or lack of knowledge can be compensated for by sufficient backups. But David set off alone, he was not dressed for immersion, and to our knowledge he carried no means of attracting outside help. In short, he had none of the backups that may have ensured his survival.

The lowest reported core temperature ever survived is 68°F (20°C). Loss of consciousness occurs at about 86°F (26.7°), and death usually occurs between 86°F (26.7°C) and 80°F (30°C). The type III PFD typically worn by kayakers usually does not keep an unconscious victim's face out of the water; in this situation, drowning would occur soon after unconsciousness. In David's case the official cause of death was drowning, but it almost certainly was the result of unconsciousness due to hypothermia.

One of the pleasure boats on the rescue scene took the kayak in tow and turned it over to the U.S. Coast Guard cutter *Pt. Doran* when it arrived a few minutes after the helicopter. Dan Crookes spotted David's paddle and picked it up. There was an inflated rescue float attached to one blade. The paddle had been about one hundred feet downwind from the body, and the kayak was floating level but upside down about one hundred feet farther downwind.

A few days later I learned from the Coast Guard that the kayak, a rental boat, had been returned to a Seattle rental agency. I called the agency and learned that the kayak was a Mariner II, a relatively narrow model (17'11" by 21½") without a rudder. At first I wondered why a novice would rent such a slender kayak and then paddle it solo, in extreme conditions, far from shore.

It turns out, however, that David had been paddling for two years and had taken several classes. He had learned to roll after only fifteen minutes of instruction, had practiced rescues and self rescues (in a swimming pool), and was considered a strong paddler. He preferred to rent rather than buy, and this was not the first time he had rented the Mariner II. Although he was not a novice, it's possible that, as a fast learner, he developed his skill level and confidence faster than he developed good judgment and knowledge about paddling in serious conditions.

From the positions of the body, paddle, and kayak, it appears that they had not been separated for more than an hour. I would assume that the paddle with the inflated paddle float attached would have drifted faster than the capsized and partially swamped kayak, so I speculate that the kayak drifted away first and David held on to the paddle until he became unconscious.

David was tall and thin and was wearing polypropylene under a Gore-Tex shell and pants. A core temperature of 72°F (22°C) indicates that he had been in the near-45°F (7°C) water for at least three or four hours. (In this estimate I am considering U.S. Navy research that indicates that for someone dressed as David was—no wetsuit, drysuit, or survival suit—heat loss may be up to twice as fast in rough and turbulent water as it is in the calm water of research tanks upon which survival times and heat loss estimates of a non-swimming victim are usually based. In turbulent water the rate of heat loss in a stationary person is roughly the same as it is in a swimmer in calm water. This makes sense; both turbulent water and movement in calm water would have the effect of replacing the partially heated water next to the skin with colder water.)

There is no way of knowing how many times David Eskimo rolled, if at all; nor is there any way of knowing if he succeeded with a self rescue or how many times he may have regained the cockpit before capsizing again. The attached paddle float points to at least one self-rescue attempt. So too does the fact that a pump usually secured under the deck was missing when the kayak was returned, suggesting that at some time David had reentered the cockpit and then tried to use the pump.

It's possible that David did not have a spray deck. One was included with his rental, but when Dan Crookes picked him up, he took note that David was not wearing one. The spray deck supplied to David had shoulder straps, so it is unlikely that it would have come off by itself. He may have removed it if he was swimming after the kayak and felt it was slowing him down. Or, if he put it in the kayak when he drove to the launch point, it may have blown out on the highway. Without a spray deck, even if David had been able to reenter his kayak, he would still have been unable to pump his cockpit faster than he took on water, considering the very rough, if not extreme, conditions.

David's kayak had float bags in both ends when found; it was properly equipped for an outrigger self rescue, and this was a method that David had practiced, at least in a pool. Nothing but the extreme conditions and possible lack of a spray skirt appear obvious as reasons for the rescue's failure; thus, it seems likely that he may have recovered from a number of capsizes before becoming too weak from cold to succeed again. Because of the close proximity of his paddle and kayak when he was picked up, I would guess that although David may not have been able to paddle his swamped kayak, he at least might have been able to keep himself partially out of the water much of the time, slowing heat loss.

Therefore, all things considered, I believe that David first capsized well before noon, at a time when local conditions were indeed extreme. During late morning there was an ebb current of up to two knots flowing south in Rosario Strait (though Dan Crookes told me he thought the current seemed to be running far faster than two knots), and a strong wind was blowing in the opposite direction, with gusts of thirty knots or more.

Crookes canceled his morning ferry runs because he was concerned about taking his very seaworthy 28-foot craft through the five-foot breaking swells that he had observed in the middle of Rosario Strait from Tide Point on Cypress Island. He had canceled runs due to weather only four other days that winter. He did report that the conditions looked less serious in other, nearby locations where the current was not running against the wind. By 2:00 P.M. the current changed direction and the water had started to calm down, so at 3:15 the *Can Do* made its run. By 4:00 P.M. the winds had dropped to ten to fifteen knots.

David paddled from Washington Park, near Anacortes, on a north (protected) shore, so even the strong wind may not have been that obvious from where he set off. As long as the conditions were within his skill level he probably continued to paddle toward his goal, and would not have come upon the most extreme conditions until he was most of the way across Rosario Strait. (The crossing distance to James Island is approximately three miles.) Even then it might have appeared to him that the conditions had deteriorated generally, not just in his location, and that the best thing to do would be to paddle toward the nearest shore. Thus, he may have continued toward James Island into an area of even worse conditions. As a paddler, David very likely lacked the experience to recognize dangerous water ahead; rough water isn't at all obvious at a distance, especially from kayak level, and the size of waves or surf is especially easy to underestimate.

Based on David's planned destination, believed to have been Decatur Island, and the location where he was picked up, he may have been crossing a notorious area of tide rips where the waters flowing out of Thatcher Pass collide with the ebbing current in Rosario Strait. This area, to the north and east of James Island, can be dangerous even on calm days. Ferry boat crews refer to it as "the Haystacks."

We don't know whether David listened to the weather reports that morning; we do know that the Weather Service was issuing small-craft advisories for winds from the south up to thirty knots. The current tables show an ebb current until afternoon in Rosario Strait. With this information, David could have predicted the wind-against-tide situation in the Strait. The charts warn of the tide rips off Thatcher and the mouths of the other passes spilling into Rosario. *The San Juan Current Guide,* published by Island Canoe Company, combines a chart with information from current stations, the *Current Atlas,* and information on currents from the Coastal Pilot. Near the area where David's body was found the chart reads, "With a S wind and ebb current, heavy tide rips will be encountered off the E entrance to Thatcher Pass." Randel Washburne's book, *Kayaking Puget Sound, the San Juans & Gulf Islands* (Mountaineers, 1990), warns about the crossing David attempted: "Southerly winds can make this an extremely dangerous body of water on a falling tide. . . . Crossings should be made only in auspicious conditions; otherwise use the San Juan Islands ferry."

I've written about many accidents in Washington's San Juan Islands—not because I happen to live nearby. The San Juans are both a popular and a treacherous area. Strong currents sieve through these islands, often combined with an opposing wind. This combination, wind against tide, seems to be the one-two punch that is most likely to catch kayakers by surprise. A change in current direction (very predictable with the correct tables) or a shift in the wind (less easily predicted, even with a weather radio) is all it takes to turn relatively calm waters into overwhelming conditions. Whenever you plan to paddle in an area where currents run strong, think about the possibility that the wind could come to blow in the opposite direction and create dangerous conditions. Know the weather report and the strength, direction, and time of the currents.

Although David's kayak was equipped with sufficient buoyancy (in the form of standard bow and stern bags), a sea sock or a well-placed set of bulkheads would have reduced the amount of water entering his boat and made it easier to pump out. David could have obtained a sea sock (and a wetsuit or drysuit) from the rental agency.

Another Exposed Crossing

Paddler Eric Soares frequently sets off on exposed crossings. Like David Kelley, he got caught in a very bad situation—but without the tragic outcome. Eric is an expert when it comes to surf paddling, survival swimming, kayak surfing, and paddling ocean rock gardens. The following is his report of the incident.

"On March 9, 1986, I was testing a borrowed Icefloe kayak (16'8" by 24"), which I planned to paddle from my home in Alameda to Schoonmaker Point in Sausalito. The distance was twelve (or so) nautical miles. After consulting tide/current charts, weather updates, and people who surveyed the bay that morning, I decided to paddle past the Naval Air Station to Yerba Buena Island

Pumping out a Kayak

How can you pump out a boat without giving up the use of your hands for boat control in extreme conditions?

Paddlers in Tasmania have used battery-operated electric bailing pumps for many years. Tom Trump, a paddler from Connecticut, developed an electric pump system for his kayak several years ago. He used a gel-cell type battery which, unlike most storage batteries, can be turned upside down without leaking acid. Eddyline Kayaks developed and market two systems, which are sealed against salt water and incorporate rechargeable gel-cell batteries capable of emptying a kayak five to ten times on one charge. The electric pumps (360 or 1,100 gallons per hour) take from five to ten minutes to empty a swamped kayak (or less if you use the larger-capacity model in a single kayak). Optional solar panels are available to recharge the batteries, which might be necessary on a long trip. Eddyline now also markets a system that is powered by D-size alkaline batteries.

The key feature of the electric pump is that it leaves the hands free for paddling and bracing. Theoretically, a foot-operated pump would provide the same benefits as an electric one, but most of the foot pumps I have seen can handle only small amounts of water picked up from paddling in rough seas or during an Eskimo roll.

I once tested a 2½-gallon-per-minute "galley pump" mounted to a bulkhead/foot-brace on a very small-volume kayak. The five gallons or so of water that entered the cockpit area during a rescue were pumped out within a few minutes, but my foot had already cramped; obviously, the process would be prolonged with a standard-volume boat. Higher-capacity diaphragm pumps are now available that make pumping out by foot practical and efficient. Always back up a foot pump or electric pump with a hand pump.

and then go either east or west around it, depending upon the conditions at the moment. None of my friends could accompany me; reasons varied from 'Too dangerous' to 'I'm going surfing with Rashad.' I decided to go alone, as I had done dozens of times in the bay under storm conditions.

"When I embarked at 14:30, the water temperature was 55°F (12.8°C), the air temperature was 57°F (14°C), the wind speed was seventeen knots from the southwest, and the tide was about two hours before maximum ebb (predicted current by Alcatraz/Angel Island was 4.7 knots). I figured the actual current speed would be six knots, due to the excessive delta runoff caused by storms. I thought the southwest wind would blow me to Sausalito, the ebb would propel me to the center of the bay, and I would boogie to Point Blunt then around to Point Knox and on to my destination. So far, so good.

"I figured that, at worst, the approaching storm front would break while I was in the middle of the bay, and the accompanying gale would blow me even faster to Sausalito. I decided to prepare for disaster—loss of boat in the middle of the bay with a strong current sweeping me out of the Golden Gate. Hence, I wore fleece underclothing, my full surfing wetsuit over that, neoprene booties, and my scuba hood. I wore my buoyancy compensator inflated all the way (thirty-four pounds flotation) and carried another life jacket between my knees. I ate a big meal and carried a huge orange and flares in my buoyancy compensator. I informed friends of my trip, told them not to worry about me, and I took off in good spirits.

"The trip to Yerba Buena Island was not intense, but the wind and fetch (the distance the wind blows unobstructed over the water) were building up. The stern kept catching the wind gusts, which caused the bow to turn windward. I had to continually engage in port sweep strokes and starboard strokes to maintain my course, using my feathered, slalom-type paddle. The waves were too big to brace on the starboard side and still maintain a four-knot speed. So I found myself wishing I was in my surf ski and could use my rudder. I decided to go west around Yerba Buena/Treasure Island and let the wind blow me through the slack on the west side of Treasure. I went under the Bay Bridge on the east side of the pillar closest to Yerba Buena. The last thing I wanted was to go too far west and then not be able to cross the bay safely. Due to the compressed current, a swirling eddy, uneven shallows, and rebounding waves, the conditions became gnarly very suddenly. I was engulfed by six- to eight-foot chaotic waves that were smashing all around from all directions. Every paddle stroke demanded a reflexive brace to preclude capsizing in the confused water. I pearled on one of the beastly waves and awkwardly tipped over. I immediately rolled up and paddled on until I was through the yucky part. I rested on a protected beach area on Treasure Island, ate my orange, and plotted the remainder of my course. I was not cold, thanks to my wetsuit.

"The time was about 15:20. I figured I would make it to Schoonmaker Point by 16:30, just as I had planned. I paddled to the northeast corner of Treasure Island and headed to Point Blunt across the shipping channel. The wind came up rather suddenly (the storm hit) and it started raining just as I entered the middle of the channel. I tried to surf on the nice-sized waves but I couldn't persuade the boat to perform the way I wanted it to. Still, I was making good progress, and the wind was really picking up fast. A 30-foot sailboat zoomed by and the skipper yelled, 'It's bad and it's going to get worse. I'll get help for you!' I yelled back, 'Thanks, I don't need help.'

"Famous last words. I was only four hundred yards from Angel Island, so I figured I could bivouac there if things really got nasty. They did. The Coast Guard told me later that the winds were blowing a steady fifty knots with gusts up to seventy. The combination of the wind, waves, swells coming through the gate, and the ebb tide caused some outrageous seas, with six- to eight-foot waves in constant breaking stage and colliding with each other from all directions. I thought, 'Oh boy, here we go again. I wish, I wish I had my old surf ski instead of this shiny new boat.' Extreme exertion was required to stay afloat.

"Out of the blue, one of the tricky bastards endoed me. I was upside down. No problem. I oriented myself. 'No current on either side, I'll come up starboard.' I tried and failed. 'Hmmm. Now is not the time to analyze, now is the time for action, while I still have air.' I rolled up starboard again—and was blown down; then I realized that the wind was not allowing me or the boat to roll up. No problem. 'I still have five seconds of air left, so I'll roll up on the port side, into the wind.' I did, but as my face broke the surface, a wave broke right into my mouth. Gasp! I thought calmly, 'To hell with this!' and pulled myself out of the cockpit and into the water.

"There is nothing like submersion in cold water to invigorate the senses, and I was thankful for the protection of my wetsuit and scuba hood. I decided to reenter and roll. I had no difficulty sliding my skinny frame into the small cockpit, but found I could not secure the spray skirt and hold my paddle at the same time. I blew my first reentry attempt. I thought about securing the paddle to the boat near the cockpit and decided. 'Naa. I might get entangled.' So I reentered again, ignored the spray skirt, and just rolled back up with so much force that I fell over the other side and slipped out of the boat again. I repeated the reentry and roll, taking care this time to finish the roll with a port brace into the wind. I was up, but couldn't figure out how to put the skirt back onto the coaming while I leaned at a forty-five-degree angle into the wind and sculled. I tried sculling with my left hand while I levered the paddle shaft behind my neck. Concurrently, I reached back with my right hand and tried to start the spray-skirt-around-the-coaming routine, which is difficult to do even on land. Splash, back in the water again.

"I reentered and rolled one last time and decided to paddle the boat full of water over to Angel Island. This was not a bad idea, because the boat is segmented by bulkheads, and only the cockpit resembled Lake Shasta. Nevertheless, given the weird wave, wind, and current interaction, I could not keep the boat upright. A sea sock would have been handy. I missed my surf ski, with which I did not have to worry about water in the cockpit.

Self Rescues

Extreme conditions such as those David Kelley probably found himself in—high wind, breaking seas, and the confused swirling waters of strong tide rips—individually are serious hazards, even to a group of expert kayakers. Combined, they create a death trap, making practiced rescues marginal at best.

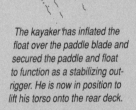

The kayaker has inflated the float over the paddle blade and secured the paddle and float to function as a stabilizing outrigger. He is now in position to lift his torso onto the rear deck.

CAM BROZE

A capsized kayaker who Eskimo rolls is still in the same conditions that capsized him or her in the first place, and with each roll he or she will take on more water, lessening the kayak's stability. Bailing won't work when waves are coming in over the cockpit, even if the kayak is somehow stabilized. Pumping by hand can be done through the waist hole of the spray deck or with a deck-mounted pump, but only if the kayak can be stabilized so that at least one hand can come off the paddle shaft for several minutes of pumping. In the case of a reentry attempt, both hands will have to come off the paddle shaft long enough for the spray deck to go on. In strong winds, even taking one hand off the paddle can cause a lost paddle or a capsize, unless a paddle tether or wind-resistant paddle park is used.

Unfortunately, for a kayak in breaking seas, there really is no such thing as "stabilized." Hanging on to a second kayak for stability is often the best option, making it possible for paddlers to ride out fairly severe conditions. But if the breaking seas are big enough to slide the rafted kayaks along before them, or dump them over when they break, the other kayak or kayaks in the raft could create a new, more immediate hazard. One of the major advantages of an outrigger self rescue is the stability it provides for pumping after reentry; but the limits of the outrigger system will be reached at about the same point as the raft of kayaks will come apart. In breaking seas, stability becomes a disadvantage if it is great enough to inhibit your ability to lean into the wave.

1. Right the kayak.
2. Inflate the paddle float (if required) and attach it to paddle blade.
3. Secure paddle to the rear deck in order to prevent it from pivoting.
4. Swim your upper body up on the stern deck.
5. Place one foot in the cockpit, then place the other foot, and pivot into the seat.
6. Reattach your spray skirt.
7. Pump out the boat.

During steps 4 to 7: Keep your center of gravity to the float side. There is a paddle-float rescue that differs from the paddle-float outrigger rescue described above, in that the paddle is not fixed to the kayak but is

(continued on page 92)

"I had used up about twenty minutes by this time and realized that I was not going to paddle the boat any more that day. I noticed two things: The current had pushed me toward Alcatraz, and while I was treading water I could feel no breeze. The waves must have protected me from the howling wind. I tied my extra life jacket and my paddle to the boat and began towing it to Alcatraz, using my left arm in a side-stroke maneuver and my feet in a whip kick. I calculated that I would reach the western tip of Alcatraz by swimming toward Treasure Island and allowing the current to sweep me toward the Golden Gate.

"I planned on abandoning the boat if it looked like it was detaining me from Alcatraz. I also decided to attract help. I glimpsed a ferry five hundred yards east of me and pulling away. I reached into my buoyancy compensator, pulled out a red Skyblazer flare, and shot it toward the ferry, hoping that a passenger would see it. No one did. I continued swimming and waited for another rescue opportunity. I saw a Channel 4 helicopter coming across the bay toward me. I shot a flare right at its nose. It banked right and split. I figured it had not seen the flare.

"I continued swimming as efficiently as possible. I began to wonder about white sharks, but put the thought out of my mind. Then an ocean-going barge passed by two hundred feet north of me. I shot a flare right across its bow, and the Pablo Island barge responded by calling the Coast Guard. They did not signal me, however, so I thought they had not noticed the flare. I swam on toward Alcatraz. Then a Red and White Fleet tour boat, *The Harbor Queen,* bore down on me and pulled alongside, sheltering me from the waves. A boatswain threw me a life ring, and I climbed up a net to the boat amidst cheers from the passengers. They got their money's worth on this Alcatraz excursion. The boatswain gaffed the boat by the grab loop and, as a man held me by the feet, I leaned down, grabbed the kayak and pulled it up to the deck. The Coast Guard boat

(continued from page 91)
held in the outrigger position by the paddler during reentry. From the evidence, it is not clear which of these two rescues David Kelley was attempting. The paddle-float rescue is performed as follows, once the float has been attached to the paddle blade:

1. Starting from the right rear quadrant, hold the paddle shaft to the rear of the coaming with your right thumb.
2. Hook the right foot over the paddle shaft.
3. Pull your chest up on the rear deck so it is resting on the paddle shaft.
4. While always keeping at least one hand or foot holding the paddle perpendicular

to the kayak, pivot around on your chest until both feet and both knees are in the cockpit.
5. Twist down into the seat.

This rescue has the advantage of creating less risk of capsize or equipment damage in surf or large breakers than a fixed outrigger would if caught by a breaker before it could be removed. It also makes a rescue possible in situations where there is no means of securing a paddle to the afterdeck. But it does not provide the hands-off stability needed for securing the spray deck and pumping out once reentry has taken place.

arrived a moment later. I was amazed at how fast and efficient everyone was.

"I drank coffee and toasted the crew with a shot of whiskey. *The Harbor Queen* picked me up about two hundred yards off Alcatraz. I had swam about five hundred yards and spent about an hour in the water. I was not cold, but I was hungry. I later wrote letters commending everyone involved."

LESSONS LEARNED

In Eric's words: "The main lesson I learned from this? I had made a rational (ha) decision to paddle alone through storm conditions. My big mistake was to paddle a boat I was not familiar with."

Eric is correct: Paddling an unfamiliar boat in serious conditions ranks high on the list of dangerous experiments. This is due both to the unpredictability of the kayak and the fact that tried-and-true self-rescue methods may no longer apply. In particular, Eric's experience dramatically points out the flaws in the reentry-and-Eskimo-roll technique that many solo paddlers believe will back up their Eskimo roll. Even though the Icefloe is 24 inches wide and equipped with bulkheads limiting water entry to the cockpit area and a built-in pump that can be operated with one hand, the kayak remained too unstable for Eric to get the spray deck refastened or pump the water out without capsizing. If Eric could have fastened his spray deck when he first reentered the kayak (upside down), and then rolled, he may have been able to stay upright long enough to empty his cockpit with a high-capacity electric pump if he'd had one.

Two things spelled the difference between Eric's frightening experience and David Kelley's tragedy. First, Eric wore a wetsuit. Second, although Eric believes he could have swum to Alcatraz, he had, and used, flares to summon help. He had the good sense to use them when they were most likely to be spotted, rather than waiting to see if he could make it to Alcatraz on his own—tempting as that might have been for a man who takes pride in his self-sufficiency.

10

The Phantom Barge

Alison Armstrong

On July 3, 1990, Ken Wade and I set sail on the Hudson River in Ken's 17-foot folding kayak. We had put in around 4:30 P.M. (just before high tide) at the Downtown Boat Club at Pier 26, near Vestry Street, to sail the kayak up river with the flood tide and paddle back down with the ebb at around 10:30 P.M. We had made numerous day trips between Saugerties and New York Harbor, and this was to be our longest sail yet.

We rigged the kayak with new leeboards, running lights, aluminum mast and boom, mainsail, and jib. We packed drybags with first-aid kit, pocket flashlight, waterproof lantern, flares, mirror, whistle, spare warm clothing, food, and drinking water. Each of us had a life jacket—a Type II PFD.

The sail up river in a stiff southwesterly wind was beautiful, and by 7:30 in the evening we had reached a tiny beach on the New Jersey shore just north of the George Washington Bridge. We stopped to stretch our legs and eat our picnic supper, then continued to sail north beyond the Cloisters. The Palisades glowed in the twilight of a perfect summer evening. The river was bathed in lavender light from the setting sun, and a nearly full moon rose over Manhattan. Colorful sparks from fireworks too far away to hear illuminated the broad, calm river. Pleasure boats of all sizes greeted us; an occasional barge pushed by a tug passed regally.

As twilight turned to darkness, I signaled other boats with the nine-volt marine lantern and shined it on the sails. We attached a red-and-green running light to the cross section of the leeboards, and Ken had a small light fixed on the stern.

Darkness grew and the moon rose high over the bridge. At 10:00 we decided to turn with the tide, which was beginning to ebb, and sail back down river for as long as we could, tacking against the wind. The new leeboards were working well and the kayak felt very stable under sail. We were making such good time that we were reluctant to switch to paddling. Since the tide had not completely turned and the wind was still coming from the southwest, we estimated that we would pass beneath the bridge sailing southward after four tacks; but in fact we made our way under the massive bridge on the second tack and got a fairly close view of the little red lighthouse that sits under the supporting steel pillars on the Manhattan shore.

A large paddle-wheeler blaring loud dance music looped around us several times. The lively passengers waved and called out to us each time they passed by us. We responded by waving our lights as we continued to tack against the wind. Feeling relaxed, competent, and fortunate, we continued to sail and made good progress.

As we approached 125th Street, Manhattan, the wind picked up and the river became turbulent and battered us with noisy chop. We made good speed heading directly into the waves on the southwesterly tacks, but shipped quite a bit of water over the coaming when tacking toward the New York shore. As we tacked, my PFD made it difficult for me to move, so I removed it and placed it between my knees. I periodically scanned the river with the lantern and illuminated our sails to warn other boats of our presence. Although we had right-of-way over motorized vessels, we were always prepared to give way to larger, faster boats.

At about midnight, after nearly an hour of intense sailing through heavy water, the waves seemed to subside a bit, but as we came about on the New Jersey side Ken decided that it would be better to finish the next southeastward tack at the 79th Street Marina, where we could rest and take down the mast and sails. We could then paddle down river, close to the Manhattan shore, to Pier 26.

As we prepared to scan the water again for other boats, Ken looked over his left shoulder and cried out, "Quick, give me my paddle!"

I swung around from my seat in the front; with my left hand I reached to untoggle Ken's paddle and at the same time lifted my lamp with my right arm. A dark wall of steel, some thirty feet high, bore down on us. It seemed to have come from nowhere. It had no lights and no one was on it to call out to. We had only an instant to act, and I called out to Ken, "Too late to change course!" Expecting to feel the crunch of a thousand tons of steel on my backbone, I rose from my seat and dove over the right leeboard.

I don't recall hitting the water, but I remember taking the first stroke toward the Jersey shore, looking up over my right shoulder, and seeing the steel wall. Then foaming water flooded over my eyes—and a sucking power pulled me back and under. Despite my attempts to swim, I was sucked into a churning vortex beneath the massive steel hull. I could hear the incessant, dull roar of the motor as it surged above me and felt the barge's hull press and rub against my back. I was afraid that my clothing might get caught.

I knew that there must be a propeller coming up soon—that I must dive or get chopped to bits by its blades. I opened my eyes and, working against instinct, exhaled and dove as deeply as I could. The filthy river water above me bubbled with a greenish glow. I fought against the impulse to breath in, amazed that I was able to keep from gasping for breath for so long. "Just this moment, keep alive *this* moment," I told myself.

At last the pressure that held me beneath the hull let up, enough so I could struggle toward the surface as the side of the barge passed over. As soon as I surfaced, I heard Ken's choking voice calling my name. I turned toward the departing roar and saw his head bobbing among the waves as the blunt back end of a huge barge, pushed on the opposite rear corner by a white tugboat, plowed down river, its crew unaware of us struggling in its wake.

Everything became very still except for the surging waves and the occasional burst of fireworks over Manhattan. As we swam toward one another, I saw that Ken could barely keep his head above water or raise his arms. I ripped open the zipper of my water-soaked jacket and tore it off my arms impatiently, thinking that I must get hold of Ken, support his head, and perhaps try to swim before we both went under. I shouted, "Where's the boat?"

Ken saw the black hull of the overturned kayak floating about ten yards away down river. His windbreaker jacket, which was tight at the wrists, was holding so much water that he could not lift his arms to swim. Dog paddling, he got to the kayak and kept calling for me until I reached his side.

Together, we managed to rock the kayak once, and it righted itself immediately. The mast and sails had become dislodged and were hanging overboard from the rigging. The kayak was half full of water but afloat, thanks to the inflated sponsons along the gunwales.

I hooked my left arm over the starboard coaming and attempted to kick myself free of the rigging, which had tangled around my legs. Ken got astride the stern and handed me the small flashlight from the pocket of his windbreaker. I shined it in the hope of attracting the attention of other boats. But by now, approximately twenty minutes past midnight, there was no river traffic—until *another* barge passed, pushed up river in the opposite channel along the Manhattan shore. We cried out, "Help!" over and over, but the barge continued up river. The possibility of being struck and run over a second time overwhelmed us with horror. We were exactly in mid-river. Using Ken's paddle, we attempted to direct the kayak toward the Manhattan side. We soon realized we would not be able to paddle to shore before the combined forces of the river current and outgoing tide swept us by Manhattan.

Ken retrieved the waterproof flares from his repair kit. As the waves inundated the boat and splashed into our faces, he attempted to read by moonlight the tiny print of the instructions. The first flare went off quickly and burned a hole in his right index finger. He fired the remaining two flares aloft, but they were no competition for the early Independence Day fireworks on the shore. With nothing left but a whistle and tiny flashlight, we decided that he should signal SOS on the whistle and I would keep shining the flashlight. We watched our large marine lantern float downstream out of reach, beaming its strong light uselessly at the sky. The waves that kept washing over us from the south did nothing to slow the pull of the outgoing tide, which moved us toward New York Harbor at four knots. We were being washed out to sea.

Ken had been struck in the back of the head by the barge, making it difficult for him to keep his balance astride the stern of the kayak while he paddled and blew SOS signals on his marine whistle. I retrieved my life jacket, the canvas waterproof food bag, and a drybag that floated nearby and stuffed them into the prow to give it some buoyancy.

We had been struck about 80th Street and we were now drifting by 34th Street, past our Greenwich Village apartments and past our put-in at the Downtown Boat Club. The waves were steadily washing away our body heat and our strength.

After about forty-five minutes on the water, we saw a cluster of lights and heard voices. A white cabin cruiser, brilliantly lit, drew near. At first I was uncertain whether anyone on it saw or heard us, but soon we realized that the motor was turned down and it was slowly and steadily circling in. Four young men leaned over the side. Their presence seemed as sudden and benevolent as the barge's appearance had been sudden and brutal. I managed to reach the prow of the kayak and retrieve its towline while the boys reached for me with a pole and pulled me up into their bright, warm craft. I handed them the line and collapsed. When they pulled Ken aboard, I saw for the first time that he was bleeding heavily from a gash on the back of his head.

We sat shivering while our rescuers alerted the Coast Guard on their radio. The Coast Guard responded their presence was not necessary since no one was killed and "only" a kayak was involved. (Their policy, we were later told, is not to investigate damage to boats worth less than $25,000.) Our four rescuers good-naturedly begged us not to put their names in the paper. They had borrowed the cabin cruiser, which belonged to one of their fathers, without permission. A thank-you and handshake were all they needed. One of the young men said, "I had this premonition it would be just our bad luck to find some-one who needed rescuing tonight when we're not supposed to be out on the river." It was our good luck that they were!

After a muffled radio conversation with the Coast Guard, the young men revved the motor and headed for Hoboken with the kayak in tow. We watched helplessly as some of our equipment washed away. They wrapped us in dry tow-els and blankets and took us inside the warm cabin. We went ashore at the Imperial Marina in Weehawken, New Jersey, where paramedics were waiting for us. We stepped into what seemed a freezing air-conditioned ambulance. The young paramedics seemed to be interested only in repeatedly taking our blood pressures, despite a blare of rock and roll coming from the ambulance radio that must have made it impossible for them to hear a pulse.

We fared no better in the emergency room—nobody seemed to understand that we were in shock, cold, and dripping with filthy water, that Ken was still bleeding from an open head wound. No one thought to get us dry, clean, and warm. The first order of protocol was to put us into wheelchairs and interview us at length about our insurance status while we sat in the air-conditioned lobby.

After twenty minutes I insisted that Ken get treatment for his bleeding head wound. When I tried to follow Ken through the flapping green doors to the emergency room, hospital staff held me back, but eventually also admitted me to the ER. A nurse joked, "How'd you hold your breath so long? Sure is a good thing you don't smoke. Anything I can get you?" I longed for a smoke and cup of coffee but I had to be content with an aspirin and cup of weak tea. After what seemed hours of intense listening for sounds of life from Ken, who lay behind the next wall, we were reunited by a sympathetic male nurse.

At 4:00 A.M. on the Fourth of July, we were released from St. Mary's emergency room. Barefoot, wearing nothing but green cotton hospital gowns (the type that tie at the back and flap open), without any money, and carrying our soaked belongings in a large, clear plastic bag, we walked out of the hospital into a taxicab. On the way to Manhattan, we announced to the driver that we had money but none with us. We persuaded him to go through the tunnel under the Hudson River and on to our apartment building and wait at the curb while Ken and I ran in turn up to our respective apartments to find what money we could to pay him.

The next day, we retrieved Ken's kayak and his water-soaked wallet from the pier where it had been dumped at the Imperial Marina in Weehawken. We dried out his personal papers and dollar bills on the dashboard, dismantled the kayak, and returned home. And began to ask questions.

Why did the barge not slow its pace or blow a horn or otherwise signal that it was bearing down from behind? Though our kayak was too low in the water to be picked up by radar, surely even from a distance the tug pilot could have *seen* our little sails. Do tug pilots look where they are going or rely only on instruments for navigation?

A Coast Guard lieutenant told Ken that there are "unlit barges engaged in illegal traffic at night on the Hudson."

The police recorded the incident as a case of "hit and run." To us, the barge remains a phantom—and a reminder of the prudence required of boaters on a large river where commercial traffic adds to the complexities of river currents and wind and tidal patterns. We continue to paddle and sail on the Hudson—but never after dark.

LESSONS LEARNED

Christopher Cunningham comments: Kayaking in commercial shipping lanes is risky business. At night, and whenever visibility is reduced, the risk is much greater. At a distance, tugs with barges and other large vessels may not seem to be moving quickly—"an occasional barge pushed by a tug passed regally"—but a kayak is no match for their speed. Large vessels have limited maneuverability; they are slow to turn and stop. Even if the tug had spotted the sails of the kayak, it might not have been able to avoid a collision.

On rivers, tugs push barges rather than tow them on the end of a cable as is the common practice in larger bodies of water. The noise of the tug's engine may be several hundred feet behind the bow of the lead barge. There may be only a faint hissing noise at the forward end of the barge—not a noise loud enough to give much warning. Tugs usually display three white lights arranged vertically to indicate that something is in tow; these lights may be your only clue to look for a barge that may have only dim kerosene lanterns for running lights. If there are other lights along shore or on the horizon (buoys, channel markers, or other vessels), you might be able to detect the presence of a nearby vessel when those distant lights "blink off" as the vessel crosses in front of them.

Alison was scanning the river and illuminating their sails with her flashlight. But the flashlight wouldn't have been bright enough to help them detect any other traffic, and its reflected glow off the sails may not have been as visible as she hoped. Using the flashlight also would have dulled Alison and Ken's night vision, making it more difficult to distinguish the faint outline of the barge among the shadows.

At night, larger vessels may be relying heavily on radar for navigation. From the bridge, the helmsman would be keeping an eye out for aids to navigation and for other vessels. A small kayak sailing across the shipping lanes at midnight isn't something a pilot would be on the lookout for. The view over the bow of a large vessel has a large blind spot extending far ahead. In this incident, the view from the tug, at the barge's stern, would have been obstructed by the barge's tall bow. The kayak could have sailed into the blind spot long before the collision.

Ken and Alison may have found the sailing exhilarating and felt they were "making good time," but their zig-zag course tacking down the river means they may not have been "making good distance." Not only would they have made quicker progress toward their destination by paddling straight into the wind, they also would have been able to keep out of the shipping lanes and close to shore where there would have been little, if any, other traffic. Even though there were two of them in the boat, a lone double kayak carries many of the same risks as a solo paddler. Without another kayak to assist in a rescue, keeping within easy reach of shore provides a margin of safety when something goes wrong.

While power is supposed to yield to sail, it is appropriate for recreational boats to yield to working vessels and for more maneuverable boats to yield to less maneuverable ones. Kayakers should also obey the commonsense "rule of greater tonnage": If it is bigger than you, stay out of its way.

11

Run-in with a Great White

Ken Kelton

Año Nuevo Island is a barren patch of rocks about sixty miles south of San Francisco. It was once the tip of a short, grassy peninsula and the site of an old Coast Guard light station. Many years ago, a storm cut through the low peninsula, isolating the light station across several hundred yards of wave-swept shallows. A huge, many-chimneyed Victorian station house dominates this treeless knoll. The gaunt, haunted-looking building streaked white with sea bird guano stands vacant. Nearby, the great steel, Eiffel-style light tower lies rusting on its side, thrown down by some long-past storm. A few dilapidated outbuildings dot the rest of the quarter-mile-long island, giving it an eerie, ghost-town look.

But the island is teeming with life. Great colonies of sea lions and seals sprawl on its beaches and rocks. Seals large and small crowd each other and struggle for space on the beaches, while mobs of seals cavort in the surf offshore. The cacophonous barking and bellowing is constant as pelicans wheel overhead and dive into the sea. A benign chaos seems to rule this mass of creatures as they jostle for space, but beneath the waves lurks a terrible predator—the great white shark.

It is unseen and therefore not to be believed. The possibility of an encounter with this four-thousand-pound killer seems as remote as being hit by a meteor. Mike Chin and I launch our kayaks through the surf for my sixth trip to Año Nuevo. Mike is a veteran river kayaker on his first open ocean trip. He asks me about the great white.

"Sharks? Nah, never seen any." After all, I think, we are only observers of the food chain, not participants.

A wave rushes toward us as we paddle out from the beach. Its green, glassy face arches up and over as we blast through its foamy crest. Cold sea water rushes down the neck of my ragged wetsuit. We paddle out past the impact zone and turn down the coast toward the island, a few miles away. Mike paddles a wash-deck surf kayak, long, sleek, and very fast, while I am in an old river kayak with a metal skeg attached with duct tape. Its plastic hull is tough as leather and turns on a dime, but it's painfully slow compared to a sea kayak; I have to struggle to keep up with Mike as he glides along.

Rusty-colored jellyfish undulate along, parachutelike a few feet down in the clear, cold water. Purple encrusted rocks loom below us as we rise and fall in the light swell, and black bull-kelp heads pop up suddenly alongside. We paddle through masses of transparent jellylike gobs, each containing a cherry-pit egg of some sort. I stop to pick one up, but a rogue wave comes out of nowhere, and I have to scramble clear.

We paddle around a big, isolated rock and startle a flock of black, long-necked cormorants. They had been sunning themselves with their wings out-stretched to dry after diving for fish. Dozens of them leap off the rock, flapping madly, but their water-logged wings won't lift them, and they dash along the surface, leaving little footprint splashes in the water as they gradually pick up speed and take off.

Pelicans cruise majestically, skimming the surface. They fly in a line along the face of a rising wave, picking up speed as they arc effortlessly into the air, where the leader wheels abruptly and dives thirty feet down into the sea to catch a hap-less fish. A seagull looking for scraps lands next to the pelican. The pelican flips its head back, and a lump moves from its baggy pouch down its throat.

We are approaching the island, and its desolation is oppressive. But we have begun to hear the seals. As we hit the crest of a wave, the din is more evident. It is punctuated by the occasional guttural fumble of the elephant seal's roar, a string of deep pops like some giant outboard motor that won't quite start. Soon we are assaulted by the pungent odor of thousands of seals digesting fish. We paddle a little farther out to sea, out of line with the breeze, and the odor disappears.

We enter the shallow straits between the island and peninsula. Seals are everywhere. All along the beaches and rocks is a seething mass of life. Great bull Stellar sea lions, some the size of grizzly bears, have staked out territories on the rocks, and they bellow at us as we paddle by. Gigantic, sluglike elephant seals undulate their blubbery bodies up the beach. A big bull rears up, inflating his grotesque schnoz and brandishing his two oddly puny-looking tusks. Small har-bor seals leave the beaches to these behemoths and discretely occupy the rocky tip of the island, while great crowds of California sea lions cavort in the surf. As we paddle by, mobs of seals dash off the beach and swarm toward us, barking furiously. We back off, but they rush at us, as if they were going to crash into our kayaks. When they are a few feet away, they dive down and pass under us. A big one pops up right behind me with a startling snort. We paddle out to the point, where the big waves break. We watch seals twisting and turning with balletlike grace, surfing inside a moving, translucent wave.

Some of the seals ignore us and wrestle, while others loll about on the sur-face, some with one flipper extended limply into the air in a languid salute. As we approach they duck beneath the surface.

By now we have been paddling about three hours. We are getting hungry and cross the straits to the mainland side. We paddle north to find somewhere to land to eat lunch and come upon a small, isolated colony of harbor seals. We are about one hundred and fifty yards out from where they are lying on the sandy beach. Just outside the surf zone, I notice that there are about forty seals on the beach and none in the water. We have the water to ourselves, and I am about to find out why.

We are paddling slowly, and Mike is about twenty feet ahead of me. He stops and turns to me, and we begin to discuss the best route around some nearby rocks. Fairly big surf is breaking there, and we should probably go around. Suddenly I hear a blast of water, and out of the corner of my eye I see something burst from the water. I hear and feel a violent impact against my kayak, right behind me. "Hey, man," I whine, remembering a previous trip when I was rammed from below by a playful seal. The seal had given me one hell of a scare, and I hadn't appreciated it. Evidently it had meant no harm, and I had managed not to capsize.

Mike watches as a huge great white shark lunges up through the surface. it latches its jaws around the kayak, just behind me, and then blasts over half of its giant bulk out of the water. My kayak is about twelve feet long, but the shark is much, much longer. I catch a glimpse over my right shoulder of a tall, shiny, black fin as high as my head. Holding my boat just behind the cockpit, the shark skims briefly across the surface on its belly. Then it begins a violent thrashing. As I struggle to stay in the cockpit, it lifts my kayak completely out of the water and slams it from side to side. Mike sees me disappear in a mass of foam and spray. "That's it, Ken's dead," he thinks. But I burst back into view, flailing at the water with my paddle, trying to stay in the boat and keep it upright.

The thrashing goes on for five to ten long seconds. I don't look back again, and I don't think. I know that some huge, vicious creature is right behind me, and my only hope is to maintain control of my kayak. My Eskimo roll is marginal in the best of conditions, so I *will not capsize!* I dig at the water furiously with my paddle, sometimes missing the surface completely as the shark swings me back and forth. Amid the foam and spray, I hear the hollow, tortured squeaking of his teeth crushing and tearing the plastic behind me.

Gradually my paddle grips the surface as the attack diminishes. As my kayak becomes more or less horizontal, I feel it slip free. My fear spurs me to paddle furiously. I know I have broken free of the shark, but I can still *feel* him; he's right with me. Warp drive. Still no time to think, and the fastest paddling posture is eyes straight ahead.

I paddle about fifty feet before I lose the sense of his presence. Only then do I know the attack has stopped, and I look back. There is a huge bite mark in the rear deck of the kayak. It is close enough to touch.

"Oh m'God, oh m'God, oh m'God," I mutter as Mike catches up to me. His eyes are wide and his mouth gapes open. *"Sh . . . Sh . . . Shaaark,"* he stammers. Then I notice that as my knees knock inside the boat, they also splash. The shark has bitten right through the heavy plastic, and I am taking on water quickly. We are now about two hundred yards out from the beach with the seal

colony. We have to get to shore fast, but I am *not* going through the same spot. We scramble a little ways north, around the rocks, and head in. By now the boat is completely awash. Not only has the shark bitten through the hull, it has slashed through the starboard inflatable flotation bag. The port float bag is still okay, so the kayak does not sink, but it is like paddling a bath tub. I move agonizingly slowly. Mike is pretty shaken up, but he stays with me.

As I reach the surf zone, it is very difficult to keep the boat upright. If I go over, I will have to exit the kayak and swim for it. There is nothing Mike can do for me, but it is very comforting to see him so close.

I'm moving too slowly! I have to get out of the water before the shark returns. In near desperation, I try to surf the clumsy tub in. As a wave forms, I turn the kayak broadside and brace my paddle through the wave face. I expect the breaking wave to pick up the boat and wash it sideways into the beach, an effective if not-so-graceful kayak surfing technique. No luck. The waterlogged craft just sinks into the wave, and I nearly capsize. As my kayak rises sluggishly back to the surface, I resume my careful and intense paddling.

In a few minutes I'm within thirty yards of the beach. The water is very shallow. Finally, with a pleasing little bump, I'm high and dry in the sand. I scramble out of the cockpit as Mike lands next to me, and together we dump the water out and drag my kayak to high ground. By now we have both begun to relax a little. We look over my boat. There is a circle of teeth cuts measuring seventeen inches in diameter and extending halfway around the kayak. We look unsuccessfully for tooth fragments. I surprise myself by my quick transition from being terrified to hunting for souvenirs.

I stand up and look back out to sea. The sun still shines brightly, and the waves roll across the blue-green surface. All seems quiet and benign, but in the distance Año Nuevo's little ghost town stands out like a warning beacon.

Soon, a mounted park ranger rides out from between the dunes toward us. She is tall, stern and proper, and wears a pistol on her hip.

"This is a restricted area; you can't land here," she snaps, reaching for her citation book. I gesture at the side of my kayak with my foot, saying nothing. The semicircle of red shredded plastic is self-explanatory. Flaps of torn plastic stick out in the sun.

"*Oh, my God . . .*" She catches on fast. And no, she won't make us paddle back out to sea.

LESSONS LEARNED

According to Sheila Heathcote's Spring 1993 *Sea Kayaker* article "Beyond 'Jaws,'" fewer than one hundred shark attacks are reported worldwide each year; only about thirty of those are fatal. Nevertheless, kayakers should be watchful in areas where seals and sea lions gather—prime feeding areas for some shark breeds. "Sharks attack when they are startled by a swimmer's approach. They also strike to protect their territory and are especially touchy during mating season. Some sharks are attracted by the scent of blood and heightened vibrations, such as those caused by injured fish."

Shark attacks most commonly occur along coastlines of North and South America, Australia, and South Africa. Research areas where you'll be paddling: Is there a history of shark activity in the area? Do seals or sea lions feed nearby? Although you may be able to ward off an attacking shark by striking it with a paddle, your best defense is avoiding these creatures in the first place.

—*Sheila Heathcote, "Beyond 'Jaws,'"* Sea Kayaker *(Spring 1993) 13–15.*

12

Double Fatality in Prince William Sound

George Gronseth

Two brothers died in a kayaking accident during the summer of 1989 in Blackstone Bay, Alaska, a glacial bay in the Prince William Sound area, about forty miles southeast of Anchorage. The victims were part of a group of six kayakers. The double kayak they were paddling, and two other single kayaks, capsized in following seas.

The group had arranged for a charter boat to drop them off that Friday evening at a beach inside Blackstone Bay. On Sunday, the charter boat would return to the same beach to pick them up. This plan gave the group, which included three who had no previous kayaking experience, the option of spending the entire weekend ashore if conditions were rough or if one of the first-time paddlers didn't feel comfortable in a kayak.

Their plans changed on Thursday, when the charter boat captain called and said he would be unable to pick them up as scheduled as he had to pick up another group of kayakers on Sunday afternoon. After some discussion, it was decided that the boat would pick them up Sunday evening at Squirrel Cove, just outside of Blackstone Bay. This would allow the group to get back to Whittier in time to make their connections for subsequent travel. Three members of the

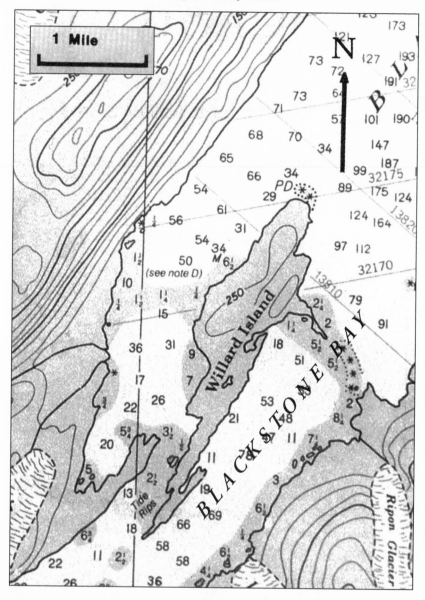

group were from California and had planned to catch the train from Whittier to reach the Anchorage Airport in time for their flight home. The rest of the group also needed to catch a train Sunday to be back at work in Anchorage on Monday.

To get to Squirrel Cove the kayakers would have to paddle around Decision Point, an area of potentially rough water that they originally had tried to avoid by planning to rendezvous with the charter boat inside Blackstone Bay. Rather than cancel the trip, they agreed to the new plan, with a provision that the captain would look for them along the north shore of the bay if they weren't at Squirrel Cove on time.

On Friday, August 18, the group took the train (there is no road) from Portage to Whittier, rented kayaks, and took the charter boat to Blackstone Bay. No one in the group owned a kayak. Bill, Judith, and Greg had never been in a kayak before. Mike, Greg's brother, had made a three-day kayak trip with some friends earlier that summer, his only previous experience. His trip had been in Culruss Passage, a more sheltered part of Prince William Sound. Carol had received some kayaking instruction while on a trip in Baja, Mexico.

Though Beth was the most experienced, she considered herself only a novice to intermediate sea kayaker. She had been to some pool sessions and had kayaked a couple of Class II (moderately easy) river trips about seven years earlier. With the exception of a previous trip to Blackstone Bay in 1984, she hadn't kayaked again until she took a sea-kayaking class in the summer of 1988. The class was composed of three evenings of lectures, which emphasized safety, and one pool session to practice wet exits and reentry techniques. Beth did well with two-person rescues but wasn't able to do a paddle-float self rescue. At the time, she thought that she didn't have the upper body strength for the self rescue. (Since the accident in Blackstone Bay, she has learned to perform self rescues and feels the high rear deck of the boat she was using in class kept her from succeeding at that time.) She also had read a book on paddling technique and watched a kayak-rescue training video at a kayak shop before renting a boat. During the last two summers, she had gone on numerous kayak trips, including two lengthy ones. Before and during the Blackstone trip, Beth and the others discussed some safety matters, especially what to do in case of a capsize.

The group's kayaks were made by a variety of manufacturers; each of the four boats was a different model but each was a relatively wide, "stable" kayak, common in the Northwest. The kayak shop where they had rented the kayaks had equipped them with front and rear flotation, spray skirts, deck lines, and rudders. A rudder pedal on the double Bill and Judith rented had been repaired with duct tape. Aside from this, all of the rented equipment was in good condition.

All the paddles used by the group were the same popular, wide-blade model; only their lengths differed. None of the paddles had been tethered to the kayaks. Everyone wore life jackets whenever they were on the water. The group had one spare paddle, two bilge pumps, and one paddle float. They kept their gear in trash-compactor bags; stuffed through hatches into bulkhead compartments, the bags kept things dry. They had a topographical map of Blackstone Bay but no nautical charts. Beth had a whistle and a signaling mirror. None of the paddlers had wetsuits or drysuits.

On Friday evening, the charter boat dropped the group off on the east side of Blackstone Bay, just east of the north tip of Willard Island. That night, the party camped at the drop-off area.

On Saturday afternoon, they began paddling southwest along the east side of Willard Island. The weather had been calm but rainy. On Saturday night, they camped on the peninsula just east of Blackstone Glacier.

On Sunday, the group paddled between the peninsula and Willard Island, fighting high winds and a two-foot chop while crossing one of the bay's shallow spots. They struggled toward Squirrel Cove, where they had planned to meet the charter boat.

Their progress toward Squirrel Cove was slow; some had trouble controlling their kayaks in the chop. (During the trip several members complained about difficulties using the rudders. At the time of the accident, the double with the repaired pedal was the only boat to reach land safely.) By about 3:00 P.M., they had gone less than two miles. Squirrel Cove was another twelve miles away. They realized they probably wouldn't get back that night and decided to make camp and wait for better weather.

That evening, as planned, the charter boat went to Squirrel Cove to pick up the kayakers. Upon not finding the kayakers at the cove, the captain looked along the north side of Blackstone Bay.

The kayakers saw a large motorboat, but it never came close enough to identify it positively, even with binoculars. They climbed on top of a twenty-five-foot-high boulder near their camp and attempted to signal the boat by waving their paddles, which probably blended in with the background. The group had no flares, horns, or smoke signals. Because of the wind and the scarcity of

Paddling in Wind

Matt Broze

A following sea is one of the trickiest conditions for a paddler and a kayak to handle. If you can stay on-line directly downwind, you'll be pushed along by the wind and pulled down the faces of the waves. When surfing, you can reach speeds you may have never though possible in a kayak. This can be both exhilarating and frightening. Unfortunately, it's not easy to hold a course downwind when the wind shifts and the waves wander. Once you've turned a little to the side of a course straight down the wave, the wind and waves combine to turn you even further sideways.

A broach begins when a kayak's stern is lifted into the air behind the crest of the wave. At this point much of the keel that had been keeping it on-line is out of the water. A rudder at the stern of the kayak also may be in the air or far enough out of the water to be ineffective at this critical time. In extreme winds, the stern may be blown to the side when it is up in the air during the early part of the broach.

Even the best paddlers can quickly find themselves yawing off course, locked into a broach. Depending as much on your kayak's design as your skill, a broach can vary from an unwanted carved turn to the side to a sideways skid down the face of the wave.

To counteract broaching once it has started, try a combination of several or all of the following techniques. If the kayak has a rudder (and the rudder is still in the water), angle it. Tilt the kayak opposite from the direction you wish to turn. Use wide, powerful sweep strokes on the up-wave side with a strong stern draw at the end to try to lift the stern back up the dry wood, their beach fire was small and may not have been visible in daylight (it wouldn't be dark until after 10:00) to the motorboat a mile or more from the beach. The fire would have been low on the horizon, where waves may have obscured it from the view of the boat.

On the side of the bay where the kayakers were camped, a submerged glacial moraine reduces the depth of the bay to 1¼ fathoms (at mean low tide); the bottom is twenty-five fathoms deep on each side of the moraine. The sudden rise accelerates the bay's currents and causes waves to steepen and break. In high winds there are steep, confused seas for about a quarter-mile around the moraine. The charter boat, a 40-footer, probably would have been at risk of hitting bottom if the captain had tried to cross the shoal. The captain later reported that it looked so rough in that part of the bay that he didn't think the kayakers would have gone into it. He turned around before crossing the shoal.

The kayakers' topographical map indicated a shoal on the west side of the island but did not show the shoal to the south or the one stretching west from the island to the shore where the paddlers were camped. The nautical chart of Blackstone Bay, which they didn't have, shows all three shoals around Willard Island and indicates tide rips over the area where the group had some trouble on Sunday. From the beach, the confused seas caused by the shoal would have been hidden by the small waves in the foreground.

wave. A stern rudder stroke on the downwind side of the wave can hold the kayak from broaching if done quickly before the kayak is skidding sideways.

On waves so steep you don't need to paddle for speed, the stern rudder is the stroke of choice to keep you on the wave. Once you're skidding sideways, do not use the stern rudder unless it has a strong bracing component that allows it to also slide over the surface. A skidding kayak can trip over the paddle and send you tumbling down the wave.

A kayak with a rudder, fin, or deep keel at the stern may have another problem: If the stern comes out of the water during a sudden broach, the stern can come back into the water when the kayak has rotated about 45 degrees. The sudden re-immersion of a rudder, fin, or stern keel can trip the kayak and initiate a roll down the face

of the wave. Be prepared for this by leaning into the face of the wave and gripping the kayak solidly by applying pressure with your down-wave knee. Use a high or low brace into the wave to support your lean.

There are other ways to arrive at your downwind destination if you prefer not to surf. Slow down or backpaddle to cut your speed whenever you are in danger of being surfed. When the waves are passing you, it is much easier to stay on course. Use the powerful stern rudder stroke to stay on course and as a brake if necessary.

You might be able to avoid broaching if you apply appropriate techniques quickly, frequently, and powerfully. Attentiveness, quick reflexes, and experience are your best bets for staying on course once gravity sends you surfing down the face of a wave.

At dusk the charter boat headed back to Whittier. The kayakers spotted another powerboat that evening, but again their attempts to signal it were unsuccessful.

None of them got much sleep that night. Since they had not planned to spend another night out, some of them hadn't packed carefully that morning and their spare clothes and sleeping bags were now wet. Their food supply was low. Worst of all, a cold wind coming down from the glaciers blew through their camp. Every few hours, the strong gusts threatened to collapse their tents.

The kayakers got up early Monday, hoping the wind would diminish enough to allow them to paddle out of the bay on the ebb. They ate some fruit and cookies and watched the waves from the beach with their binoculars for several hours.

The captain of the charter boat was also up early that morning. He was concerned about the group and by 5:50 was on his way from Whittier to look for them again. He retraced his route into Blackstone Bay, again going only as far as the shoal of the moraine. The wind and current would have made the sea rough over the moraine. When the kayakers saw the powerboat, they climbed up on the boulder again and waved their paddles, but again they were unsuccessful in signaling the boat. The charter boat turned and was soon out of sight.

The kayakers thought the boat had left the bay again. (In fact, the captain, continuing his search, was on his way to circumnavigate Willard Island, clockwise.) The wind seemed to have eased a bit and, from the beach, the waves appeared to be smaller than those they had encountered on Sunday. They decided to paddle to Decision Point, at the entrance of the bay, in hopes of getting picked up. They left the beach about 9:00 A.M. Bill and Judith, in a double, were the first off the beach. Beth, in her single, went last. The kayak at the tail end of a group is often in a good position to "sweep"—that is, watch and help the others if they have trouble. Unfortunately, Beth would be the first to capsize.

The wind direction varied, but as they tried to follow the shoreline, they had to beat into the wind. The lead double couldn't make headway, and the side component of the wind pushed all of them away from shore. The group was getting spread out. Beth yelled for the others to hug the shore, but the group had separated too much to hear one another over the wind and waves. Beth headed toward the mainland shore, hoping the others would see her and do the same. Instead, the group continued to get fanned out. Bill and Judith's double was pointed downwind toward Willard Island across the channel. The others were paddling parallel to shore but drifting farther from it. Beth turned around and headed out to rejoin the others. On this course the waves came at her from astern.

The waves seemed to get very big all of a sudden; soon they were breaking. This could have been because the shoal was causing the waves to steepen. Ahead of her, Beth could see the other kayaks struggling to keep upright. Greg and Mike, in a kayak with closely spaced cockpits that required them to paddle synchronously, were having trouble coordinating their efforts in the rough conditions. With the waves coming from behind her, Beth couldn't anticipate them. It wasn't long before a wave caught her off guard and capsized her. After she bailed out she was too low in the water to see the other kayaks beyond the waves. She blew her whistle, but no one heard.

Carol, paddling the other single kayak, capsized as well. She tried to get back in the cockpit several times, but each time a wave knocked her over. She gave up trying to reenter the kayak and pulled herself partway out of the water over the middle of the boat and kicked her way to the shore of Willard Island upright. She got ashore before Beth, but Carol was the more hypothermic of the two, probably because she was smaller and leaner. They were wearing similar clothing: synthetic long underwear tops and bottoms, nylon shorts, and wool socks. Beth also had a pile hat, a coated nylon windbreaker, and a hood that she wore over her hat. Both were barefoot when they got to shore.

Meanwhile, Bill and Judith struggled to keep their double from capsizing; they felt they would tip over if they did anything but go with the waves. They managed to reach Willard Island. They had been separated by a great distance from their friends and might not have been able to see that the others were in trouble. The severity of the waves would have precluded them from paddling back out without capsizing.

By the time the charter boat reached the southwest side of the island, the capsizes had occurred. The charter boat passed to the west of them, close enough for Beth to see it when she wasn't down in a wave trough. No doubt the choppy water obscured the powerboat's view of the kayaks and swimmers. The captain was alone and probably was looking mostly to the northwest, in the direction of the shore where the group was supposed to be. Beth waved her arms from the water. Bill and Judith tried to signal from the shore of Willard Island, but all in vain.

Beth said later that the waves were at least five feet high and very steep. Though it's difficult for anyone to accurately judge wave height, the fact that green water was washing over her bow and hitting her is a clear indication that the conditions were indeed very rough. (The rescuers who would eventually find the group on the island reported that the waves in this area were so big that spray came over the bow and windshield of their 25-foot Boston Whaler.)

When Beth surfaced after her capsize and wet exit, she was about five feet upwind from her kayak, and her paddle was gone. She tried to swim to her boat before the wind pushed it away from her, but her knee-high boots prevented her from swimming very fast, and she stopped to remove them. By the time she got them off, the wind and waves had carried her kayak twenty-five feet away. She swam after it, but the kayak was being carried away about as fast as she could swim.

Beth realized that she was losing a lot of heat trying to catch her kayak and decided it was better to avoid thrashing around in the water. She gave up on her boat and started swimming toward Willard Island, the nearest shore in the direction of the waves. She alternated between swimming and resting, curling herself up in the fetal position to conserve heat, a tip she remembered from a kayaking class. Along the way, she found a paddle in the water. She held it

Survival Rafts

Matt Broze

One piece of equipment that might have made the difference between life and death for the Blackstone Bay paddlers is a small raft, air mattress, or Sea Seat. Since water conducts heat away from the body twenty-seven times faster than air, getting out of the water significantly slows cooling, even though the victim may feel colder.

In the U.S. Navy's study of hypothermia, subjects wearing various garments were immersed in 32°F (0°C) water for ten minutes and then climbed into a small, open liferaft for the remainder of two hours. The air temperature was 0°F (-17.8°C), with fifteen- to twenty-mile-per-hour winds. (These Arctic conditions are far worse than anything most kayakers encounter but illustrate the effectiveness of a raft.) All the insulated garments, including wetsuits, drysuits, survival suits, float coats, and insulated coveralls, allowed the test subjects to maintain a core temperature well above 95°F (35°C) for two hours in these extreme conditions. The only subjects whose core temperature dropped to 95°F (35°C) before two hours had passed wore non-insulating flight suits with thermal underwear.

Years ago I purchased a one-person U.S. Air Force survival raft at a surplus store. It has some great features, including a CO_2 inflation system, sea anchor, built-in poncho-style cover that is bright silvered pink on the inside to reflect radiant heat and create a signal visible from overhead. It has pouches that will fill with water to hold it to the surface of the sea in extreme conditions. About the size of a rolled up backpacker's tent, it weighs ten pounds and definitely will not accommodate more

than one person. It is difficult to quickly deflate, lacks insulation on the floor, and is very slow to paddle or row because of the pouches. A raft this size must be carried in the kayak rather than attached to the paddler, which means it might not be available if the kayak blows away or sinks after a capsize. Its biggest disadvantage as a kayak safety device is this: It is virtually unavailable. I had been lucky to find it.

I have used this raft as a backup when leading club trips or paddling solo. I take it if setting off along a coastline where I might have to spend the night offshore. I keep it wrapped around my EPIRB to protect it from hard knocks and because if I ever need the raft, I probably also will need the EPIRB.

The Sea Seat is a large, lightweight inflatable cushion developed by hypothermia researchers at the University of Victoria, British Columbia. You can easily attach the Sea Seat to you or tuck it in a pouch on the back of some (non–U.S. Coast Guard–approved) PFDs. As the name implies, you can sit on the inflated cushion, which provides enough buoyancy to keep most of your body out of the water. You can also use the Sea Seat as a paddle outrigger for support during reentry. It had a few disadvantages: It takes about four minutes to inflate, and some practice is required to get up on it and stay on it. (According to one of the developers, the long inflation time was actually built into the design in the interest of preventing hyperventilation [rapid breathing], which can be a danger to a recently immersed victim.)

Some kayak shops have sold a child's (60-pound capacity) inflatable vinyl raft as a cheap alternative to the Sea Seat. It inflates in about a minute, appears to offer about the same buoyancy and hypothermia protection as the Sea Seat, and I found it in front of her with her elbows tucked in close to her body. The steep waves pushed against the paddle and propelled her toward shore while she stayed curled up. When she got to shore, her legs were so numb that she could not stand or walk without using the paddle for support.

Beth and Carol had spent about a half an hour in the water before reaching shore. In summer, Blackstone Bay is chilled by glacial run-off to a temperature reported by various sources to be between 33°F and 45°F (.6°C to 7.2°C). Beth was hypothermic and hyperventilating when she got out of the water. She made her way to Carol, who was so hypothermic that all she wanted to do was get into the sunshine and warm up. About fifteen minutes after they had moved to a warmer spot on the beach, they saw one of the doubles floating upside down. Then Beth saw the bodies of the two brothers drifting near shore. Greg was face down. Carol was too hypothermic to help, so Beth pulled Greg in and found that he had no pulse. She pumped his chest, but his lungs were full of water. Then she spotted Mike twenty to thirty feet offshore. His life jacket was missing. (He may have removed it, thinking it hindered his swimming.) Beth went back into the cold water and retrieved Mike's body.

Afraid that Carol might die, too, Beth went up the beach to look for her kayak, which had a thermos of hot tea and a sleeping bag in it. On the way to her kayak, she met up with Bill and Judith, who had landed safely at the south end of the island. Bill was a medical student and worked as a hospital intern.

---

easier than the Sea Seat to climb up on and stay on. It is heavier and bulkier than the Sea Seat, however, and may not be as durable.

For me, at 190 pounds, the next size vinyl raft (180-pound capacity) was almost as quick to blow up (1.5 minutes) and much "drier." Unfortunately, its size and weight roughly compare to those of my survival raft, and it offers far fewer features. It is, however, readily available, relatively inexpensive, and can be used as a bed.

Some tour operators carry several small liferafts in case more capsizes occur than the guides can quickly handle. (Even the standard six-man liferaft, once removed from its rigid casing, can be carried in a two-seater, although care must be taken to provide it with a water-proof bag designed not to interfere with the raft's deployment.)

The biggest problem with liferafts, air mattresses, and Sea Seats is that they are unlikely to be in the possession of those who are most likely to need them. If a kayak sinks because of lack of flotation, the paddler involved probably will have given little or no thought to the backups he or she might need after the loss or sinking of a kayak. But even paddlers who do observe buoyancy requirements may need to be reminded that secure buoyancy fore and aft would not prevent the loss of their kayak to wind, breaking waves, waves against cliffs, strong current, direct encounters with powerboat traffic, or rambunctious gray whales. What would they (you) do without a boat, unable to swim to shore?

He and Beth immediately began cardiopulmonary resuscitation on the brothers, while Judith treated Carol's hypothermia by getting in a sleeping bag with her and giving her hot tea. Carol revived, but the brothers did not respond. After several hours of CPR, efforts to resuscitate them were ceased. Bill and Judith hiked across the island where they hoped to have a better chance of signaling a boat. Beth stayed with Carol and waited for rescue.

Both the kayak shop and the charter-boat captain notified the Coast Guard that the group was overdue. About 3:00 P.M. on Monday, Corporal Lester of the Alaska Fish and Wildlife Department and his partner were on patrol about forty miles from Blackstone Bay when they heard a Coast Guard announcement on the marine radio (VHF Channel 16): "Pan-Pan" (a radio code—pronounced "pon-pon"—indicating a life-threatening situation), six kayakers are overdue in Blackstone Bay—any mariners in the area contact Valdez Coast Guard. The Corporal had done a little kayaking and had rescued kayakers on other occasions. He knew that the weather conditions—high pressure system inland, low pressure offshore, and bright sunshine warming the land mass—could create strong local winds, and he understood how serious these conditions could be for a kayaker. Lester radioed his intention to search for the kayakers to both the Coast Guard and his base ship, and set his 25-foot Boston Whaler on a course for Blackstone Bay.

Most of the Prince William Sound area was calm that day, except where the winds were blowing down off the glaciers. In those places the winds are typically strong and gusty. Lester and his partner reached Blackstone Bay at 5:20 P.M. and began their search on the west side of the bay. When they got to the submerged moraine, the glacial winds were blowing forty to forty-five knots. Around the shoal the waves were large and steep, forcing them to cut their speed.

Continuing around Willard Island, the rescuers soon spotted some clothes hanging up in bushes above the high tide line and then noticed two people on shore waving at them. They came ashore and found Beth and Carol in relatively good physical condition, although Carol appeared to be in mild shock. Sitting in the sun in a spot protected from the wind, the two had warmed up.

Bill and Judith were still hiking across the island to signal for help. Corporal Lester instructed Beth to look after Carol while he and his partner collected the kayaks and gear that were still adrift. After they had secured the kayaks and gear, the rescuers took to their boat and circumnavigated the island in search of the other two survivors. In the meantime, Bill and Judith spotted the rescue boat and made their way back to the beach on the west side of the island.

When the rescuers returned, the group carried the kayaks above the high tide line and secured them. All the survivors, gear, and the bodies of the two victims were loaded into the rescue boat. They left Willard Island at 7:10 P.M. and arrived in Whittier at 8:00. En route, Lester contacted Whittier Public Safety via VHF radio and requested assistance. The survivors were taken to the Whittier fire station for medical treatment. All of the survivors were in good condition by Tuesday. The death certificates issued for Mike and Greg listed drowning/hypothermia as the cause of death.

LESSONS LEARNED

Looking back, Beth offers the following safety suggestions: Be prepared to wait indefinitely for conditions you are sure you can handle, and if you're scared by conditions, you shouldn't be out there. Don't be afraid to cancel a trip if things don't work out as planned or seem too difficult.

All paddlers, even those renting kayaks, should invest in signaling devices and keep them accessible when paddling. *Keep them dry* and learn how to handle them safely. Don't rely on rental shops to provide pyrotechnic signaling devices. For obvious safety reasons, it is illegal to bring pyrotechnics aboard a commercial aircraft. If you intend to fly to your paddling area, check ahead to see if you can purchase flares from a source in that area.

When paddling in cold waters, don't bet your life on your ability to roll or make a speedy reentry. Wear a drysuit or wetsuit, especially when making crossings or paddling in questionable weather. We can't know exactly what happened to Mike and Greg, but wetsuits or drysuits would have allowed them—and the others in the group—more time before the effects of hypothermia prevented them from making a rescue or reentry or swimming to shore.

"Safety in numbers" can lead to a false sense of security. As in this case, rough conditions and varied skill levels can lead to group separation, and once a member is out of sight, he or she essentially is paddling solo. Paddling in a group is a skill in itself: Don't wait until things get rough to practice it. Further, learn self rescues and rolls as well as assisted rescues so you'll have a backup in case of separation. And be aware that different boats will handle best at different angles to the wind; the group may have to set a course to accommodate the least able paddler.

As these paddlers discovered, the apparent condition of the water can be deceiving, especially when observed at a distance or from a protected shore. The lee of a land mass creates a calm that is no indication of what the conditions offshore might be. Be conservative, especially when the wind is strong and blowing offshore. In an offshore wind, the farther you paddle or drift from shore the greater the fetch (the distance the wind blows over the water) and the bigger the waves will be. When looking out over a lee, the larger waves offshore will be masked both by the curvature of the earth and by the small waves in the middle distance.

Although sea kayakers seldom pay any attention to the ocean bottom unless they can see it, the bottom contours can have dramatic effects on currents and waves. Had this group referred to nautical charts, they would have seen the shoals around Willard Island; given the wind and current, a knowledgeable sea kayaker would have anticipated the steep, breaking waves in the area. Only nautical charts provide bathymetric information and indicate hazards like tide rips and shipping lanes. Topographical maps, although they lack important information about the water, often show the shoreline and landmarks in greater detail, which can be useful for taking bearings and for selecting possible campsites. Charts are essential; topos can be a useful supplement.

When paddling *with* the waves, a kayak generally is less stable, and therefore at greater risk of capsize, than when paddling *into* the waves. Don't use your upwind paddling experience to judge your ability to handle following seas. One reason a kayak is at greater risk of capsize in following seas is that it may start surfing whether you like it or not. Unless you take preventive action, a surfing sea kayak will turn sideways to the wave, or broach. This can happen quite fast. An unexpected broach is probably the most common cause of accidental capsizes. To keep your kayak from surfing while traveling downwind, make a deliberate effort to go more slowly than the waves—backpaddle if necessary. Unfortunately, many kayakers react to surfing by speeding up; in following seas this increases the probability that your kayak will broach. The best way to prevent all this is to learn to surf your kayak so you will know your limits, stay relaxed, and have the skills to deal with broaching when it happens.

13

Happy Endings

George Gronseth

I sometimes wonder how many stories the Eskimos must have told their children about the sea, kayaks, and kayaking tragedies: the equivalent of industrial society parents warning their children to look both ways before crossing the street. We are reinventing this mode of water transportation without the benefit of such an oral tradition or community knowledge. To keep from learning everything the hard way, we must try to gain experience, skill, and judgment without taking unnecessary risks.

Whitewater Kayaker Rescues Sea Kayaker

Saturday, January 6, 1990, was a windy day in western Washington. Small-craft warnings were posted over most of the area. Off the Mukilteo shore, the wind howled and whipped Possession Sound into steep whitecaps. Carlos had brought his whitewater kayak to surf along the beach south of a Coast Guard Light Station and the Mukilteo Ferry dock. His wife stayed on shore and watched.

After he had been surfing for a while, Carlos spotted two sea kayakers about one hundred yards offshore on the southwest side of the ferry dock. He paddled out to them. The conditions made it hard to get very close to the other kayakers; the wind was so strong they could barely communicate with each other. One of the sea kayaks was a recently completed home-built model. Its owner and builder had been kayaking for several years. The other sea kayaker was relatively new to the sport.

Carlos surfed back to the beach. While he and his wife were eating lunch, they saw that one of the sea kayaks had capsized. Carlos jumped into his kayak and paddled out to help.

The capsized kayaker had held onto his paddle when he wet exited, but the wind had blown his new home-built kayak away from him. Fortunately, his life jacket had fallen out of the kayak and he was able to grab it. (He hadn't been wearing his life jacket because he didn't think he'd need it.) When Carlos reached the capsized paddler, the other sea kayaker was in pursuit of the drifting kayak. Carlos told the swimmer to grab the handle on the back of his river kayak so he could tow him to shore, a rescue technique often used by whitewater kayakers on rivers. Carlos tried paddling for shore this way, but the wind

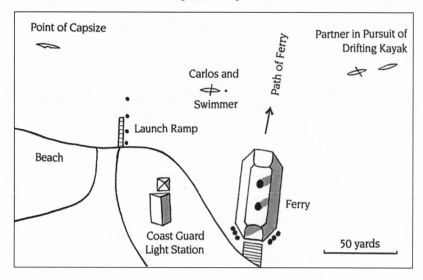

was so strong that his kayak just pivoted around the swimmer at the stern and faced downwind.

Carlos told the swimmer to let go of the paddle and put the life jacket on so they could make better progress. The swimmer let his paddle go but continued to hold the life jacket under his chest instead of wearing it. Again they tried to head for shore, with Carlos paddling and the swimmer kicking his feet behind the kayak. The southwest wind pushed them away from shore and toward the path of the ferry, which was preparing to depart. No matter how hard they tried, they couldn't make any progress toward the beach.

It was impossible for the swimmer to climb onto the rear deck of Carlos's kayak because, weighing over two hundred pounds, he would have sunk the stern of the low-volume river kayak. Carlos asked him to let go of the kayak and try swimming to shore. He stayed at the swimmer's side, but their progress through the steep waves and against the current was slow. As they struggled, they drifted toward the ferry's path.

The swimmer's partner had paddled far to the north in pursuit of the drifting kayak. There seemed to be no way of getting the swimmer to shore. Carlos paddled upwind of the swimmer and again had him grab the whitewater kayak's back handle. By paddling and swimming into the wind, they could at least hold their position and stay out of the ferry's path. Carlos waved his paddle as a signal to his wife, who notified the Coast Guard at the Light Station. The shore siren sounded, and request for assistance was broadcast on the marine band (VHF) radio. Though there weren't many boats out because of the rough conditions, a sportfisherman responded to the call and picked up the swimmer.

There was an ambulance waiting on shore. In spite of spending about twenty minutes in the 45°F to 50°F (7.2°C to 10°C) water wearing only street clothes, the capsized kayaker warmed up and required no medical attention. His large size may have been to his advantage; a smaller or slimmer person, similarly dressed, might not have fared as well.

Rescue at Shilshole

Even when the weather is much milder than it was that January day in Possession Sound, kayakers must be prepared for wind and temperature changes—as was discovered by two paddlers on a summer day trip in Seattle's Shilshole Bay. One of the kayakers, who had been sea kayaking for about a year and had some class II+ whitewater experience, capsized. Fortunately, the two kayakers had practiced rescues together, and their teamwork made for a quick reentry rescue. Both had paddle floats, bilge pumps, and paddle leashes.

Because the day started out so warm and the trip was so short, neither of the paddlers had brought a wet- or drysuit. One wore shorts without a shirt, and the other wore a medium-weight polypropylene shirt and pants under a pair of shorts. Both paddlers had life jackets.

They paddled north to a beach where local Native Americans were competing in dugout canoe races. After watching some races from their kayaks, they went ashore to take a closer look at the canoes.

The high-pressure system that brought the fair weather also brought strong northerly winds, and as the day progressed, the wind grew stronger and colder. By about 3:00 the wind and chop were severe enough that the races were canceled. The two kayakers decided to paddle back to the put-in.

The tide had begun to fall, and the ebb flowed against the wind, building up steep wind waves about two and a half feet high. In spite of the chop, it seemed safer to avoid all the sail- and powerboats heading into the marina, so the kayakers went on the outside of the marina, about fifty yards out from the breakwater. The clapotis, or interference of crossing waves, caused by waves reflected off the breakwater made for a very confused sea.

The wind waves hit the right rear quarters of both kayaks. The waves were much higher near the breakwater, but neither paddler considered the conditions

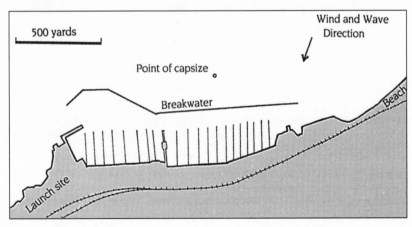

intimidating. One of the paddlers wanted to try a little surfing, and she took a few hard strokes to catch a wave. Unfortunately, she leaned the wrong way and capsized. She had rolled river kayaks before, but her sea kayak didn't fit her properly, and her foot braces, even though they were set as far aft as they would go, were too far forward for her to lock herself into the kayak. After two attempts to roll, she had to wet exit.

Two other kayakers paddling in the area saw the capsize. One paddled up and yelled, "Do you know what you're doing?"

A bit embarrassed, she replied, "Yes, thank you," as she righted her kayak.

"Have you practiced this before?" he asked.

"Yes, thank you," her partner replied while maneuvering alongside her boat.

"Well, how do you want to do this?" the other rescuer asked.

"It's handled," her partner replied as he set up the paddles for the rescue.

The would-be rescuer took a second look and said, "Oh, your kayak is so narrow. You'll never get back into that. It's too tippy! I've never seen anyone get back into one of those!"

The capsized paddler got in her "tippy" boat without trouble. She later mentioned that, had a bazooka been handy, there would be one less nautical-design critic in the world. She and her partner paddled the short distance back to their put-in.

When the Tide Steals Your Kayak

I'm sure if we all could overcome our embarrassment and tell the truth, volumes of stories could be written on ways we've lost our kayaks to the tide. Unfortunately, it seems we must experience this for ourselves before we can be humble enough to religiously protect our boats from the tide's silent thievery.

Most of these stories are amusing after we get our boats back. But with the rapid growth of our sport we may need to look at this problem from another perspective. When someone finds a kayak floating around unoccupied, what is he or she likely to conclude? Search and rescue efforts might be wasted on a mere inconvenience. If the idea of losing your kayak isn't incentive enough to tie it up

or carry it well above the high tide line, consider your responsibility to those who must go in search of missing paddlers when an empty kayak is found.

Wind and low pressure systems can change the height of the tide significantly from what tide tables predict. Even though the tide table may show that a high tide will be lower than the previous high tide, it is no guarantee that local conditions will not push the tide above the mark left by the last tide.

When sleeping on the beach, put your kayak on ground higher than your tent or tie a line between your tent and the kayak. If the tide is higher than predicted, you will find out before you lose your kayak.

We can prevent false alarms of lost kayakers if we put cockpit covers on our kayaks or tie the body tubes of our spray skirts closed whenever we get out of our kayaks.

LESSONS LEARNED

Practice paddling and rescue skills in conditions at least as rough as those you consider acceptable for trips. In the case of the accident in Shilshole Bay, the rough water outside the breakwater clearly was not a good spot for testing one's skill. Practice in controlled conditions by getting together with other kayakers on a windy day and picking a suitable beach with the wind blowing toward shore. Wear a wet- or drysuit if the water is cold. Another way to practice in a controlled environment is to take a river kayaking class; in most whitewater rivers, the shore is never far away, and in a training class there will be plenty of help nearby. Always spend some time practicing rescues with anyone you'll be paddling with—and possibly relying on in a rescue situation. The Shilshole Bay incident ended well because the paddlers had recently practiced rescues together.

None of the capsized kayakers in these incidents were dressed appropriately. The capsized kayaker in Possession Sound was lucky to have escaped the effects of hypothermia in the January cold. In the Shilshole accident, the wind was cool even though it was a warm day—and the water in most parts of northern Puget Sound is always cold. Given the water temperature and weather conditions, all these paddlers should have been wearing farmer-john wetsuit bottoms or drysuits. Had the rescues not been effective, the cold water would have quickly become a serious problem.

Finally, if you are going to help rescue someone, do it! If you are unsure of his or her emotional state, at least get close enough to properly assess the situation. An underdressed person in cold water does not have time to discuss the relative merits of boat design. Any discussion should focus on setting up the rescue. A capsized kayaker needs encouragement and fast action.

The contrasts between these two accidents illustrate the need to hang on to both your kayak and paddle during a wet exit. Consider tethering the paddle to the kayak as a backup.

Two-Person Rescue at La Push

One of the events at the annual Surf Frolic is a circumnavigation of James Island, just offshore from La Push, Washington. On January 21, 1990, I paddled with three other sea kayakers and one whitewater kayaker out the mouth of the Quillayute River to do the circumnavigation.

Paddling conditions were difficult: There were ten- to twelve-foot swells and twenty- to thirty-knot winds. Everyone in the group was wearing a wet- or dry-suit, and all said they had a roll, knew some deep-water kayak rescues, and had practiced in surf.

By starting in the river, we were able to avoid the shore break and had only to deal with the wind and swells. After fighting a strong headwind to get out of the river mouth, the group tightened its formation and headed around the island. Everyone seemed to be doing well.

After passing the first boomer, or offshore breaker, I led the group closer to the island to some of the birds and nests that cling to the cliffs surrounding the island. Without warning, one paddler suddenly capsized when a wave reflecting off the cliffs met an incoming wave and the two combined to make a wave much taller and steeper than the other swells. Our companion happened to be in the wrong place at the wrong time when the waves met. When the water settled, he found himself upside down.

The capsized paddler tried to roll a couple times, but apparently he needed more practice. I could see that he wasn't likely to roll up, so I yelled to his buddy, who was about fifteen feet away from him but looking the other way, to

Reenter and Roll Problems

The weekend of January 20, 1990, was the annual Surf Frolic at La Push, Washington. I'd bought a new sea kayak and I was eager to give it the ultimate test—pummeling it in the surf. If a sea kayak can surf well and hold up to the pounding waves, then it can't be all bad. The back of the boat was packed with all the emergency gear for a serious day trip along the exposed ocean coast.

After catching a few gentle rides on the steepening swells outside the hot surfing spots, I realized that I still had my paddle leash on. Loose lines such as a paddle leash can be dangerous in the surf, so I stopped to remove it. When I opened my spray skirt to put the leash away, a wave suddenly broke on top of me and pummeled me around and around.

The violent forces within the plunging wave pulled me most of the way out of my kayak. As I was getting pulled out, I kept spreading my legs until my feet hooked under the cockpit deck.

When the forces eased, I tried to pull myself back into the cockpit of my capsized kayak to prepare to roll up. I couldn't find the foot braces, and my thighs couldn't get a grip on the thigh braces—rolling would be tough. My first attempt failed. I pushed against the inside of the kayak as hard as

I could with my feet and knees to develop as much friction as possible to help grip the kayak with my lower body and thus roll it up. It worked. Once upright, I found out why I couldn't get my feet on the foot braces: I was too far forward in the cockpit. I tried to move aft, but the seat back had flipped forward and pinned me against the front of the cockpit. There wasn't enough room to straighten out the seat back.

The inverted seat back was quite uncomfortable. In spite of the front and rear airbags, the kayak had water up to the coaming. It would be hard to control a flooded kayak under the best of conditions; to handle it swamped in the surf I needed the use of my foot and thigh braces. I flipped the kayak over so I could get far enough out of it to flip the seat back into its proper position, but my gear and the stern airbag had slid forward, locking the seat back in its inverted position. I pulled gear from behind the seat and held on to it while I straightened the seat back. Then I pulled myself back in again, stuffed the loose gear between my legs, rolled up, and breathed. Ah—the joy of rolling!

Floppy seat backs can be a problem during a reentry rescue (whether it's a reentry and roll, paddle-float, or assisted rescue) after righting the kayak. You can add a shock cord with a snap hook to hold such seat backs in place while allowing access to storage behind the seat.

help rescue his friend. This paddler seemed to freeze when he saw his friend's boat upside down. I paddled around him and got into position for an assisted reentry rescue as the capsized paddler did a wet exit.

When the swimmer righted his boat, I was relieved to see his kayak was fitted with a sea sock, limiting the amount of water that got in to only a few gallons. I also was glad to see that the boat had a low, flat aft deck, which generally makes it easy to get back in.

I laid the paddles across the decks of the two kayaks. Then I leaned my kayak over as far as I could in order to put my weight onto the other kayak and thus stabilize it with a firm grip on his coaming. The capsized paddler could then get back in by lunging out of the water and across the decks of both kayaks. But, because the boat I was using was practically new and was not equipped with any deck lines or fittings (other than handles at the ends), the swimmer couldn't get a grip on my boat. Without anything to hold onto, he couldn't pull himself far enough out of the water to complete the rescue.

Although I carry a piece of one-inch webbing (inside my paddle-float rescue bag) that he could have used for a stirrup, we didn't have the time to set it up. The current was quickly taking us close to a huge boomer near the end of the island. I was about to put off the reentry and start towing the swimmer and his kayak away from the boomer when he finally succeeded in getting up onto the decks of our kayaks. The rest of the rescue went smoothly. I continued to stabilize his kayak while he pumped most of the water out with his bilge pump. We then paddled quickly away from the hazardous boomer and returned to the put-in.

LESSONS LEARNED

With more roll practice, this tense rescue could have been avoided. When practicing rescues, try simulating as many situations as you can think of. Practice without grabbing deck lines. There are lots of tricks for getting out of the water and across the kayak deck. Some people push themselves deeper into the water just before pulling themselves out, giving them more momentum. Others prefer to first push against the kayak by kicking with their feet until their body is horizontal; they can then use most of the power from the lunge to move horizontally across the deck without having to lift themselves very much. Practice and find out what works best for you.

Deck lines are an important accessory even if you don't think you'll need them yourself. They can make it easier to rescue others by giving them something to grip. Ideally, all manufacturers would include deck lines that run along the perimeter, but you can easily retro-fit such ropes (rather than bungies) to a kayak that does not have them.

14

Surf Zone Accidents

George Gronseth

The following stories by survivors of close calls and long swims in the surf raise the possibility of drowning due to exhaustion and/or cramps—even with the buoyancy of a wetsuit and PFD.

In May of 1991, at Kalaloch Beach on Washington's Pacific coast, two kayaking accidents occurred within a week of each other. The incidents were so similar that the editor of *Sea Kayaker* and I thought we were comparing notes on the same close call when we first discussed them. Both the similarities and the differences provide valuable insight into surf zone accidents. Contrary to the impression these two stories may give, the beach at Kalaloch is not a popular place for kayak surfing.

The average water temperature off the Washington coast in May is in the low 50s. In *Oceanography of the British Columbia Coast* (Canadian Department of Fisheries and Oceans, 1981), author Richard Thomson writes, "While body surfing off . . . Kalaloch Beach, the author has been aware of fairly strong long shore currents, and distinct rip currents in the lee of offshore rocks and shoals."

A Close Call

Carey Worthen, of Bellingham, Washington, told us his story:

"My family and I were camping at Kalaloch Campground in Olympic National Park south of Forks, Washington. From past experience, I had decided not to carry a float bag or pump, as reentry rescues in the surf would be nearly impossible and would surely be followed by another capsize before the boat could be pumped out. I wore a ⅛-inch farmer-john wetsuit,

PFD, neoprene spray skirt, helmet, and water-sport sandals.

"I started about an hour into an incoming tide [about five hundred yards north of the Kalaloch River. The wave faces in the surf were six to eight feet high.] I thought that when I spilled I would simply swim the boat to shore as I had done in the past. I did spill, quite far out [seventy-five yards] on the last couple breakers. After a quick wet exit, I began swimming for the beach with both hands on the stern of my boat. After a while it appeared my effort had been wasted; I was no closer to the beach. Resting occasionally, I had made several attempts to swim to shore when my unsecured stern flotation bag popped out of the cockpit, allowing the stern to fill with water. All this time breakers were crashing over my head, putting a severe damper on consistent breathing and making for a high intake of salt water. As the bow of my kayak turned skyward, I decided it was time for my boat and I to part. Having heard that you can use a paddle to propel your body

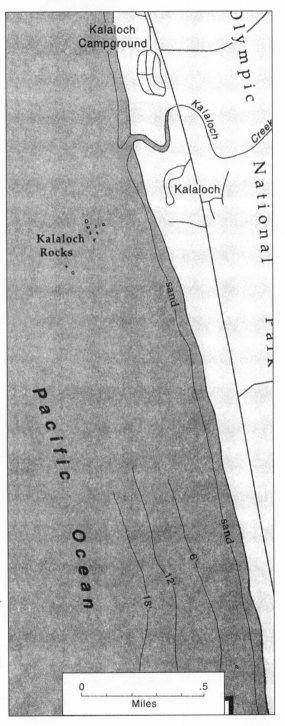

A Kayak Surfing Accident

Eric Konheim, 27, died on June 12, 1991, while kayak surfing alone on the coast of Coos County, Oregon. Eric was a skilled kayaker, proud of his ability to roll and to read moving water. He was an avid reader of *Sea Kayaker;* he was one of us.

In 1987, Eric bought a folding sea kayak and began taking trips, including a 450-mile expedition along the Gulf Coast from Belize to Cancun, Mexico. He also paddled in the Sea of Cortez, the Bahamas, and along the coast of Venezuela. In 1988 he took a river kayaking class in Colorado and bought a white-water kayak. He kayaked many whitewater rivers and was a commercial raft guide.

Most kayakers who have both a white-water kayak and a sea kayak use white-water kayaks for ocean surfing because these generally are tougher and more maneuverable than the typical sea kayak. Eric was using his river kayak on the day of his accident, but the accident could just as easily have happened with a sea kayak.

Eric's kayak was a Prijon T-Slalom, a popular river kayak featuring a large keyhole-shaped cockpit. The keyhole cockpit combines ample thigh braces with the ease of entry and exit of a large cockpit.

Eric was traveling through Oregon with Dave, another kayaker. Unfortunately, Dave was feeling ill and didn't paddle on the afternoon of June 12. Eric told Dave he would surf for only a short while and went out alone at about 4:00 P.M. Dave took a nap and awoke about a half hour later. He began looking for Eric and around 5 P.M. found his friend's kayak floating in the surf. Unable to find Eric, he called for help.

About 6:00 P.M., a Coast Guard helicopter found Eric floating face down, just 150 yards offshore from the area where Dave had found the kayak. The height of the breaking waves had made it impossible to see Eric from shore. A diver from the helicopter crew recovered the victim, who was flown to an ambulance and taken to a hospital. Eric had no vital signs. At 10:00 P.M., CPR and hypothermia treatment were discontinued.

When Eric was found, he was wearing a helmet, a PFD with a whistle and knife attached,a neoprene spray skirt, shorts, a pullover pile jacket, and a long-sleeve paddle jacket. Eric's kayak and paddle were found in good condition. He had not worn either his wetsuit or his drysuit, though he had both in his van.

Eric had EMT and river-guide training and knew about hypothermia. Ironically, in his van were notes he had made on hypothermia, along with literature on the subject from a river safety course he had recently taken.

This accident was the first kayaking fatality at Bastendorf Beach, but it was by no means the first drowning there. The beach's combination of large, unpredictable waves and rip currents have contributed to many deaths. According to Sergeant Craig Zanni of the Coos County Sheriff's Department, one or two people drown there every year. Sergeant Zanni, who was part of the search-and-rescue team that found Eric, reported the waves were breaking "pretty good for that time of year."

A sign at the beach warns of "sneaker waves," sudden large waves that can come from any direction. *Soggy Sneakers* (Mountaineers, 1994), an Oregon kayak through the water, I kept mine [a feathered paddle] in hand. I soon decided that method worked better in theory and disposed of my paddle and started to swim. [Note: As illustrated by the next incident discussed, there are techniques for swimming successfully with a paddle.] By this time about forty minutes had passed, and I still wasn't making much progress.

"I should have realized sooner that I was caught in a rip current and begun swimming across the current parallel with the beach until it released me. I believe cold shock was at the root of my confusion and breathing problems.

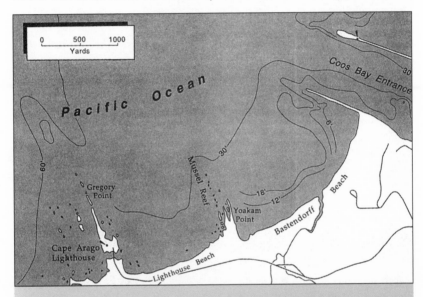

guidebook that Eric and his friend used to find the beach, cautions: "Large ocean swells close out much of the central part of Bastendorf Beach with freight train walls that often break in only a few feet of water."

A Coos County sheriff's deputy said the currents at Bastendorf Beach flow away from shore and then set southwest toward the lighthouse south of the jetty. Because of this pattern of drift, the bodies of drowning victims are usually found near the lighthouse, where Eric's body was recovered. Rip currents and along-shore currents are a common hazard at surf beaches.

Since no one witnessed the accident, we will never know the exact cause or sequence of events that lead to Eric's death. The official cause of death listed on the medical examiner's report is "asphyxia by drowning, immersion hypothermia." This is reasonable, considering that the water temperature was 50°F to 53°F (10°C to 11.7°C) and that Eric was tall and thin and was not wearing much thermal protection. His core temperature was 73°F (22.8°C).

Although we'll never know for sure, there's some speculation that Eric was knocked out by his paddle—a danger when paddling in surf.

After about an hour in the water, my legs were badly cramped and I was nearing total exhaustion. My body became so deeply chilled I knew my survival depended on one final struggle for the beach. I blocked out the pain in my legs and began a hard crawl stroke toward the beach. I don't know if it was that last-ditch rush of adrenaline or a sudden subsiding of the current that allowed me to inch forward until I could see I was making progress. But that little bit of progress renewed my hope and strength. After swimming several more yards, I met up with Ranger Clay Butler clad in a wetsuit, helmet, and life jacket and tethered to a long rope. As it turned out, his assistance was not needed, but I appreciated a shoulder to lean on as I walked to shore. Despite my blue lips, cramps, total fatigue, and chattering teeth, it felt good to be alive.

"A couple on the beach had seen me enter the water and had called 911 after deciding I needed help. At the same time, my wife and our friends grew concerned and went in search of park personnel. In addition to Ranger Butler, a helicopter had been sent in case I couldn't be reached from shore. Many well-wishers awaited me on the beach with outstretched arms, blankets, and tears.

"Please don't put your family through this! Be more prepared than I was. The most important piece of advice I have is *don't give up!* Moments before I escaped the rip current, I very nearly said, 'What's the use?'

"I would also say don't hesitate to discard your gear at the right moment. I should have removed my skirt and sandals much earlier."

A Long Swim

One week after Carey Worthen's incident, Bill (who's last name is withheld at his request) and his family rented a cabin at Kalaloch. While his wife stayed in the cabin with their kids, Bill headed out by himself to practice kayaking in the

A Broken Paddle

My paddle once broke from water pressure alone when I was somersaulted (pitchpoled) by a breaking wave. Since the water was very turbulent and the paddle shaft had broken outside of where my hands gripped it, I didn't figure out what had happened until after three unsuccessful roll attempts and a wet exit. Then I discovered the broken paddle. The one-piece aluminum shaft was permanently bowed over the full length: It didn't just break because of a weak spot.

Later, I ran some calculations on the force it would have taken to break the paddle this way, using figures that I use in my profession to check the strength of airplane wings. I discovered that it took only the equivalent of bench-pressing about two hundred pounds to break the paddle shaft.

The lesson: I now have less faith in the indestructibility of my equipment and more respect for the hydraulic forces at work in the ocean.

Hazards of Rip Currents and Breaking Waves

Oceanographers assure us that there isn't any such thing as an undertow—a current that pulls people under and takes them out to sea. However, the combination of breaking waves and rip currents can give you the feeling that you are caught in an "undertow." This is probably how the undertow myth got started.

Rip Currents

Rip currents are found only at surf beaches. Breaking surf transports water into shore, and rip currents—streams of water that flow away from shore—return the water back to the sea. Rip currents are sometimes referred to as "rip tides," a misleading name easily confused with tide rip (an area of rough water caused by tidal currents). Rip currents are neither tides nor the direct result of a tide.

Water piled up on shore by the waves will seek paths of least resistance while flowing back to sea. There is less resistance to the movement of water in deep channels than in shallow areas. Water carried in by the broken waves flows along the shore until it reaches the deeper channels, which cut through the offshore sandbars. This sets up "alongshore currents," which flow parallel to the beach before feeding into the rip channel. Rip currents dissipate outside of the area where the waves begin to steepen.

Reported speeds of rip currents vary, but it is safe to say they often are faster than we can swim. Even rip currents that are slow enough to be imperceptible to a paddler may be a significant threat to a swimmer. Remember, you won't be setting any speed records when encumbered with kayaking gear and struggling just to get air between breaking waves. Survival swimming expert Eric Soares advises that you not swim against any current faster than a half-knot.

Because rip currents run out through rip channels, which are deeper than the adjacent bottom, the waves in rip channels will generally not be as rough nor as big as they are between channels. The area with the biggest waves, although it seems intimidating, will probably be the best bet for making headway toward shore. Trying to swim toward shore against a rip current can be a futile and exhausting task. The standard advice is to swim perpendicular to the current (parallel to the beach) to get across the rip, and then head for shore. However, if you are too close to the rip, the along-shore current and/or sideways motion of the backwash could push you back into the rip current. It would be better to clear the rip current by a safe distance (ideally, halfway between it and the next rip current) before turning in toward shore.

When swimming alone in breaking waves that obscure your view, you can't always tell if you're making headway. If there are rocks or points protruding out from the beach, use these landmarks to check your progress. Carey Worthen suggests checking a watch to see how quickly you're making headway.

It is unlikely that you will actually feel a rip current. It doesn't take a very strong current to push a swimmer backward. Unless a current is turbulent, you feel the movement only when you enter the current.

(continued on page 130)

surf. He was unaware of Worthen's mishap. Bill had kayaked in rough wave conditions a few times. He had once played in a rip current north of Shilshole (near Seattle), a shallow area that has frequent, steep boat wakes, and he had been out in ocean swells on a trip in Barkley Sound, British Columbia. But this was his first time kayaking in ocean surf. Bill couldn't do a roll, but he thought he could perform a self rescue or swim to shore if he capsized.

Bill is a strong, formerly competitive swimmer with scuba diving experience. He is very comfortable in and around the water. His kayak had front and rear

(continued from page 129)
Once you've been in the current for a few seconds, the feeling of movement is lost just as it would be if you closed your eyes a few seconds after stepping onto an escalator.

Breaking Waves

The wash of broken waves up and down the beach may threaten to sweep you off your feet. For adults, this is only a problem on steep beaches where waves break directly on the beach. If you lose your footing, the backwash can carry you into the next breaker. You could get beaten to exhaustion if this process continues. If the beach is so steep that you can't regain your footing, swim out away from shore until you are outside the shore break. Once free of the pounding shore break, you can catch your breath and pick a better place to go in or call for help. At more desirable surfing beaches, the waves begin to steepen and break offshore. (Waves breaking over coral reefs or other rough beach elements present special problems. The discussion here is limited to hazards from moderate-sized waves at a sandy surfing beach.)

When you are swimming in steep or breaking waves, the wave crests will go over you; you need to wait until you come out the other side of the passing wave before you can breathe again. Breaking waves can also turn a swimmer head over heels. Either situation may give you the feeling that you are being pulled down, but you are not. You are not being sucked down by a mysterious force; your own inertia prevents you from rising with the wave fast enough to stay on top. Don't panic; swim back to the surface and breathe when you are in the wave troughs. In the froth, if you are careful, you may be able to breathe without inhaling water by clenching your teeth and putting your tongue against your front teeth to filter some air out of the foamy water. (This breathing technique is also useful while riding waves in your kayak.)

Kayak surfing is a growing part of sea kayaking. For the advancing intermediate sea kayaker who wants to try surfing, start with a kayak surfing class; river kayaking classes also help because they usually include practice surfing on standing waves in rivers. Standing waves don't go anywhere. In a river you can surf all day on even a three-inch-high standing wave. After conquering such a molehill, you can progress to bigger and bigger waves to play on. Even the easier grades of rivers provide a variety of surfing opportunities without the need to launch or land through the surf. However, river kayaking experience will not completely prepare you for ocean surfing, so find some experienced ocean kayak surfers to accompany you while you learn the ropes.

bulkheads providing buoyancy in both ends. He wore a ¼-inch-thick, full wetsuit (the same suit he would wear for scuba diving in water of this temperature), polypropylene long underwear, neoprene booties, neoprene diver's hood, paddling jacket, and PFD. He was carrying a bilge pump and a self-rescue float and had some flares in the pocket of his paddle jacket.

Bill launched in the lee of some offshore rocks south of the Kalaloch River and then paddled out through a surf with four- to five-foot-high wave faces. He was almost past the surf zone, about two hundred yards offshore, when his troubles began. At the outer edge of the surf zone, most waves pass by as harmless swells, but exceptionally big waves will break there. Bill was hit by two eight-foot breakers. The first one broke on top of him, but he somehow emerged upright. The second breaker capsized him, and he did a wet exit.

Three waves later his kayak was yanked away from him, but he swam and caught it. He tried in vain to reenter the kayak using a paddle-float outrigger self-rescue technique. He could get only halfway in before another wave would hit and knock him over.

After about ten minutes of unsuccessful self-rescue attempts, he realized he and his kayak were drifting dangerously close to the rocks. He took a flare from his paddle jacket and fired it. He watched with dismay as two beachcombers pointed at the flare but did nothing—obviously he would have to get himself out of trouble. A breaking wave pulled the kayak from his hands again.

As he drifted closer to the rocks, he figured he was better off letting go of his kayak. Like Carey Worthen, he had heard a paddle can be useful when swimming. He retrieved his paddle and the paddle float and began swimming toward shore with the paddle float under his chest. After about a half hour of swimming, he realized he was losing ground. He was about three hundred yards from shore and quickly becoming exhausted. Waves broke over his head and tumbled him; he struggled to get air. He had one thing in his favor: His wetsuit was keeping him warm.

Finally, he mustered all his strength and determination and began body surfing toward shore for all he was worth. He discovered that if he held the paddle against his chest the waves would push it and carry him toward shore. (Swimming a crawl stroke works well with an unfeathered paddle; users of feathered paddles often feel it is easier to use while swimming a backstroke. This technique is similar to back-paddling in a kayak.) Bill soon found he could steer across the waves by shifting the paddle in his hands; this allowed him to angle away from the rocks. It worked so well that he landed about two miles south of where he started. Angling away from the rocks also probably got him out of the rip current described in Richard Thomson's book.

Eventually, Bill got to where it was shallow enough to stand up. Again he found his paddle to be a great help. By sinking the paddle into the sand at about a 45-degree angle, he was able to keep the backwash from pushing him out to sea. Exhausted but relieved, he made his way to shore. Bill found his kayak about two miles north of where he landed. The damage indicated the kayak had gone straight into the rocks.

LESSONS LEARNED

Both Carey and Bill underestimated the effects of breaking waves and rip currents when kayaking in the surf zone and were surprised at the difficulty of swimming alone in this situation. If you capsize and end up swimming toward shore against a rip current, do what Bill did: Try to swim parallel to shore until you get across the rip, and then turn and continue toward shore. For more specifics on rip currents and breaking waves, see the sidebar on page 129.

In a kayak without a rear bulkhead, add a means to secure the rear float bag. This can be done with a strap or a shock cord and clip from the seat to a fitting installed on the underside of the rear deck. Sea socks are primarily used to keep water out of the kayak, but in a kayak without front and rear bulkheads, a sea sock also helps keep the float bags from slipping out.

While Carey Worthen became chilled and mildly hypothermic in his ⅛-inch farmer-john wetsuit, Bill was actually too warm in his ¼-inch-thick full suit, booties, and hood. Soon after Bill got to shore, he removed some of his wetsuit clothing to cool off. In the water, Bill worried only about exhaustion and the rocks, whereas Carey knew his time was limited by the effects of hypothermia. In my experience, ⅛-inch-thick farmer-john wetsuits are not adequate protection for prolonged immersion in 50°F (10°C) water. Unfortunately, ¼-inch-thick wetsuits are not often found in kayak stores (at least in the Northwest). They are, however, available at scuba diving shops.

15

Saved by a Drysuit

George Gronseth

In November 1992, Larry Kaiser, Jr., 31, survived a two- to three-hour swim in the 50°F (10°C) waters of Washington state's San Juan Islands. Fortunately, his partner had loaned him a drysuit of the type generally used for scuba diving. Larry probably can thank the drysuit for saving his life.

On Friday, November 6, Larry and his friend Saul Kinderis launched their kayaks at Washington Beach Park near Anacortes, Washington. They paddled four miles north up Rosario Strait to Strawberry Island, where they planned to stay through Sunday.

Both men are very athletic and experienced in wilderness sports, but neither had much kayaking experience. Saul had been on a couple of kayak trips in the area and had sailed to Strawberry Island. While he had practiced wet exits on his own, he had never taken a kayaking class. Neither man had practiced two-person rescues or paddle-float self rescues. Larry had kayaked on lakes a few times, but this was his first kayak camping trip and his first experience paddling in salt water and tidal currents.

This was also the first time Larry had paddled the Nimbus Puffin kayak, which he had borrowed from Saul. Neither wore spray skirts; in fact, Larry's was packed away because it fit the cockpit so tightly that Saul felt his friend, who had never practiced a capsize and wet exit, would be safer without it. Larry wore Saul's drysuit, and Saul wore a wetsuit.

They put in at 9:00 P.M. While their night crossing was successful, it was not uneventful. The choppy waves made Larry seasick, and when they got to Strawberry Island, the current swept them past the only beach on the island. They crash-landed in the dark on a steep, rocky part of Strawberry Island. Waves pounded the kayaks while the men struggled to lift them up the bank. Water leaked through the hatches of Larry's kayak and soaked his sleeping bag and clothes—the men had packed in haste and darkness, and his drybags had not been properly sealed.

They toughed it out through a windy and rainy night. Saul slept in his clothes so Larry could use the one dry sleeping bag. The next morning, the two woke early and evaluated their situation. The wind was blowing strong out of the south-southeast, but because Strawberry Island is somewhat sheltered by

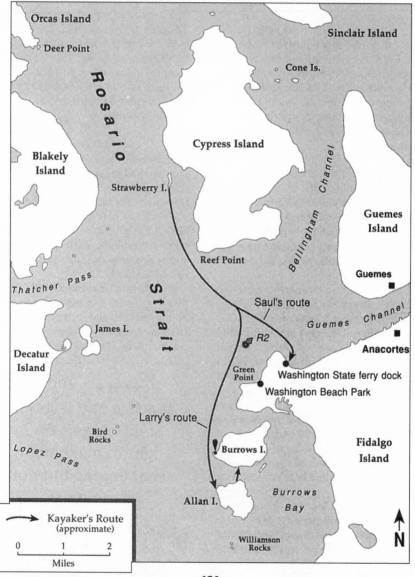

Cypress Island from winds in this direction, the nearby water didn't look too rough. They knew that the flood current was going with the wind and that the waves would get much rougher when the current changed in the afternoon. They listened to Saul's weather radio—the forecast for their area (Camano Island to Point Roberts) called for "a small-craft advisory, southwest winds fifteen to twenty-five knots, wind becoming northwest in the north part this afternoon." They talked over their options:

1) Leave soon and go with the wind and current, continuing north to Orcas Island as originally planned.

2) Paddle the half mile to Cypress Island and ask for help (directly east of them was one of the few inhabited parts of Cypress Island, and they could see smoke coming out a chimney of a cabin there).

3) Stay put until the weather improved.

4) Paddle around the south end of Cypress Island, cross to Guemes Island, and take the ferry from Guemes to Anacortes.

5) Wait for the afternoon slack before ebb and return to Washington Beach.

Larry ruled out continuing the trip. Going to Cypress would involve finding someone with a powerboat who was willing to give them a ride to Anacortes (there's no public transportation to Cypress Island), and they didn't feel their situation was dire enough to warrant such an imposition. They stayed put that morning, but by early afternoon the sun was out and the conditions didn't seem that bad. They decided to paddle around the south end of Cypress Island and then choose between crossing to Guemes Island or Washington Beach Park, depending on the conditions.

They departed Strawberry Island an hour prior to slack tide. As they rounded Reef Point at the southwest tip of Cypress Island, things changed for the worse. Saul felt confident he could handle the waves, but he was less sure about his partner. Larry kept paddling toward Washington Beach Park, and the two ended up going back the way they came.

Soon the seas were so rough they frequently lost sight of each other when waves passed between them. Larry had trouble keeping his kayak on course and was soon trailing behind Saul. Larry's kayak started to take on water. Although neither wore a spray skirt, Saul's kayak (an off-brand, Saul didn't know the name) had more freeboard than the Puffin; that, combined with Saul's tactic of angling with the waves kept him from taking on water. Saul yelled to Larry to head downwind, but Larry was afraid he would capsize if he went with the waves. Instead, Larry took most of the waves from the side so he could turn into the bigger ones.

As Larry's kayak filled with more water, it became more tippy and moved more slowly. Larry yelled to Saul to wait up, but Saul was out of voice range. Larry's troubles slowed them down so much that at the turn of the tide they were only about one mile into the two-and-a-half-mile crossing. Saul estimated their progress was only about one knot. At that rate, they wouldn't make it to shore because the two-and-a-half-knot ebb current coming out of Bellingham and Guemes Channels would soon take them out into the middle of Rosario Strait. Even if they turned back, the result would be the same. They were now battling forty-knot winds and six-foot waves coming from both the south and southwest. Saul thought it was too rough for towing and yelled back to Larry that he would get help. But Larry was too far away to hear him.

Saul sped up and kept angling with the waves until he landed near the Washington State ferry dock, three-quarters of a mile east of their put-in. At 4:03 P.M., Saul called 911 from the ferry terminal office. The Anacortes police started a search and rescue for Larry, but conditions were too rough for the police department's boat, and the Coast Guard took over the search. Saul later heard that it was so rough that some of the crew aboard the Coast Guard cutter became seasick during the search.

Meanwhile, Larry kept paddling and made it to within seven-tenths of a mile from shore. By then his kayak's cockpit was completely swamped and he was making almost no progress. With his drysuit to keep him warm and his experience swimming triathlons, he felt sure he could swim the rest of the way. Just as he was considering getting out of the kayak to swim for shore, a big wave slowly rolled his kayak and he fell out. Abandoning the kayak, he swam toward shore.

After a while, he noticed that the shore was moving—the current was sweeping him sideways, out toward Rosario Strait. He tried swimming against the current, but he still lost ground. A sight-seeing excursion boat went by within about fifty yards of him, close enough that he could almost make out the faces of passengers, but no one saw or heard him. Another small boat went by farther out. He saw that he was drifting toward a big, red navigational buoy (R2, three-quarters of a mile north of Green Point). Thinking he could climb up on the buoy, he swam toward it, but the current swept him past it. (This buoy is located at the edge of a shoal where the current is much faster than in the surrounding waters.) He got his first real sense of the speed of the current, and he was shocked. For the first time, he thought, "I'm not going to make it. I'm going to drown."

Larry floated at the mercy of the current, which took him southwest out into Rosario Strait and then south. Darkness was setting in when he saw a helicopter with a searchlight. He assumed it was looking for him and did his best to signal it, but the helicopter was too far north.

By now Larry was feeling cold and shivering. He had resigned himself to dying, but then he saw the lighthouse on Burrows Island and thought there might be a lightkeeper there. He swam within about a hundred yards of the lighthouse before the current swept him south past Burrows Island and on toward Allan Island. He quit swimming again and floated along, watching search crews scan the shore and water north of him. When he saw the shore of Allan Island, he realized that it was the closest he had come to land. His hope was renewed, and he started swimming again. Soon he could see that he was making real progress.

Larry thanked God as he reached the shore of Allan Island. Although he was cold, he didn't think he was seriously hypothermic. The wind and rain on land made it seem colder than being in the water, so he headed into the woods for shelter. He covered himself with fir branches and exercised to stay warm. He wore the drysuit all night and stayed awake watching and waiting for search-and-rescue crews. When the helicopter or one of the rescue boats passed near Allan Island, he ran down to the beach and waved his orange life jacket. He did this about twenty times during the night, but they never saw him. At about 11:00 P.M., a rescue boat passed close to shore near his location. He was sure they would see him, but they were searching the water. That was the closest the rescuers came to him all night.

At about 9:00 P.M., the search crew found Larry's kayak washed up on Burrows Island. The rear hatch cover was missing, and no sleeping bag was found in the kayak; this inspired a false hope that Larry had landed on Burrows Island and pulled some of his gear out to spend the night.

Sometime before dawn the searchers left, but Larry didn't give up hope. As a volunteer fireman, he had experience with rescue operations; he felt confident the search would resume at daybreak. He felt it was ironic to be the one waiting to be rescued.

As soon as there was enough daylight, Larry hiked through the woods to the north end of the island. Bushwhacking across the island was a strenuous workout, but at least it warmed him up. For almost an hour he rested and stood facing Burrows Island. He watched for signs of the search-and-rescue crews, but saw none and decided they must have given up the search. Larry assumed Allan Island was uninhabited (in fact, there is a caretaker at the other end of the island), but he still hoped there might be a lighthouse keeper on Burrows Island. He considered swimming the three-tenths-mile crossing to Burrows Island. He threw sticks in the water to check the current in the channel. It looked slack, so he went for it.

Larry made it to Burrows Island only to find the old lightkeeper's house boarded up. Unfortunately, the light on Burrows is automated. About that time he saw a Navy helicopter hovering over the part of Allan Island that he had just left. He ran out into the open lawn in front of the lighthouse and waved at the helicopter; this time he was spotted. The helicopter circled and landed in front of the lighthouse. Larry was flown to Island Hospital in Anacortes. When he arrived, his core temperature was 92°F (33°C). He was warmed up and released.

LESSONS LEARNED

Larry believes he could have succeeded in paddling to shore if he had been wearing a spray skirt and had tried going with the waves as Saul did. (However, for unskilled paddlers, going with the waves often causes capsizes.) He regrets not having taken a flashlight, matches, and other survival gear with him when he abandoned his kayak.

Saul says that from now on he will have people practice wet exits and rescues before going to places like the San Juan Islands—even in the summer. He has put flares in his PFDs and added a pump holder to the kayak Larry used. When buying a kayak he would choose a more visible color than the Puffin's dark green top and bottom.

The real lesson is that novices need to learn a lot about sea kayaking before they are ready to go out by themselves on overnight trips, especially during stormy seasons or to places with strong currents, long fetches, or long crossings. In my opinion, both these men are lucky to be alive. Larry's luck was aided by the protection of the drysuit that Saul had loaned him. My first reaction was that they should have stayed together, but they were so lacking in skill, knowledge, and experience that they wouldn't have known what to do if they had stayed together. There just isn't any good solution when novices get themselves into this kind of trouble.

Education and practice go a long way toward eliminating this kind of accident. Larry and Saul were not merely caught off guard by a sudden change in the weather; rather, they made a number of mistakes because of a lack of knowledge and experience. As Saul later put it, "You end up making decisions based on what you know or don't know." When it is windy, it is dangerous to base your decision to paddle only on whether or not you think you would capsize; you must also consider whether or not you could turn around, rescue yourself if you capsize (and not become hypothermic in the process), rescue others if they capsize, stay within voice range of each other (which may be only a few boat lengths apart), and tow a sick or injured kayaker or swimmer to shore.

If your answer to any of these questions is "I don't know," or "I'm not sure," you should not go farther than a short swimming distance from a safe beach. If the current predictions or weather forecast suggest that conditions could get worse while you are out paddling, ask yourself these questions with the worst conditions in mind. If that sounds too limiting, it is time to improve your skills so you can safely handle the conditions you want to paddle in.

Although knowledge and experience will help reduce errors in judgment, we all make them occasionally. When this happens, you need skills you can count on to get you out of trouble. For example, if Saul had been skilled enough to raft up safely to Larry's kayak, they would have had several better options than separating to go for help: They could have pumped out Larry's kayak and both paddled the final three-quarters of a mile to shore, or they could have stayed rafted up and ridden out the storm. (At around 11:00 P.M. the current reversed and would have taken them back north. More importantly, with the wind and current going the same way, the waves would have been less steep. Eventually high winds pass. They were not in danger of being blown out to sea or getting hypothermic or dehydrated.)

Many kayakers worry about rafting up in rough conditions. Although there is a risk of injury from getting close to another kayak in rough conditions, once you are rafted up it is mostly a matter of watching out that you don't get a hand or finger smashed between kayaks. Practice and test your ability to raft up in conditions that are challenging but not dangerous. Certainly there are extreme conditions—such as surf—that would make rafting up impossible for anyone, but I have rafted up with others for up to fifteen minutes at a time in some very rough conditions.

Once they had rafted together, a skilled paddler could have set up a towline

Seasickness

One summer day after work, Alice took her friend Jennifer out on Lake Washington to introduce her to sea kayaking. The day was warm, sunny, and calm, a perfect day for Jennifer's first kayak lesson. The lake was as close to dead calm as it gets. Jennifer, a whitewater rafter and a competent swimmer, was looking forward to paddling a sea kayak.

Alice explained how to perform a wet exit if the kayak tipped over. Jennifer practiced releasing the spray skirt several times until she felt confident that she could do it while upside down. Next, Alice showed her some basic paddling strokes and described the reentry rescue technique they would use in case of a capsize.

All went well, and Jennifer was having fun. They paddled at an easy pace along the shore. After they had gone only about five hundred feet, Jennifer suddenly became seasick. They stopped paddling, hoping the nausea would pass. It didn't. They turned around and paddled back. They did not have to paddle far: The beach where they put in was still in sight.

Alice was glad they had done this practice paddle before she had taken Jennifer along on a group or overnight trip where it would not have been as easy to change their plans. Had Jennifer been disabled by nausea in more severe conditions offshore, the consequences could have been much more serious.

Jennifer had a long history of motion sickness in cars and boats; neither she nor Alice had thought kayaking would be a problem, especially on such a nice day. Jennifer decided to get a prescription for motion sickness medication and try paddling again.

In her book *Keep It Moving*, Valerie Fons tells of getting seasick every day at the beginning of her trip with Verlen Kruger around the Baja Peninsula. Later, anti-nausea medication allowed her to continue until she became accustomed to the ocean swells and the problem went away.

You can prevent and prepare for many problems by taking a number of shake-down trips to work up to longer and more difficult cruises. In the event that someone gets seasick, he or she will probably need to be towed. A rope suitable for towing a kayak should be a part of every sea kayaker's equipment, and as with other gear it is important to test it before you need it. Besides towing sick or injured paddlers, tow ropes are valuable for retrieving a kayak that gets loose during a wet exit. To keep the towing kayak from pivoting downwind of the tow, fasten the towline near the middle of the towing kayak. If there isn't a deck cleat handy, make a loop around the cockpit coaming, your waist, or over one shoulder. The over-the-shoulder method makes it easier to slip out of the loop quickly if necessary. The rope used as the towline should float (or have a float attached to it) and should be readily accessible at all times.

on Larry's kayak and given him a tow. If necessary, Larry could have used a paddle float or two (one on each end of his paddle) to keep himself upright while being towed. Another device that would have helped stabilize Larry's kayak is a set of sponsons (these would have to have been set up on the kayak ahead of time). In a larger group, one person could have stayed rafted with Larry while another paddler towed the two.

Adequate practice will lead not only to strong skills, but to a better understanding—and appropriate use—of paddling equipment. Without a properly fitting spray skirt, an open-cockpit kayak is unseaworthy. While in some cases it may be prudent for a novice *not* to use a spray skirt, or to use one with a very loose fit around the cockpit until the paddler has practiced a wet exit, a person of this skill level should not be in a paddling situation where a spray skirt might be necessary.

Larry's Puffin kayak features a "cockpit pod" that keeps the floodable volume of the cockpit to a minimum and prevents water from getting from the cockpit to the rest of the boat. However, Larry was taking on water through the hatches because the kayak was missing the neoprene inner hatch covers and had only the plastic outer hatch covers, which Larry didn't realize were required to make a watertight seal.

Marine weather radios provide both forecasts and observations, but interpreting this information to decide whether or not to head out on a windy day takes experience, familiarity with the local geography, and an understanding of how wind is channeled by land forms. For example, the two weather stations nearest Strawberry Island are at Bellingham, sixteen miles northeast of Reef Point, and at Smith Island, fourteen miles to the south-southwest. On the day of this incident, the wind in Bellingham had been less than ten knots all day, and at Smith Island the wind was from the west to southwest at around twenty knots. Twenty-knot winds would give many if not most sea kayakers trouble, but Saul and Larry found themselves in even stronger wind. Where did it come from? By visualizing a twenty-knot wind accelerating as it funnels through the land that surrounds Rosario Strait, you begin to get the answer.

Other clues might come from reports of conditions in even more remote areas. At 4:00 P.M., observations taken at Dungeness Spit reported west winds at thirty knots with gusts to thirty-eight knots. Dungeness Spit is twice the distance from Strawberry Island as Smith Island, but if the winds are that strong in one area, you need to be wary—all that wind has to go somewhere.

Once ashore, a kayaker waiting to be rescued can improve his odds by making a signal to attract attention and show his location. Larry's situation demonstrates the prudence of carrying some survival gear in the pockets of a PFD. As a minimum, consider storing distress flares, whistles, and waterproof matches there.

16

Vanished

George Gronseth

On the eve of Memorial Day, 1992, a solo kayaker disappeared in the San Juan Islands of Washington. Bryan Maybee's body was never recovered, and he was presumed drowned. The weather that day in the San Juans was hot and clear with only a five- to ten-knot breeze. Nine hours passed between the last sighting of the kayaker and the recovery of his kayak; during that time the tidal exchanges were moderate for the area.

B ryan Maybee was a 45-year-old chiropractor reportedly in good health. He had rented a kayak, taken a ferry to San Juan Island, and driven to San Juan County Park, where he parked his car and set up his tent. A witness at the park said Bryan launched his kayak between 6:00 and 7:00 P.M.; he was wearing a red T-shirt, blue shorts, Nike Aquasocks, and sunglasses. His kayak was dark green and he wore a blue spray skirt. His life jacket was stowed under the shock cords in front of the cockpit.

An experienced kayaker who was also staying at the county park met Bryan on the water that evening. Bryan had asked him how far it was to Limekiln State Park and told him he was planning to paddle there and then return to the county park. The kayaker thought Bryan appeared to be a rather inexperienced kayaker.

Limekiln State Park is a popular spot for whale watching, and that evening about thirty people had gathered on the shore. Around 7:30 P.M., people at the park saw a lone paddler whose kayak, clothing, hair, and build matched Bryan's. He was just offshore, near the lighthouse. A short time later a pod of seven orca whales appeared near the kayaker, who was observed paddling toward the pod until he was in their midst (a violation of marine mammal protection laws). Several people on shore yelled to the kayaker to move away from the whales. One of the whales repeatedly breached very close to the kayaker. Many of the observers felt the kayaker was placing himself in danger.

According to these witnesses, the whales were putting on quite a show,

141

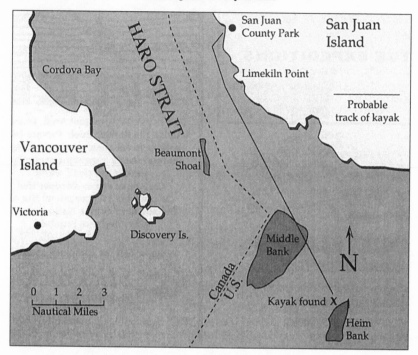

breaching, rolling, and poking their heads above water; they seemed to be looking at the people on shore and at the kayaker. There was a young calf in the pod; it stayed close to its mother. The biggest male stayed several hundred yards offshore, but the rest of the pod was close to shore.

The kayaker was last seen at about 9:30 P.M. By then the sun had set, but there was still enough light to see the kayaker paddling south toward open water with the whales. The waning quarter moon would not rise until 2:51 A.M.

At 6:50 A.M. the next day, a motorboater recovered Bryan's kayak six and a half miles south of the shore where he was last seen. The empty kayak was floating upside down near a shoal called Heim Bank. The life jacket was still secured under the front shock cords, and a wetsuit was under the shock cords aft of the cockpit.

Both the United States and Canadian Coast Guards sent helicopters to search the water, and the San Juan County sheriff's boat searched the shoreline on the west side of San Juan Island. At 10:15 the caretaker of San Juan County Park notified the sheriff that a kayaker staying at the park had not returned from the previous evening. The search was canceled at 5:15 P.M.

The owner of the store where Bryan rented the kayak reported that the boat, a rotomolded plastic Chinook by Aquaterra, had no signs of damage, and there was virtually no water in either of the bulkheaded compartments. The paddle and spray skirt were not found. When he rented the kayak, Bryan indicated on the release form that he had watched the required safety video; however, he declined the free use of a bilge pump, spare paddle, and paddle float.

Working toward a New Wildlife Ethic for Kayakers

Chris Amato

It's no secret that kayaking is one of the best ways to view wildlife. The kayaker enjoys the dual advantage of silent propulsion and a close-to-the-water profile. However, while we humans may treasure those moments when we are nose to nose with wildlife, it doesn't necessarily follow that the birds or marine mammals we're viewing share our enthusiasm for such close encounters. In fact, in some instances our presence can actually harm wildlife.

A popular myth is that kayaks do not disturb wildlife because they lack noisy outboard motors. But the mere presence of humans, no matter how silent, may be perceived as a threat. The kayak's increased navigability also allows kayakers access to sensitive wildlife areas not navigable by motorboats.

Contrary to popular belief, wildlife do not somehow sense that kayakers are peaceful, well-intentioned observers. A friend of mine was fortunate to sight a pod of orcas in British Columbia's Johnstone Strait, and with a strong stroke he soon drew even with the pod. For some time Rob cruised within a paddle's length of the nearest whales, unaware that he was violating regulations by making such a close approach. Eventually, he wearied of the pace, and began to head back to shore.

Suddenly he noticed the orcas had turned and were following him. Several orcas edged closer to the kayak. Rob began to get nervous. He angled his kayak toward the nearest island. His adrenaline began pumping when a few of the whales peeled off from the pod and, with a burst of speed, cut off his line of retreat to the island. Rob was convinced he was about to become the first documented case of orcas attacking a kayaker. "When those orcas were closing in on me, I had no idea what their intentions were, and I expected the worst. Yet afterward I realized I had done the same thing to them. I probably scared them as much as they scared me."

Like humans, different species of wildlife vary in their ability to tolerate disturbance. Scientists do not yet completely understand why some species (and even some individuals within a species) are more tolerant of humans than others.

Nearly all species are extremely sensitive to human disturbance during the breeding season, which for most wildlife occurs in the spring and summer—when most kayakers are on the water. Intrusion into nesting areas can have serious consequences. For instance, seals and sea lions haul out on land to form colonies where they give birth and nurse their young. Even one kayak venturing too close to a haul-out site can start a panicked stampede by the adults, resulting in pups being crushed to death during the rush to the water's safety. Those pups lucky enough to survive are left vulnerable to predation. Studies of seabird nesting colonies have shown human intrusion can cause widespread nest abandonment by adults, leading to significant mortality among nestlings due to predation and other causes associated with adult absence from the nest.

Human disturbance during the fall and winter can have equally significant, though less readily observable, negative effects on

(continued on page 144)

(continued from page 143)
wildlife. These other, more subtle effects relate to what biologists call the "energy budget." All wildlife (and humans) have a limited supply of energy, and one of the challenges of life is budgeting this limited energy supply among competing but essential activities such as breeding, foraging, and predator avoidance. The more energy a surf scoter spends on predator (or human) avoidance, the less energy is available to the bird for other activities such as foraging.

Kayakers should be aware of two federal laws, the Endangered Species Act (ESA) and the Marine Mammal Protection Act (MMPA), which afford special protection to certain wildlife species. Under the ESA it is illegal to harm or harass any species listed by the U.S. Fish and Wildlife Service or the National Marine Fisheries Service as endangered or threatened. ESA-protected species include the bald eagle, peregrine falcon, brown pelican, marbled murrelet, Aleutian Canada goose, snowy plover, piping plover, least tern, Everglade snail kite, Stellar's sea lion, humpback whales, and Florida manatee. Check with your local branch of the U.S. Fish and Wildlife Service to get a complete list of protected species in your area. Like the ESA, the MMPA prohibits the harming or harassment of protected species. The MMPA's protection extends to all marine mammals, which includes whales, dolphins, seals, and sea lions. In both the ESA and the MMPA, "harassment is broadly defined to include virtually any disturbance of the protected species' breeding, foraging, or other behaviors."

The general rule of thumb is to maintain a buffer zone of at least one hundred yards between kayakers and wildlife. In certain instances, such as during the breeding season or when observing a particularly disturbance-sensitive species, a larger buffer will be required. If your presence is changing wildlife behavior, then you've overstepped the boundary.

Many seabird areas are already protected as sanctuaries, and kayakers should take care to obey any signs that limit or prohibit access to such sites. Should you come upon an unposted site, remain at least one hundred yards offshore. If you observe changes in behavior at one hundred yards, you should increase the distance to where the birds no longer react in a disturbed manner.

Among seals and sea lions, the most easily recognized indication of disturbance is lifting the head. This is a sign of increased alertness caused by the kayaker's presence, and is in many cases the only indicative behavior prior to a stampede into the water.

Since whales and dolphins do not haul out on land to rest or breed as seals and sea lions do, the opportunities for disturbance are less apparent. Nevertheless, the MMPA's one-hundred-yard buffer requirement applies to encounters with whales and dolphins. Kayakers should avoid approaching whales and dolphins directly, and instead paddle on a parallel course that maintains the required buffer. Of course, if the pod of orcas you're watching decides to swim next to or under your kayak, you need not paddle furiously to reestablish the buffer. Be particularly careful about approaching orca pods that appear to be moving very slowly, or not moving at all, since the orcas may be napping and could easily be disturbed by your approach.

There are three basic and easy-to-follow guidelines for wildlife viewing that can be the starting point for developing your individual ethic for wildlife interactions: Use binoculars;observe the one-hundred-yard rule; and educate yourself about the wildlife you are likely to encounter while paddling. These three simple rules will help you maintain a balance between your desire for wildlife encounters and the needs of birds and mammals with which you share the water.

LESSONS LEARNED

Due to the frequent appearances of orcas, this area is a popular destination for both private and commercial kayak trips. The orcas here have had frequent encounters with kayakers for many years and have never shown aggression toward them. There are no documented attacks on kayakers by orcas, but still one wonders if the animals had something to do with Brian's troubles—an accidental bump, perhaps?

We may never know what happened to Bryan. Even if the orcas were not a factor, many things can go wrong even in seemingly benign weather. For example, there are many shoals both near shore and miles offshore in the area between where Bryan was last seen and where his kayak was found. During the flood tide the maximum currents in this area (away from the shoals) would have hit 1.5 knots around 10:00 P.M.; the maximum ebb current was 2.3 knots around 5:00 A.M. Though these currents are only moderate for this area, they are fast enough to create turbulence near shoals and points, where local currents would be faster. Perhaps in his enthusiasm to follow the pod, Bryan encountered conditions beyond his skill, capsized, and became separated from his kayak. He may have succumbed to cold shock (sudden drowning) or hypothermia.

17

Ferry Rescue in the San Juans

George Gronseth

On Sunday, December 13, 1992, friends dropped four kayakers off near the Lummi Island ferry dock at Gooseberry Point near Washington's San Juan Islands. The paddlers made arrangements to be picked up four days later in Anacortes.

They had rented two double kayaks (Seascape I's, made by Northwest Kayaks) from Western Washington University in Bellingham. Both kayaks were equipped with front and rear bulkheads for flotation and hand-held pumps for bailing. Also included with the rental were spray skirts, PFDs (each with a whistle and rocket flare in a pocket), self-rescue paddle floats, and one spare paddle for the group.

Lorene, the least experienced kayaker, shared a kayak with Ian, the most experienced. Mike and Scott shared the other double. All four are in their early twenties, physically fit, and experienced wilderness campers. All had been kayaking before, and all but Lorene had read books on sea kayaking. Ian and Scott had both been on more than ten multi-day kayak trips, paddled in wind waves up to three feet high, and done some reentry rescue practice—although not together and not in rough water. Ian had practiced group rescues, including dumping the water out of a kayak before getting back in, but his practice was limited to one-person kayaks. Scott and another friend had once practiced wet exits and self rescues in a double kayak, but they had not tried rescuing other kayakers.

The group didn't have a weather radio, but Mike and Scott had checked the TV weather forecast, which predicted fair weather for the first three days of their trip followed by rain and windy weather on the last day. They were unaware of the

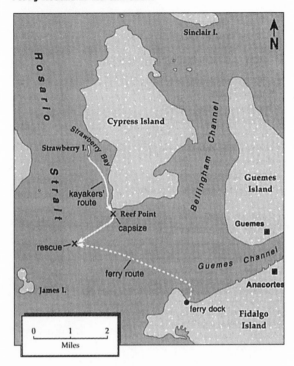

marine forecast, which called for "a small-craft advisory and winds becoming southeast at twenty knots in the afternoon" on their first day and "increasing clouds, rain, and gusting wind developing late" on the fourth day.

During the first day of their trip, the kayakers discussed what to do in case of a capsize. They also agreed they would head for shore and wait things out anytime conditions got too rough. Their plan for the first day was to paddle five miles southeast from Goosebery Point and spend the night at a campground near the south end of Lummi Island. This meant they would be paddling into the southeast wind all the way. Fighting the headwind proved harder than they had expected, and they ended up camping in a bay a little north of their goal for that night.

The next day was much calmer, and they had no trouble paddling south to Guemes Island, where they camped for the night. On the third day they paddled eight miles around the south side of Cypress Island and over to tiny Strawberry Island, where they camped for their final night of the trip. The weather again was calm, but Ian pointed out to the others that there were signs that the weather was changing. While the previous day had been clear, there was now a dark band of high clouds moving in from the west, and cumulus clouds were building at lower elevations.

The next morning was windy, and the whole sky was heavily overcast. The marine forecast called for "small-craft warnings; southeast winds fifteen to thirty knots, with the strongest winds in the afternoon; rain and snow mixed." But without a weather radio, all they had to go by was what they could see—and from their perspective on Strawberry Island, the conditions, despite the wind, didn't look too rough. Apparently they were somewhat sheltered from the wind by the nearby bluffs of Cypress Island and the short distance between Strawberry Island and Cypress Island.

They considered several options that morning. They could stay put and wait for the wind to calm down (they had plenty of food and water), or they could hug the shore around the south end of Cypress Island, cross to Guemes Island, and then cross Guemes Channel to Anacortes (a seven-mile trip). They also considered heading north along the west side of Cypress Island, which they felt would provide more shelter before crossing to Guemes but would add four miles to the trip.

The conditions didn't seem bad enough to warrant staying put, and they didn't want to add extra miles to what was already one of their longer days, so they decided to head to Anacortes via the south end of Cypress Island. They had been up since about 8:00 A.M., but chose to wait until 11:15 to leave Strawberry Island. Leaving earlier would have meant fighting both the wind and the flood current on their way south to Reef Point at the southwest end of Cypress Island; instead, they caught the beginning of the ebb, which helped take them to the south end of Cypress Island. However, waves get much rougher when the wind and current are in opposition. So even without a change in weather, they were bound to run into worsening conditions as the ebb current sped up. When they departed Strawberry Island, the waves were only about one foot high. In Scott's words, "It was a little choppy at first, but not bad at all." But things worsened as they headed south. Upon rounding Reef Point, they suddenly felt the full force of the wind and found themselves in steep, three-foot waves.

Realizing they weren't going to make it to Anacortes, Ian and Lorene headed for the first beach they saw. They made it into shallow water near the point and

Doubles and Sea Socks

Matt Broze

I have become concerned about the rescuability of double kayaks as they are usually paddled. I have had little experience with doubles and have never personally tried a rescue after capsizing one, but after watching a demonstration by NOLS at the West Coast Sea Kayaking Symposium, it became obvious to me that almost any swamped double would be difficult to bail.

One boat used in the demonstration had float bags in bow and stern and, once swamped, floated level without anyone in it; however, it was so low in the water that bailing would have been difficult even in calm conditions. Such bailing would have had to be done from the water, as the cockpits, if occupied, would most likely disappear below the surface, even in calm water

Even a double with bulkheads at bow and stern can fail to lift the coamings sufficiently above the waves. The amount of water to bail from a double is immense compared to that in a single. In a loaded double, there is an even greater need to stow gear in waterproof bags to maximize overall buoyancy.

I recommend that anyone paddling a rigid double with individual cockpits fit them with sea socks. A sea sock is a large waterproof bag that your lower body fits into; the top of the sock seals around the coaming with shock cord. In the event of a capsize, the kayak floats high and water intake is limited to the sea sock's volume (though the intake usually turns out to be could have landed but thought they should wait for their friends. Mike and Scott had been on the outside as the group came around the point, and now were a hundred or more yards offshore—well beyond voice range given the conditions. Fortunately, Mike and Scott also decided to head in, but it was rougher in their location and they had difficulty turning their kayak around.

Ian and Lorene let their kayak drift while they waited for their friends. The wind and current swiftly carried them away from shore. Ian, who was in the back and had control of the rudder, tried to keep the kayak from turning sideways to the waves, but without forward speed the rudder was ineffective. It wasn't long before a couple of big waves hit their kayak from the side. One wave knocked them off balance and the next flipped them over.

Ian and Lorene surfaced on the same side of the kayak. Lorene seemed to be in shock, but Ian was confident they could rescue themselves. He righted the kayak by himself and climbed back in his cockpit. He then steadied the kayak with his paddle so Lorene could get in. But she couldn't pull herself up out of the water; she was in pain and couldn't move her left arm. (They later learned she had dislocated her shoulder during the capsize.) Lorene's paddle was lost; then Ian capsized again and lost his paddle. They had been only about twenty yards from shore at the point of their first capsize, but now they were much farther out. In the 50°F (10°C) water, a swimmer could die of hypothermia before reaching shore. Ian knew the risks of hypothermia and soon

much less because a kayak equipped with sea socks is so buoyant that not much water gets in it when the kayak is righted).

I use a sea sock when practicing in surf, both to keep water weight out of the ends of my kayak for quicker maneuverability, and to keep the kayak riding high if I bail out. Floating virtually empty, the boat can get tossed around in the surf, speared into the beach, or banged around on rocks with a lot less chance of damage than might be sustained by the same kayak containing several hundred pounds of water. In hot weather, sea socks have the disadvantage of being a little warmer and more humid. They also make knee braces slipperier, requiring the use of knee braces that don't depend on friction for their effectiveness (you can also coat the knee area on both sides with contact cement and let it

dry thoroughly). A sea sock also separates you from the contents of your kayak: If you don't keep it in the sock or on deck, you have to open the top to get at your snack or camera (on the up side, you are less likely to lose things in the event of a capsize).

It takes a while to get used to them, but because they maximize flotation, sea socks provide an extra safety margin. They also keep a kayak's interior clean. I consider sea socks a safety essential in most double kayaks.

The decision to use sea socks should be based on your own experience. As with any equipment, you should practice with and without them, in all kinds of conditions, both with help from other kayakers and solo (but with help nearby). Give yourself adequate information with which to make an informed, intelligent decision.

realized their survival depended on staying together, with the kayak.

Meanwhile, Mike and Scott managed to get their kayak turned around, only to discover that their friends needed help. They recovered Ian's paddle and then rafted the kayaks together. They decided to try dumping the water out of the swamped kayak before getting Ian and Lorene back in but were unable to lift the loaded double. They rafted up again and, with Ian's help, pulled Lorene up out of the water. Ian then climbed back in his cockpit. Lorene managed to sit in her cockpit but was too incapacitated by her shoulder injury to pull her feet into the kayak.

In spite of having front and rear bulkheads for flotation, the kayak was so swamped that Ian's cockpit coaming was below the surface of the water. There was still hope—if Ian's spray skirt could seal his cockpit well enough to keep water from coming in, the kayak could be pumped out. However, every time Ian fastened his spray skirt, a wave would wash over the kayak and pop the spray skirt off.

With so much going wrong, the paddlers began to get really scared. Nevertheless, they stayed calm enough to keep thinking of new things to try. They gave up on bailing the swamped kayak and decided to try paddling to shore. Lorene was unable to paddle, and they were not equipped for towing, so Ian and Lorene kept the kayaks rafted up while Mike and Scott paddled the two kayaks forward. The swamped kayak was positioned just enough ahead of the other one that Mike was able to paddle on both sides. Scott, on the other hand, could paddle only on one side. Scott said later that they "paddled like hell," but their progress was negligible and they had difficulty keeping the kayaks on course.

The combination of wind and current continued to take them west into Rosario Straight, farther away from land. They decided it was time to signal for help and shot one flare toward the cabins along Strawberry Bay on Cypress Island and two toward Anacortes. They soon used the remaining flare to try to signal a ferry boat headed west for the San Juan Islands. All the flares fired properly but none attracted help.

The ebb current in Rosario Straight was now running at about two knots, and the wind was blowing around forty knots. It was raining, but that didn't matter—they already were drenched by the breaking waves. Some of the waves were now so big they washed over their heads. Mike and Scott's kayak started taking on water, apparently through the spray skirts, which had loose-fitting nylon body tubes. Holding onto the swamped kayak seemed to pull them deeper into the waves, which in turn caused them to take on more water—or so they thought. After about an hour of riding things out with the kayaks rafted up, they decided to abandon the swamped kayak in hopes they might be able to paddle faster that way and get to shore.

Lorene straddled the center of Mike and Scott's kayak, and Ian climbed up on the bow. But Ian's weight on the foredeck pushed the bow down so low that the front cockpit was submerged. Scott felt water rushing into his cockpit, so Ian got off and moved to the stern. This arrangement worked for a while, but the waves kept getting bigger. Before long Mike and Scott's kayak was again taking on water, making the kayak unstable. To improve their stability, Ian moved to the center, and he and Lorene laid across the kayak facing each other with their legs in the water.

None of the paddlers had wetsuits or drysuits, but all wore wool hats and gloves, long underwear tops and bottoms, and rain gear over wool sweaters and pants. Nevertheless, hypothermia was becoming a serious threat to their lives, and they knew it. Ian later said he didn't shiver or feel any numbness, but he recalled times when he just wanted to close his eyes and go to sleep. In spite of their lowering body temperatures, they managed to stay alert by talking to each other continuously.

At 1:20 P.M., another ferry boat left the Anacortes dock on Fidalgo Island and headed west. Fifteen minutes into the trip, the captain saw what at first looked like a log, but moments later he realized it was someone in need of help. The kayakers had seen the ferry and were waving their paddles. The captain blew the ferry's horn and headed toward them.

The thought of being rescued was such a relief that the paddlers let their guards down, and they capsized. This time they didn't even try to get back in the kayak; they just clung to it and waited for help. Although they were exhausted and hypothermic, Scott recalled later that they all were still able to talk coherently at this time.

Paddling in the Lee

Christopher Cunningham

When an offshore breeze is blowing, the land slows the wind and lifts it over the water. In the lee of the land, the air can be still and the water deceptively calm, even glassy smooth. There is little to indicate the true strength of the wind. Farther out, the wind touches down on the water and begins to generate waves. From shore you may see only the smooth, dark backs of the waves. Because you can't see the white, breaking faces of the waves, the water may appear much less rough than it really is.

You can paddle safely in the shelter of the lee, as long as you take care to stay in the corridor of calm air along shore. Many accidents are the result of paddling or drifting out of the lee and into the wind. At the downwind edge of the lee, the wind can hit hard and fast, even though you may still be on fairly smooth water. By the time you feel the wind's full force, you may find it difficult to get the kayak turned back toward land. During the time you are trying to turn around, the wind will push you farther offshore into stronger wind and more powerful waves.

In an offshore wind, the width of the lee is determined by the height of the land along shore. Beware of breaks in the contour of the land—wherever the land ends or decreases in elevation, the wind is likely to increase in intensity. It is easy to get lulled into complacency paddling in the lee. Before paddling away from shore, across the mouth of a bay, or beyond a point of land, stop and make a thorough assessment of the conditions. If you have any doubts about the severity of the conditions offshore, paddle back into the safety of the lee.

The ferry captain estimated the wave height at six to eight feet; his instruments measured wind gusts of sixty-six miles per hour. In spite of the conditions, two crew members, David Lawton and Gordon Brewster, volunteered to rescue the kayakers. The ferry's lifeboats aren't motorized, so David and Gordon launched the ferry's work skiff, a 12-foot Livingston. Meanwhile, the captain positioned the ferry boat upwind of the kayakers to help block the wind and waves.

Miraculously, David and Gordon managed to reach the kayakers. Scott and Ian held the bow of the motorboat while David pulled Lorene out of the water. Ian was next, then Scott, but Mike and the kayak drifted away. The rescuers waited a couple minutes for a lull and then went after Mike. David needed help pulling Mike in, but Scott was too weak so Ian moved to the bow. Together Dave and Ian pulled Mike into the tiny boat. The rescuers took them to the side of the ferry where Lorene and Mike were hoisted up with a winch. Scott and Ian used a ladder on the side of the ferry to climb up to the deck. The rescue took only thirteen minutes.

Once on the ferry, the rescuers removed the kayakers' clothes, and some of the passengers warmed the victims under blankets. The captain turned the ferry back to the Anacortes terminal where two ambulances waited to take the kayakers to the hospital. Lorene had trouble breathing and was given oxygen, and Mike was put on monitors. Scott and Ian were wrapped in heated blankets. All recovered and were released by the next day.

LESSONS LEARNED

After the accident, Scott said, "We should have had a VHF/weather radio. We also should have stayed closer together while paddling."

Ian commented, "The limited rescue practice some of us had may have contributed to a general overconfidence. Every member of a group should practice rescues before such a trip, and practice in waves would be best."

Besides being cool, winter is a stormy time of year in the Northwest. This makes the risk of getting caught in rough conditions much higher, especially during multi-day trips. Winter also means shorter days and less boat traffic, both of which reduce the chance of being rescued.

In my own subsequent trips to Strawberry Island, I have observed that during the ebb current, the island is in a slow back eddy that flows off Tide Point (to the north on Cypress Island). Thus, when the wind is out of the south and the current is ebbing, it can look deceptively calm near Strawberry Island because locally the wind and the current are not in opposition. But farther out in Rosario Strait or to the south around Reef Point, conditions will be much more severe.

This was the second time in a little over a month that a group of kayakers got in trouble at Reef Point (See Chapter 15). The paddlers in both accidents had these things in common: They were not well prepared in terms of equipment or skill; they went out in windy conditions; they were caught off guard when conditions suddenly changed as they rounded a point; they took too long to realize conditions were getting beyond their ability; they were not prepared to deal with a capsize in the conditions they had paddled into; they used borrowed or rented kayaks; they paddled with only two kayaks in the group; and they had poorly fitted or maladjusted spray skirts, which compounded their other problems and errors.

This group lacked the following equipment: a weather radio or a two-way VHF radio (to receive the marine weather report); adequate flotation; properly adjusted spray skirts (which might have allowed them to pump the water out after getting back in); wetsuits or drysuits; and tow ropes (which may have allowed them to paddle fast enough to reach shore).

Even wide, "stable," two-person kayaks can capsize when waves get steep. And when a fiberglass double kayak swamps, the amount of water that gets in can be so immense it is exhausting to pump out. Worse yet, the buoyancy in bulkheaded compartments of a swamped double is often insufficient to keep the cockpit coamings above water. To solve these problems, some two-person kayaks are built with a center flotation compartment. Another solution is to add a pair of sea socks—waterproof nylon bags that line the cockpits and seal around the coaming; they greatly reduce the amount of water that can get into the kayak.

This group demonstrated that it is possible to raft up and stay rafted even in quite rough conditions. If they had worn wetsuits or drysuits, they might have been able to ride out the storm by staying rafted up. Wetsuits could also have allowed them to stay in the water long enough to pump the kayak out before getting back in it, using their spray skirts to seal up the cockpits while pumping.

Better paddling skills could have prevented or minimized these paddlers' problems. For example, leaning and bracing into the waves could have prevented the capsize. Good bracing skills also make it possible to paddle a swamped kayak—even in rough conditions. Try this the next time you practice rescues. If you can't brace well enough to stay upright in a swamped kayak, try bracing with paddle floats on both ends of your paddle—this would at least allow you to stay upright while being towed. A pair of sponsons attached at either side of the cockpit would also provide additional stability.

Fortunately, shoulder dislocations are rare in sea kayaking. However, the possibility that these injuries can occur should cause everyone to take capsizes more seriously, especially solo paddlers and pairs of paddlers who go by themselves in two-person kayaks. Try practicing wet exits and rescues using only one arm. Although loose spray skirts are hazardous because of leakage, it is also dangerous to use a spray skirt that is so tight it requires a strong arm or both arms to open it. Be sure you can open your spray skirt with either hand before leaving shore. If you have trouble getting out of the water during reentry rescues using one arm, try using a rescue technique that uses a "stirrup" (a rope or webbing sling to step into). And consider what you would do after getting an injured person back into his or her kayak. If a group consists of more than two kayaks, one could stabilize the injured person's kayak while the other kayak tows them.

If this group had decided to go ashore a little sooner, they would have avoided the whole incident. However, as is often the case, they didn't know enough about their limits to make this judgment in time. The conservative approach would be to avoid paddling in conditions that are worse than those in which you've successfully practiced rescues (including rolling, for those who know how). In other words, if you want to paddle in rough conditions, first find ways to practice safely in challenging but controlled situations.

18

Rosario Strait Rescue

George Gronseth

On March 10, 1993, three kayakers capsized while on a guided tour in Washington's San Juan Islands. The guide sent out a distress call on a hand-held VHF radio. At the time of their rescue, all three were suffering from hypothermia—none had dressed for immersion.

The tour started from Doe Bay on Orcas Island. The group consisted of four paddlers in two doubles and Joe, the guide, in a single. (The types of kayaks could not be verified.) James West, nineteen, and Monique Sicard, twenty, were students at the University of Portland, and Rob Hildum and Debi Tribe were staff members at the university.

The weather that afternoon was clear, but a cold north wind had been blowing all day. The marine weather forecast included a small-craft advisory due to winds greater than twenty knots. The seas would get rougher during the afternoon, when the currents of the flood tide would oppose the wind, making the waves steeper and taller.

The group had in their favor a guide who was familiar with the area and had many years of kayaking experience. They also had a low client-to-guide ratio, and all were physically fit. The kayaks and paddling equipment were in good condition, and Joe had a variety of emergency signaling devices: VHF radio, whistles, air horn, and flares. Visibility was good, and there was enough daylight left to allow for search-and-rescue operations in case of trouble.

Before the group launched, Joe spent about an hour teaching the four how to paddle and what to do in a capsize. He gave them directions for releasing spray skirts, wet exiting, and reentering the kayaks. They practiced releasing their spray skirts until they were confident they wouldn't become trapped.

Around 1:00 P.M., the party launched and began paddling northeast along the shore of Orcas Island. After about twenty minutes, they attempted to make the crossing out to the Peapod Islands, a half-mile offshore from Orcas Island. The waves soon got bigger, so Joe had them turn back toward Orcas. Rob felt Joe was being too conservative; it didn't seem that rough to him.

Debi and Rob were the faster of the two pairs in the double kayaks. They were more athletic (both lift weights and run marathons) than their friends, and both had kayaked on lakes. James and Monique, who had never been in a kayak before, had trouble just keeping their paddles synchronized. Nonetheless, Joe was able to keep everyone together.

Once the paddlers were closer to Orcas Island, they continued along its shore to the northeast. A short while later they rafted up for lunch, drifting farther northeast toward Lawrence Point while they ate. The waves off the point made it obvious that it was much windier and rougher there. The steep terrain to the north had partly sheltered them from the north wind, but to the east or north of Lawrence Point they would lose this shelter and become exposed to a long fetch (the distance the wind blows unobstructed over the water) and rougher seas. There was a clear boundary line between the lee they were in and the tide rip off the point.

As they drifted closer to the tide rip, Joe told the group they should either paddle back along the shore of Orcas or head directly out to the Peapod Islands; they decided to go to the Peapods.

They paddled south for about ten minutes without making much headway. The current had moved them eastward and into the tide rip. They were now in waves about two feet high. Joe decided they should head back to Orcas and instructed the kayakers to point toward a specific beach and paddle harder for a while. Rob estimated later that at that point the group was a hundred yards offshore and sixty yards away from the calm water. To avoid the roughest part

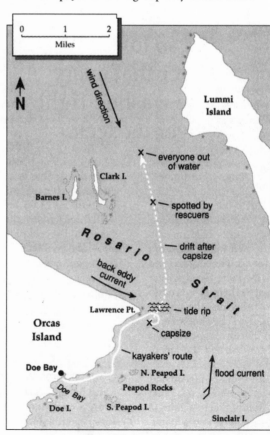

of the tide rip, they had to paddle with a ferry angle against a very fast current. (Remember: Where the current is funneled or deflected by a point, it speeds up.)

By now the kayakers were, according to Rob, "paddling like mad but only inching our way out of the rough water." He kept track of their progress by lining up the point with the terrain behind it—sometimes they advanced and sometimes they lost ground. He and Debi made better progress than the others. As they passed Joe, he told Rob and Debi to keep paddling hard until they crossed the eddy line. Joe stayed back with Monique and James.

It took another twenty minutes or more for Rob and Debi to clear the tide rip. During most of that time they could hear Joe encouraging their friends. James later guessed that he and Monique got within twenty feet of the edge of the tide rip, but in spite of their best efforts they weren't able to reach calm water (the smooth water just upstream of a tide rip is where the current is fastest). James and Monique were getting tired and scared. James said later, "I'll never forget the taste in my mouth when I realized how much trouble we were in. I felt helpless and at the mercy of the ocean."

Monique and James were inadequately dressed for the conditions. Spray from the waves soaked through their nylon wind breakers and saturated the cotton clothes they wore over their polypropylene long underwear. The wind chill cooled them further. As the waves grew bigger, it became increasingly difficult for James to steer the kayak (the waves may have been lifting the rudder out of the water), and the wind and waves kept turning the kayak sideways to the waves. Eventually a wave hit them, and the double flipped. Joe later told the paddlers that he estimated the waves to be about two or three feet high.

James panicked for a moment before remembering Joe's instructions for wet exiting. Joe, who was only about ten feet away when the capsize occurred, jumped into the water, but by the time he swam to the double kayak, both James and Monique were out. They surfaced on the side away from Joe. Monique, more shaken by the experience than James, grabbed him from behind and climbed over him on her way to the kayak. They were both gasping for air and shocked by the cold water. According to James, the water was so cold it seemed to "knock the wind out of your lungs." Fortunately, all were wearing PFDs.

Meanwhile, although Debi and Rob had made it out of the rough water, they were still in a strong current when Rob looked back and saw the bottom of their friend's double; the capsized kayak was about one or two hundred yards offshore and almost hidden by the waves. Rob couldn't see Joe or their friends. Rob and Debi were faced with a difficult decision: Should they try to rescue their friends, or go for help? They had only seconds to decide, because the current was sweeping them back toward the tide rip. They knew Joe was with their friends, and they feared that an attempt to help might result in another capsize. Rob turned the kayak away from the point in search of help.

As soon as James got out of the double kayak, he turned and saw Joe in the water. James asked what he should do; Joe told him not to panic. Then the guide, holding on to his single kayak, tried shooting an emergency signal flare.

It was a dud. James saw a couple other flares floating in the water, but he didn't think he should let go of the kayak to get them. The air horn Joe carried on his PFD had been lost. They blew the whistles attached to their PFDs, but no one heard them.

Meanwhile, the waves rolled the double over a few more times. With Joe steadying the kayak from the water, James quickly climbed into the front cockpit. Joe then had James hold the single kayak. Joe had a two-way VHF marine band radio packed with other emergency gear in his kayak's aft buoyancy compartment. Opening the hatch to get the emergency gear meant risking filling the rear compartment with water, but Joe opened the hatch. Inside were drybags full of clothes; he handed these to James, telling him not to lose them. He pulled out the radio and held it with his teeth to keep it from sinking. Just then, a wave swamped the rear compartment, and Joe's kayak went vertical. Joe called for help on the radio but didn't hear any response.

By now Joe's kayak was on Monique's side of the double and was hitting her. Her legs were numb, and she was unable to get out of the water. Seeing her struggle, Joe swam over to give her a boost. She managed to get back in, but she still had no feeling in her legs.

Although neither of them had shivered while in the water, once they were out of the water both Monique and James started shivering uncontrollably. (It's common for people to feel colder after getting out of the water, but don't be fooled by this sensation. Tests show that immersion will chill you faster than spray.) James said later that his shivering "felt almost like an epileptic seizure" he had experienced as a child.

Joe pulled himself over the middle of the double to get partway out of the water. But because his weight made the double less stable, he dropped back in the water whenever a big wave hit the kayak. He again tried to summon help with his radio and again heard no reply.

All three had lost their paddles. The water inside the double kayak was up to the cockpit coamings, making the kayak tippy and so low in the water that every wave washed right over its deck. The bigger waves were hitting them neck high.

Joe told James to let go of the single kayak and start pumping out the double. Since the cockpits were awash, they had to pump with the spray skirts sealed. Monique and James slid the pumps between the spray skirts' body tubes and their bellies. James soon discovered that cold hands can turn a simple task, such as putting on a spray skirt, into a monumental one. His hands were so numb "they felt like boards." Nevertheless, James managed to seal his spray skirt by coordinating his movements visually. Joe then told them to pump for all they were worth. Unfortunately, it wasn't long before a wave submerged the kayak, popped open the spray skirts, and filled the kayak again. They tried pumping numerous times, but the spray skirts kept coming off.

It was about 3:00 when Joe made his first mayday call on the VHF radio. The radio signal was broken and difficult to understand, but his distress call was heard. The Coast Guard radio operator continuously tried to answer the kayaker's call, but Joe's radio didn't receive the Coast Guard's reply and requests for more information. At about the same time, Rob and Debi made it to a house and had the residents call 911 and the office at the resort where they started the trip. The Coast Guard diverted three of their ships and a helicopter (which took only twenty-one minutes to reach the area) to search for the kayakers. Several local private boaters also went to help. The search focused on the area around Lawrence Point, but the kayakers, carried upwind by the current, were well north of the point.

Mike Ryan and his twelve-year-old son, Casey, were among the volunteers who joined the search. Mike has responded to many distress calls and knew from the tone of the voice that the person on the radio was in serious trouble. He could also "hear the waves in the background and water splashing on the radio's microphone." Mike and Casey sped past the north end of Lummi Island and then continued south toward Lawrence Point.

Joe's calls were sounding progressively more desperate. In the last call that Mike's scanner picked up, fifteen minutes after the first call Mike heard, the guide's voice was getting weak and he had to catch his breath between words.

James and Monique kept pumping. James also held onto the drybags containing the dry clothes they would need if they got to shore. James felt colder and colder; eventually his shivering subsided (a sign of a more severe state of hypothermia). His right calf cramped. He later estimated that about fifteen minutes before their rescue, his thinking started to get foggy and his vision blurry. He thought he was going to die and mentally said his good-byes to his family. He told Monique that he "loved her and really cared about her." He asked Monique to help him say the Lord's Prayer, but she didn't respond. She hadn't said much since the capsize.

About that time, Joe told James he was worried he (Joe) might not make it. Until then James had been counting on Joe to tell them what to do and to encourage him and Monique. James told Joe, "It's OK, we're going to make it." Secretly, James began wondering who would be the first to die. For him that thought was the worst part of the ordeal.

By this time they had drifted a considerable distance north of Lawrence Point, where the searchers were still looking for them. Luckily, Mike and Casey Ryan were coming from the north. On their way to Lawrence Point, Casey saw the bow of a boat on the crest of a wave and yelled to his dad. Mike's attention was focused on the safety of his own boat and he didn't see the kayak, but he took his son's word and circled around. Mike estimated later that the wind was blowing at twenty to thirty knots from the north; this combined with a 2.3-knot current from the south made conditions quite rough (steep four- to five-foot waves), even for his 30-foot salvage boat. The waves made it hard to see the kayakers, and Casey lost sight of them. Mike radioed the Coast Guard about the sighting off Clark Island. The kayak's blue deck and white hull were perfectly camouflaged by the whitecaps, blue water, and blue sky. Mike and Casey didn't see it again until they happened to come up alongside it and found all three kayakers clinging to it. Mike radioed the Coast Guard with their location.

Not long before the rescue, the double had capsized again. There was less panic this time, because the swamped kayak flipped more slowly, giving James and Monique time to bail out before they were completely upside down. No one had the strength to get back in, so all three clung to the inverted double. Moments later they saw Mike's boat circle around and started cheering and waving their pumps.

The deck of Mike's boat was too high for him to reach the kayakers, so he launched his inflatable lifeboat. At about the same time, the Coast Guard helicopter arrived and dropped frogman Chris Kemper in the water next to the kayakers. Chris asked who needed the most help; James and Joe indicated that Monique did. The frogman had Monique hoisted into the helicopter. Next, James and Joe swam the five or ten feet to the raft; Joe climbed in by himself, but James had to be pulled in by the frogman and blacked out shortly thereafter. Chris asked Joe if he knew CPR; when Joe said yes, the frogman told him to perform CPR on James. Meanwhile, Chris rowed the raft to the Coast Guard vessel that had just arrived. James remembers coming to as Joe was giving him mouth-to-mouth resuscitation.

From the liferaft, Joe and James were assisted onto the 41-foot Coast Guard vessel. On board, the two kayakers were laid on the cabin floor in front of a heater and stripped of their clothes. Chris Kemper, an EMT, continued to supervise their care. The cabin was so hot the crew members were sweating heavily; yet Joe, now shaking violently, asked if he was out of the water yet. James was shaking too, but he could feel the heat and said, "Yeah, that's really good, keep that on!" James's teeth were chattering, his hands were shaking, his breathing was difficult, and his vision was blurry—partly because his head was shaking so much.

The helicopter had room for one more person. To determine who was in the worst shape, the crew asked James and Joe questions such as, "Who is the president of the United States?" While James had difficulty answering the questions, Joe didn't even seem to understand them, so he was hauled up in the helicopter and flown with Monique to ambulances that took them to hospitals in Bellingham.

About fifteen minutes had elapsed from the time Mike and Casey Ryan located the kayakers until they were all either in the helicopter or on the Coast Guard vessel. During that time, the current had carried them another mile upwind (for a total drift of about 3.5 miles).

James remained on the ship until the helicopter returned for him. Meanwhile, the ship set a course for Bellingham. The crew tried to give James oxygen, but it made him feel like he couldn't breathe so he pushed it away. James feared he wasn't going to survive, but then he thought, "If I want to live, I can will myself to make it." He told Chris, "I really want to live, tell me what to do."

The helicopter returned, and the ship's crew put James in Chris's survival suit before hoisting him up to the helicopter. Even with the suit on, James couldn't help but scream from the pain of the wind chill outside the heated cabin. The crew huddled around James to block the wind from the downwash of the helicopter blades while they put him in the stretcher. James blacked out from then until the landing. He remembers that Chris helped load him into the ambulance and wished him well. James thanked him for saving his life, and the ambulance sped off to the hospital. The medics started an I.V. and checked his core temperature, which was 85°F (29.4 °C).

Monique's core temperature was 80°F (26.7 °C.) The last thing she remembered was the frogman telling her to let go of the kayak—she had stayed conscious just long enough to be saved.

In the hospital, the kayakers were treated for hypothermia. They were slowly rewarmed with a machine called a Bear Hugger, which circulates warm air through baffles in a special blanket. After a couple hours they were ready to be released from the hospital, but it took several more days to fully recover.

Joe had been in water the longest (about fifty minutes) and had a core temperature of 77°F (25°C), which is often fatal. Yet he managed to be the most functional of the three until they all were out of the water. The hospital staff had to rewarm him more slowly than the others to prevent him from going into shock. The doctors and nurses were amazed that he was still alive. James believes Joe's concern for saving the others wouldn't allow him to let go of his own will to survive.

LESSONS LEARNED

James took several lessons from the incident. He later said, "One thing I learned from this experience is to always keep your head and not panic." He cautions paddlers not to put absolute faith in everything a guide tells you; if you see a potential hazard or problem, let the guide know right away. He feels that wetsuits should be used on such trips. He is glad Joe had the group practice releasing their spray skirts before they launched.

Monique stresses that "people should be in good shape before going on a kayak trip. I can't imagine someone who wasn't in good shape surviving what we went through."

This accident was the third time in four months that kayakers had to be rescued in Rosario Strait (see Chapters 15 and 17). These accidents point out the need to be especially alert to winds and currents that may carry you into conditions beyond your ability, and the need for properly fitted spray skirts.

Shoreline trips often become more difficult than anticipated. As these paddlers discovered, wind and/or current can carry a group away from shore; at other times a group may decide to go farther out to avoid a tide rip at a point, waves reflecting off a cliff, or surf near a beach or just to explore. The trip leader must consider these possibilities when deciding whether or not to cancel the trip.

The decision of whether or not to kayak in windy conditions should be based on more than just the estimated probability of capsizing. Can the group stay together, turn around, raft up, perform rescues, deal with a (completely) swamped kayak, and paddle to safety? Is it likely the conditions will worsen? Will the speed of the current be increasing or decreasing? Will the current switch and oppose the wind? Are there squalls or increasing winds in the weather forecast? Remember that winter is a stormy season in many areas, and extra caution is needed. Winter also means shorter days and less boat traffic, both of which reduce the chance of being rescued.

Lawrence Point is a typical example of topography that creates tide rips— areas of rough water resulting from tidal currents flowing around a point, over a shoal, or through a narrows. Wind waves or boat wakes add to the roughness at tide rips. You can usually see and hear a tide rip from a considerable distance; however, the current accelerates upstream of the rough water and often carries kayakers into a tide rip they thought was avoidable.

If you are getting carried toward a tide rip, act quickly. First try paddling faster and increasing your ferry angle (point more upstream of your destination). A fast paddler may be able to keep a slower paddler out of the rip by assisting with a tow rope, but for this to work towlines should be stored so they're easily deployed. If your group can't avoid a tide rip, change tactics. If everyone has practiced rescues, stay together. Turn your kayaks to face oncoming waves and paddle through them. If there are any large boils (upwellings) or whirlpools, steer around them if possible. The good news about tide rips is they usually cover a relatively small area. The current that creates a tide rip will gen-

Releasing a Spray Skirt

No one wants a spray skirt that pops off too easily; in rough conditions you need a skirt that stays on and keeps the waves out. But what if you capsize and your spray skirt won't release?

There can be a fine line between a shock cord being tight enough to keep the spray skirt on in rough conditions and relaxed enough to release easily if a wet exti becomes necessary. Opening your spray skirt by pushing the release handle forward and quickly pulling it up over your head, rather than pulling the handle straight back, allows you to remove much tighter spray skirts. This method also reduces wear and tear on the spray skirt. Finding and gripping the loop is easier if you lash a piece of dowel or a ball at the end of the loop. This is an especially good idea if you sometimes wear gloves or have a slippery release handle. For handles made of webbing, sewing folds into the end of the webbing can prevent your hand from slipping. Be sure your modifications are sturdy and lashed or sewn securely enough to hold up under load.

Now and then you hear of paddlers tearing the release handle off their spray skirt or discovering after capsizing that they tucked the handle inside while putting the spray skirt on. Checking that the release

erally carry you out of the rip (this is not the case with hazards such as wind waves). If you feel unable to negotiate a tide rip, you may be better off rafting up with one or more kayaks and simply riding it out. Once the current has carried you through the rip, conditions will settle down.

If you do choose to paddle in challenging conditions, dress for immersion; drysuits or wetsuits would have given James, Monique, and Joe more time to try other rescue options. Maximize your kayak's flotation and back it up with airbags or sea socks. Make sure each kayak has a spare paddle, tow rope, and flares. And don't take people who haven't practiced wet exits and deep-water rescues.

Luckily for Monique and James, Joe had packed his VHF radio. These are the only radios designated by the FCC for marine use. The Coast Guard and other boaters monitor VHF Channel 16 for emergencies. A two-way VHF radio can also be used to talk with other ships and make phone calls (similar to using a cellular phone). Now that the price of hand-held VHF radios has dropped into the $100 range, there is little excuse for anyone who leads private or commercial sea kayak trips not to carry one. There are special waterproof bags that allow you to operate these radios through the bags.

Other signaling devices can be just as important as a radio. This group knows the sinking feeling of firing off a flare only to discover that it's a dud. Keep flares dry and inspect them regularly for signs of moisture. Their whistles weren't of much help either; the sound of a whistle doesn't carry much farther than a loud scream, and wind and waves can drown out both in about fifty feet. The main advantage of a whistle is that you can still make noise after your voice is gone.

Joe was forced to open his kayak's rear hatch to retrieve his radio. Safety gear,

handle is on the outside and that the stitching holding it to the spray skirt is in good condition should be part of your routine each time you get in a kayak.

Practice releasing your spray skirt without using the release handle—just in case. When pulling the spray skirt off without the handle, it's easier to start from the side than from the front. Grab the spray skirt along the side of the coaming and yank it off directly or pull it over the lip of the coaming enough to get your fingers between the spray skirt and the coaming. If your spray skirt adjusts with a knot at the rear of the coaming, this knot and the tail of excess shock cord can also be used as a backup release handle. You can also try reaching down the spray

skirt tube and pull up from the inside.

Try all these methods one-handed, with each hand. Also try releasing your spray skirt with your eyes closed: Find the release handle by starting with your hands along the sides of the coaming and then sliding them forward.

Always test your ability to release the spray skirt when borrowing, renting, or testing new gear. Even a kayak–spray skirt combination that works fine for one person may be too tight for another. Also watch out for beginners in your group, since they are more likely to tuck the release handle inside or panic and pull straight back on the release handle, and since they often use equipment other than their own.

which may be needed on the water, should not be stored inside the kayak's primary flotation. If the kayak relies on a closed compartment or cockpit pod for flotation (this is true for most sit-on-top kayak designs), do not store emergency gear inside the compartment. Similarly, in kayaks that rely on airbags for flotation, do not store emergency gear inside the airbag or drybag serving as the main flotation for that end of the kayak.

Consider storing flares in waterproof bags inside a fanny pack worn around your PFD, or buy one of the newer Coast Guard–approved PFDs with pockets. Bigger items are best stored in the cockpit behind the seat and clipped into the kayak. If the kayak has an airbag for flotation in the stern, let out just enough air to make room for the emergency gear. If your kayak does not have enough room behind the seat, seal the gear in a drybag and lash it securely (with ropes, not bungee cords) to the rear deck. If some emergency gear must go inside a hatch, fill the remainder of that compartment with an airbag so the kayak will still have flotation even if water gets into the compartment. In general, it is prudent to back up flotation chambers by putting airbags inside them in case of a leak in the hull, the bulkhead, or the hatch. Kayak airbags are cheap insurance.

I used to stow my tow rope on the rear deck, but recently I've been carrying it in one of the front pockets of my PFD. This has already paid off—once when a member of my group didn't quite have the speed needed to ferry across the upstream side of a tide rip. If it had taken me too long to access my tow rope, this paddler would have been carried into the rough water. But because my tow system was so handy and quick to deploy (clips at both ends; rope stowed in a sack), it took only seconds to get my rope out, clip it to her bow, and begin assisting her (she kept paddling, too). Less than a minute later we were out of the fast water and she could paddle to safety on her own.

Monique and Rob found out that even wide two-person kayaks can capsize. What's more, the amount of water that gets into a double can be exhausting to pump out. The buoyancy of the end compartments of a double kayak is often insufficient to keep coamings above water when the kayak is swamped. When this happens, it is unlikely the water can be pumped out with the paddlers in the kayak. It may be necessary to pump some water out of the kayak before getting back in; the swimmers' spray skirts can be put on to seal the cockpits while pumping. If there's one upright kayaker in the group, that person should try spilling some of the water out of the swamped double before paddlers reenter. To do this, the swimmers right the kayak and move to its stern. Then the rescuer grabs the bow of the swamped kayak with both hands and positions it perpendicular to her own kayak. She pulls the bow across her lap and turns the swamped kayak on its side so water spills out of the cockpits. The capsized paddlers may be able to assist by pushing down on the stern of the swamped kayak or by stabilizing the rescuer's kayak.

Some two-person kayaks are built with a center flotation compartment in addition to bow and stern flotation. A pair of sea socks can greatly reduce the amount of water that gets into a double lacking such a compartment. Battery-powered bilge pumps made for kayaks can be especially helpful in emptying a double kayak. These electric pumps have much higher flow rates than hand pumps and can be used in conjunction with hand pumps or while paddling to safety.

A rescuer can generally be more effective in his kayak than in the water. If everyone in a group has capsized, the most experienced and/or skilled kayaker should be the first to get back in his kayak. Generally, it is not necessary to get out of your kayak to help someone exit a capsized kayak. Paddle alongside the overturned kayak and then reach over it and pull up on the cockpit coaming while pushing down on the other side to right his kayak. Even if you can't completely right the kayak, just turning it onto its side is usually enough to let the person breathe; after he has caught his breath, he generally will relax enough to get himself out of his kayak. Once the kayak is on its side, you can reach over and grab the paddler by the arm and pull him upright or, if necessary, release his spray skirt. If you must jump in the water to pull the person out, be aware that he is probably panic stricken and may pull you under.

Although it is rare for someone to get trapped in a capsized kayak, it does occasionally happen. Entrapment is sometimes caused by an excessively tight spray skirt. A spray skirt must be secure enough to stay on when hit by waves, but you should still be able to release it with either hand (or one-handed, in the case of a shoulder dislocation).

Panic is the most common cause of difficulty while trying to wet exit. Practice wet exits until they become boring. If you can't bring yourself to do this, trade your kayak in for a sit-on-top model.

19

Nighttime Accident on Willapa Bay

George Gronseth

Sometime after midnight on the moonless night of July 17, 1993, James Wiegardt set out alone in Washington's Willapa Bay. The night was warm and clear with light winds. James was commuting by kayak from his residence on the Long Beach Peninsula to his family's shellfish farm on Long Island. There was a low tide in the morning, so harvesting would begin early the next day. His co-workers were already camped at the bunkhouse near the oyster beds. James, who was 23 and reportedly a strong paddler, had soloed this three-mile crossing many times.

The following afternoon, recreational boaters discovered James's body—floating face-down in the water near shore at the north end of Long Island (about two miles north of his probable route). He was wearing a cotton shirt,

Wind and Shallows

In December 1996, another kayak fatality occurred on Willapa Bay. This time the incident involved two kayakers who became separated because of the wind. One made it to shore; the other perished.

Even relatively sheltered waters such as Willapa Bay can be hazardous when it is windy. In fact, the shallowness of the water in Willapa Bay makes it especially treacherous in windy conditions, because waves in shallow water are steeper than they would be in a deeper body of water. And as we all know, steep waves are the ones that capsize kayakers.

shorts, socks, and glasses, and no PFD. There were no visible signs of trauma.

James's kayak was found floating upside down five miles farther north, caught in tall spartina grass near the western shore of the bay. The wind was out of the north, so James's body and the kayak apparently had drifted with the ebb current. The kayak was undamaged, and the airbags that gave it buoyancy were still in place in both ends.

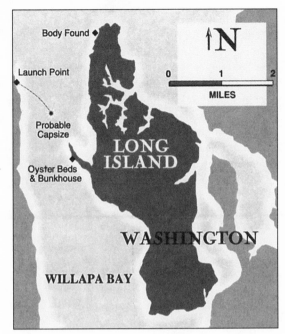

The water temperature in this part of Willapa Bay was about 66°F (18.9°C), so hypothermia was not as immediate a threat as it is in most marine areas of Washington. Even without thermal protection, a good swimmer or someone wearing a PFD should have at least several hours in water of this temperature before the effects of hypothermia become fatal.

LESSONS LEARNED

It is quite unusual to have a sea kayaking fatality in water as warm as that of Willapa Bay in midsummer. Although we'll never know the details of James's death, we can discuss some general safety precautions that might have saved him. If it hadn't been dark, or if other kayakers were with him, the incident may not have cost James his life.

When something goes wrong, a solo paddler has fewer options than he would have if paddling with a group of skilled kayakers. If you paddle alone, take extra precautions with regard to safety equipment (distress signals, self-rescue devices, etc.) and backup gear (carry a spare paddle, extra flashlight, etc.), and be more conservative about paddling challenging conditions—in this case, darkness—than you would be when paddling with others.

There is always a chance of losing your paddle or kayak in a capsize, especially in the dark. You can greatly reduce the risk of losing your paddle by tethering it to your kayak or your wrist.

At night, kayakers are required by the Coast Guard to carry a flashlight or other light source and visual distress signals—either an electric distress light that flashes SOS (for inland waters, a light flashing fifty to seventy times per minute is acceptable) or at least three red flares. By making yourself visible, you can help prevent collisions. But a waterproof flashlight has many other safety uses, including making it easier to retrieve lost gear. Putting reflective tape on your kayak, bilge pump, and
paddle blades is another simple step you can take to improve your night safety.

Fatal accidents such as this should remind us of the inherent risks of our sport. Even on day trips, it's wise to prepare for the possibility of night paddling. Sea kayaking is only as safe as you make it.

20

Lessons in Judgment

George Gronseth

O n November 8, 1992, John Gaulding launched in Bowman Bay, Washington, going out alone in his kayak to spend the day fishing off Deception Island. The morning started out fairly calm, but a big storm had passed through the area the day before, and the weather was still unsettled.

The area where John was fishing is best known for the eight-knot tidal currents in nearby Deception Pass, Washington. The bridge over this pass and the adjoining Deception Pass State Park are popular tourist attractions. John lived less than an hour from the pass and had paddled through its turbulent currents on previous trips. On this day he planned to stay well outside the pass and fish off Deception Island.

Although the currents near Deception Island are no match for those in the pass, they are quite strong. Furthermore, Deception Island has no beaches to land on; it is lined with rock cliffs and is exposed to the winds and swells of Juan de Fuca Strait. Despite the exposed nature of his destination, John was not wearing a wetsuit or drysuit and he had no flares or other distress signals.

After putting in at the public boat launch in Bowman Bay, John paddled southwest for about a mile to Deception Island. To keep from drifting while fishing, he tied his kayak to some kelp just south of the island. Before long, the weather started to deteriorate, but John was fishing and didn't pay much attention to the change in the wind until the waves began to crest.

By the time John decided to head back, the waves were three to four feet high and the wind was blowing at twenty-five knots from the southwest. John capsized and came out of his kayak. It was so rough he thought it would be futile to get back in his kayak. Instead he started swimming for Deception Island. At about 40°F (4.4°C), the water was excruciatingly cold. Fortunately, he was wearing his PFD. He later estimated that it took him thirty to forty-five minutes to reach the island; when he did, he was so exhausted and hypothermic that he had to use his arms to lift his legs for each step.

Luckily, some tourists on shore saw John's accident and called for help. The Navy Air Station on nearby Whidbey Island diverted a helicopter to the area, and the Coast Guard sent another helicopter and a ship. The Navy rescuers were the first to locate John; they coordinated with the Coast Guard helicopter, which lowered a rescuer to assist with John's evacuation. He was flown to an ambulance and taken to a hospital where he was treated for hypothermia and released later that evening.

LESSONS LEARNED

John had nearly twenty years of paddling experience, yet until that day he had never been in a life-threatening situation while kayaking. He later felt that it was his lack of good judgment that caused this accident. This experience taught him to be more attuned to the weather and sea conditions and to reevaluate his decision-making process for judging whether or not to paddle, what clothing to wear, and what emergency equipment to bring. He has since acquired a wetsuit.

Calm conditions tempt sea kayakers to let down many of their safety guards (such as wearing wetsuits or drysuits, bringing emergency equipment, traveling in groups rather than solo, etc.), but as John discovered, conditions can change quickly. When conditions get rough, an unprepared sea kayaker may pay for carelessness with his or her life.

Luckily for John, someone happened to see he was in trouble and got help. He set off without emergency signaling devices—a minimal step toward being prepared to survive an accident. You can double-wrap a set of flares in plastic sandwich bags and store them inside your self-rescue paddle-float bag. I keep another set of flares in an emergency plastic bottle clipped behind my seat. This bottle is a convenient way to carry and protect many small items of emergency equipment, such as small first-aid items, lighter, fire-starter, water purification tablets, high-energy food bar, batteries, spare

Cold-Weather Paddling

If you paddle in cold weather, it can be a valuable learning experience to take an oral thermometer along on a trip. Check your temperature throughout the day—especially during rest breaks. I've had days where my temperature dropped 3 degrees even though I didn't get wet. Though I was able to keep myself from shivering, this temperature drop was enough to begin affecting my speech and navigation mathematics. As for my judgment, who knows?

It is also worth observing how long it takes to bring your temperature back to normal once you are indoors. Tracking this kind of information on test runs will help you understand your limits and know what to expect of your body during cold-weather paddling excursions.

flashlight bulbs, and fishing lures, etc. One of the best signaling devices is a two-way VHF radio, which can be stored and operated inside a clear, waterproof bag made especially for hand-held radios. The Coast Guard monitors VHF channel 16 twenty-four hours.

John was lucky to have withstood the brutally cold water he found himself in. It is crucial to dress properly for the conditions, which in winter in the Northwest means wearing a wetsuit or drysuit. In cold water, even good swimmers are usually better off staying with their boat than trying to swim for shore. In spite of the heat your body generates from the exertion, swimming hastens the progression of hypothermia and so shortens your survival time. If you ever consider swimming for shore without your kayak, keep in mind that the strength-sapping effects of hypothermia will greatly reduce the distance you can swim. When a sea kayaker drowns, it is most likely because he succumbed to the effects of hypothermia and was no longer able to stay conscious enough to keep from inhaling water.

No one's judgment is always perfect. To make matters worse, loss of good judgment is one of the early symptoms of hypothermia. Sea kayakers often seem to forget or ignore the fact that you don't need to capsize to become hypothermic. In cool weather, if you are not dressed properly for the conditions and your level of activity, some degree of hypothermia is practically assured. Lacking a wetsuit or drysuit, it is unlikely that anyone could have stayed warm on a winter day while sitting in a kayak and fishing. John's lack of attentiveness to the changing weather may have had more to do with hypothermia than his being distracted by fishing.

Good judgment is not something a person is born with. Nor is it something you can learn in a purely academic way. Books and lectures are expedient methods of learning about hazards to watch out for, but when making decisions about safety, your judgment will be based on a combination of your knowledge and experience. Experience is often the result of having survived the consequences of past mistakes. To improve the odds of your living to learn from your mistakes, develop good paddling and rescue skills (rolling included), dress for immersion, bring emergency equipment, and paddle in groups with other skilled kayakers.

21

Ice Fall in Blackstone Bay

George Gronseth

The spring and summer of 1993 were unusually warm in most parts of Southeast Alaska. In the bays of Prince William Sound, the higher temperatures caused more glacial calving than normal. The combination of warm, dry weather and glacial activity would seem like a kayaker's dream, but for one group, the dream turned into a nightmare.

On the morning of June 16, 1993, a group of five friends rode the train from Alyeska to Whittier to begin a four-day kayak trip in Blackstone Bay, part of Prince William Sound. Three of the five had kayaked there before and knew the routine. They had arranged to rent kayaks from the local outfitter and to be dropped off by a charter boat on the south side of the entrance to Blackstone Bay.

From the beach where the charter boat dropped them off, the kayakers followed the shore for about eight miles before making camp near the Ripon Glacier. At this latitude (60 degrees north), the summer days are very long. Encouraged by the extended daylight, the group stayed up late sharing conversation around a fire. They planned to spend at least another night at this camp, so they had no pressing schedule for the next day.

The following morning, James Rustamier was the first one out of his tent. He was eager to get going and was tempted to go paddling alone. But by the

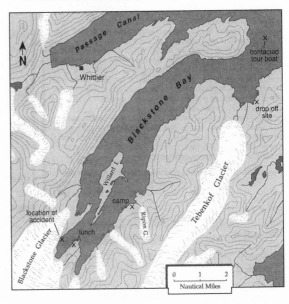

time he made break-
fast, William Quie and
Katherine Horrigan
were rising, so he
waited for them to
join him. The other
two members of the
group, Eugene
Weschenfelder and
Susan Putt, wanted to
sleep in and said they
would wait until the
afternoon to go out
paddling. So James,
William, and Kather-
ine launched their
kayaks around 10:00
A.M. and followed the
shore toward the head of the bay.

After going about three miles, the group reached the Blackstone Glacier and
toured around both forks of its terminus. After watching the glacial activity for

Survival Sense for Sea Kayakers

Tom Watson

Living through any life-threatening situation is often a matter of attitude, common sense, and just plain willpower. Sea kayakers can adopt the "Seven Steps to Survival" developed by the military and the commercial fishing industry through many years of assessing actual survival situations.

Knowing the steps, applying them, and being able to accurately reassess your status after every completed task can significantly increase your chances of survival—and in some cases even allow you to await rescue quite comfortably. At the very least they offer you some positive alternatives.

Reality Check

Recognition is the first step. Having lost your kayak and some or all of your gear, or having been forced to beach on some remote shore, you'll realize you are in trouble. But what you must understand, even though you may be injured, wet, and disoriented, is that you are in a life-threatening situation.

Accept your circumstances and try to stay positive. Knowing you are in trouble should be the first step in triggering your survival routine into action.

Take Stock

The second and critical step is the inventory. You need to assess your situation in terms of personal safety, salvageable gear, and available resources. Your first concern should be injuries. Heavy clothing, PFDs, and wet- or drysuits can mask signs of injury and even prevent bleeding from being (continued on page 174) a while, they went ashore and ate lunch on the peninsula between the north and south forks of the glacier. The beach they were on faced a long rock cliff below the main body of the Blackstone Glacier. The runoff from the glacier created many waterfalls along the cliff. Occasionally, large chunks of glacial debris carried down by the runoff would go over the falls and plunge into the bay below. Around 4:00 or 5:00 P.M., the kayakers began paddling back to camp. A short while later, they ran into their two companions. The five took a snack break in their kayaks before the group split up again, with the early group continuing back to camp while Eugene and Susan went on to explore the parts of the bay where their friends had just been.

Eugene and Susan paddled over to a cliff with waterfalls to fill a water bottle with runoff. The spray from the falls was so cold it chilled Eugene's hands before he could finish filling the bottle. He paddled over to Susan to have her finish. Just as he handed the bottle to her, bits of ice started falling from the cliff above them. At first it felt like snow; then, before they had time to move, big chunks of ice came down on top of them. Susan received only minor cuts, mostly to her hand, but Eugene, who was right beside her, was knocked unconscious. Susan grabbed him and held their kayaks together while she paddled them both to shore.

Susan landed at the first beach she could find and got out of her kayak to help Eugene, who was fading in and out of consciousness. He had been struck

(continued from page 173)
noticed. Attend immediately to any injuries.

Your second level of inventory should be to assess equipment that can be salvaged. Did any of your gear make it to shore? What are you carrying on your person? You should have a survival kit with you—and that means on your person, not stuck behind the seat of your kayak or stowed under a hatch. A pocket on your PFD is one good place to carry a basic survival kit. The rule is, If you don't have it on you, you don't have it.

The third level of inventory is to scout the surrounding shoreline for anything useful. Don't dismiss scraps of rope, a chunk of planking, or a crumpled container. Initially, consider everything. The activity of finding usable materials will generate body heat and give survivors a sense of purpose.

Seeking Shelter

The materials accumulated can be a vital part of the next step, establishing shelter. Shelter means anything that will help conserve body heat in cold and wet conditions. In warmer, sunny areas your shelter should provide shade.

It is very important to make shelter a priority. A fire is not a primary concern at this stage because it can be too time-consuming. If an impending storm would mean you'd get drenched in a half hour, a dry shelter would be much more valuable than a comforting fire.

Signaling for Help

If you have a VHF radio, you may be able to call for a quick rescue. Otherwise you need a signaling device to draw the attention of boats or planes.

You should always carry a small

on the head, and blood was coming out of his ear. The ice had also crushed and partially dislocated his left shoulder and broken his left arm. Susan, a nurse, reduced Eugene's shoulder dislocation and used a bilge pump as a splint to immobilize his broken arm.

Given Eugene's condition, Susan couldn't leave him to get help. And she couldn't tow him back to camp because his kayak was too badly damaged. The ice had not punctured the deck of the kayak, but the crushing force had caused its seams to rupture and had made foot-long cracks along both chines in the rear part of the hull. This damage allowed water to flood into the rear flotation/storage chamber, making the kayak unseaworthy.

Susan found a quick fix. After doing what she could to stabilize Eugene's condition, Susan took the kayak's bow-flotation airbag and put it inside his rear hatch to keep the stern afloat. Next, she cut a line off her kayak to lash the bow of Eugene's kayak to her kayak's stern in such a way that she could paddle on both sides.

Susan began towing Eugene, but the current from the incoming tide was too strong for her to paddle against. After a long struggle, she eventually pulled ashore and waited for the current to slow.

It was late, sometime between 1:00 and 3:00 A.M., when James was awakened by Susan's yell that Eugene was hurt. James got out of his tent and saw Susan paddling toward shore. He started to launch his kayak, but Susan made it to

packet of flares. A signaling mirror is also effective in drawing attention; in its place you could also use a wet panel of plastic or a flat piece of polished metal. Marking a beach or meadow with contrasting-colored objects is another way to signal for help. Make your ground-to-air signal at least fifteen feet in length so it can be read from the air. A series of three signals—three fires, three piles of debris, or three flashes of a mirror, for example—is usually recognized as a distress signal. In timbered country, attach a rope close to the top of a tree and pull vigorously when a plane appears to be approaching. A lone tree whipping back and forth will be out of place and worth a closer look.

H_2O

Finding a safe source of drinking water should be part of your inventory search.

The average survival rate without water is about three days, and you need to drink six pints of water each day. Beyond the obvious initial symptom of thirst, more serious signs of dehydration include headache and loss of concentration. If you don't have water, don't eat. Digestion robs water from other vital maintenance needs.

Food

Once you are safe and warm, you can begin to think about food. Foraging for and preparing food can take your mind off waiting. If you are injured, you need to eat for your own well-being. You can, however, go without food for about thirty days. Learning to identify beach and shoreline edibles could be a part of your ordinary kayaking experience. Use caution: If you (continued on page 176) shore first, with Eugene and his kayak in tow. She explained that the ice had fallen on them, and that Eugene had head and back injuries. She said he had been in severe pain for a while.

James, a physician's assistant, observed that Eugene was stuporous but still alive. James made a quick check of Eugene's pulse and found it "thready." James saw that the cockpit of Eugene's kayak was full of water and figured Eugene was hypothermic. Susan was cold, too. The group pulled Eugene out of his kayak, removed his wet clothing, and put him into sleeping bags with Susan so they could rewarm each other.

James stayed with Eugene and kept checking for a pulse while the others built a fire to help warm the two. Eugene, meanwhile, lost consciousness. James thought he felt a pulse, but he wasn't sure whether it was Eugene's or his own in his fingertips. Later, Eugene had seizures and stopped breathing. James tried to bring him back with CPR, but Eugene never responded—no breath, no pulse, no reflexes. (The autopsy concluded that Eugene's death was due to internal injuries to the head and chest.) Eventually CPR was stopped, and the group's focus shifted to getting outside help and stabilizing Susan, who was now hysterical.

No one in the group had a VHF radio, but they knew another group of kayakers was camped about a mile away. James, the fastest paddler, paddled over to the other group to see if they had a radio. They didn't. James then returned to check on Susan. It was now very late and they all were exhausted, so they decided to stay together with Susan and wait until morning to paddle out for help. At 9:00 A.M., James paddled out alone to get help. He saw some large boats, but none of them saw him until he reached the mouth of the bay where he flagged down a tour boat named *Misty*. The captain got help for the kayakers by radioing the Coast Guard in Valdez.

(continued from page 175)
don't know what it is, don't eat it.

Make It Fun

While play is the last step on the survival list, it can be critical in the long run because it keeps people busy and helps nurture a positive attitude. Play can be used to achieve some vital tasks of surviving. Creativity and caution will be your best companions as you strive to survive.

Always plan for extremes. Don't assume that your modest day trip won't develop into anything more serious. Use your head. Develop an awareness of what can happen and try to prepare for it. You are your best and often your only resource.

LESSONS LEARNED

Susan's ability to find creative solutions to the problems she faced after the accident is something we can all admire and learn from.

Although it may not have made a real difference in this case, an accident where one member is seriously injured illustrates the safety advantage of traveling in a party larger than two—one or more members can go for help while others tend to the injured person.

Calm conditions tempt sea kayakers to become careless about group size, separation, and other safety precautions, but as this accident demonstrates, there is more to sea kayak safety than just avoiding rough seas. As river kayakers often say, "most kayak-related accidents happen on land." One of the most valuable things I learned from first-aid training was that in a wilderness situation, one can easily die from an injury that would not be considered life threatening if it happened somewhere less remote. Regardless of whether we are on the water or on shore, the remote nature of most kayak trips demands we be even more careful about preventing injury accidents.

Still, accidents will happen, so it also pays to be prepared. With the ability to call for help, this group might have been able to get medical assistance in time to save Eugene's life. A hand-held, two-way VHF radio, monitored twenty-four hours by the Coast Guard, can make the wilderness much less remote in an emergency. These radios (which also receive marine weather forecasts) are now available for around $100—cheap insurance.

22

Carried to Safety

George Gronseth

In the late afternoon of February 12, 1994, a Bellingham, Washington, resident looked out his dining room window and saw two kayakers paddling in whitecaps out in Chuckanut Bay. On his way to the kitchen, he told his guests, "Call me when those guys go over; it's way too rough out there." It wasn't long before one of the kayakers did indeed capsize. Soon it became apparent that both paddlers were having difficulty getting to shore, and the dinner party guests phoned the Coast Guard.

The two kayakers, whom I will call Smith and Jones (they asked us not to use their real names), had started out about a mile and a half south of where the capsize occurred. Because of the strong southerly wind, they decided to make this a one-way trip and ride the waves for the five-mile stretch between Wildcat Cove and Marine Park. Smith arranged for his wife to pick them up at the other end of the park.

To Smith and Jones, sea kayaking is a sport for all seasons. They both go out in the winter, often together, and Smith, who is the better and stronger paddler of the two, paddles solo in the winter as well. Both men have ten or more years of kayaking experience, including numerous extended trips. Although both have successfully executed a few Eskimo rolls, neither had practiced rolling enough to rely on it. Instead, they rely on their ability to perform rescues (assisted and paddle-float self rescues). Neither had ever capsized accidentally before.

The men were using their own kayaks (Eddyline Wind Dancers, which have front and rear bulkheads), and each carried a hand pump and self-rescue paddle-float bag. Both were 36 years old. Smith is 6'4" and weighs about 210 pounds; Jones is 5'10" and weighs 165 pounds. Neither wore a wetsuit or drysuit, and only Jones started out wearing a PFD. They were dressed in medium-weight synthetic (polypropylene-type) tops and bottoms. Jones also wore a pile jacket and a neoprene cap, and Smith wore a windbreaker.

Jones remarked later, "As soon as we got out of Wildcat Cove and headed north, it was obvious that we were in real heavy-duty weather." The seas were in the three- to four-foot range, and the wind (probably thirty knots or more) was strong enough to pick up spray from the waves and blow it around. When they got to the entrance of Chuckanut Bay, they ducked around the point at the south end of the bay and stopped to look things over. Jones says it was fairly calm there, but elsewhere it was "rockin' and rollin'." They could have followed the shore around to the other side of the bay, but that would have added another mile to the trip, and the direct route didn't look any rougher than some of the stormy conditions they had been out in before. Jones remarked later that, until then, "We were having a pretty good time." They discussed their options and what they would do if they capsized. Then they headed north.

As they crossed the bay, the wind shifted to the southwest, so now they were in quartering seas. They were getting hit pretty hard by waves coming from be-

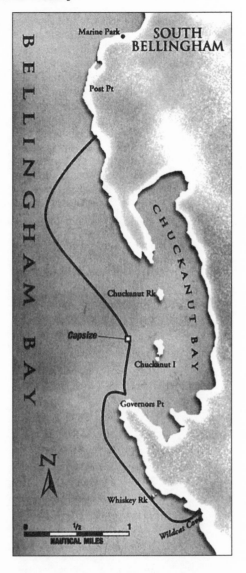

hind, over their left shoulders. Jones said later, "It wasn't too big of a problem, but the farther we got into the bay, the bigger the waves got. And they got big, real big!" Later, they were blasted by gusts of wind from the southeast, and the seas became confused. Jones couldn't tell where things were coming from. "I'll admit I got scared and dropped my cadence. As I finished a stroke on my left side, I got hit hard by a wave on my right and fell over to the left."

Jones exited and surfaced on the upwind side of his kayak, about two feet away from it. He held onto his paddle (neither man had a paddle leash) and reached for his kayak but didn't connect. "By the time I swam a couple strokes, my kayak was four feet away. It became a race, and I lost. I'm a pretty strong swimmer, but the wind just took the kayak." Smith, about twenty-five yards downwind of Jones, paddled to the kayak and got hold of it, but as soon as he stopped paddling, he started drifting faster than Jones could swim. Jones kept swimming but couldn't gain on Smith. Soon Smith ditched the kayak and paddled over to save Jones. After reaching Jones, Smith put on his PFD.

After a short conversation, they decided that Jones would climb up on the back of Smith's kayak. Jones told Smith, "My life is in your hands." Jones straddled the back of Smith's kayak, trying to be "damned careful" not to flip him. They continued talking the whole time until they reached shore. When they got hit by big waves, Jones slid back into the water to lower their center of gravity and help prevent Smith from capsizing. The wind continued to pick up and pushed them farther from shore. Smith cranked his rudder to turn toward land, but the wind kept pivoting the bow downwind. Jones even tried dragging his legs off the right side of Smith's kayak to add more turning power, with little success. By the time they crossed the bay, they were about three-quarters mile offshore.

Once they were about a half-mile past the point at the north end of Chuckanut Bay, the wind became more southerly again, and they were able to make progress toward shore. However, because of the effect of Jones's weight on the boat trim, they never had the ability to steer straight in.

They landed in a residential area about a mile north of Chuckanut Bay. It was almost dark, and Jones's legs were so numb that Smith had to help him walk. Jones says he was still coherent even though he was very cold and had been shivering for a long time. After helping Jones ashore, Smith gave him his windbreaker and walked to a house to call for help.

The Coast Guard had begun searching for the two kayakers, but Smith and Jones made it to shore before the Coast Guard could find them. When the

A Ride to Shore

Matt Broze

During one January Surf Frolic at La Push, Washington, a sea kayaker capsized in the surf; he and the kayak he was holding on to were being swept by the alongshore current toward the huge, jagged boulders of the jetty. He didn't seem to be making much progress toward shore on his own, so I paddled over to him and told him I could get him to shore on my back deck—but not if he held on to his kayak. He realized how fast he was drifting toward the jetty and decided to abandon his kayak

and accept the ride before it was too late. Meanwhile, other paddlers came by and said they would try to push his kayak between breakers to shore.

I instructed the victim that if we capsized, he must let go and swim clear so I could roll upright again. He slipped easily up into the low back deck from the stern and grabbed the back of my cockpit. With him straddling the back deck, the passing waves kept pushing the bow around toward shore rather than broaching my kayak as they usually would. This made me feel I had especially good medics arrived, the kayakers asked them to notify the authorities in case there was a search. The medics treated Smith and Jones for hypothermia and then gave them a ride to the park where they had planned to take out. It was dark and they were two hours overdue; when they arrived—with Smith's kayak tied on top of the fire department's aid car—Smith's wife was there waiting for them.

Jones said the belated rendezvous was the toughest part of the ordeal. He later recovered his kayak through a classified ad in the local newspaper.

LESSONS LEARNED

Jones said later, "How we prepared mentally was part of the problem. This was supposed to be a little afternoon jaunt: Leave at three, do a little surfing, and be back by six. We had paddled this area so many times that it felt like it was our backyard." Although he carried a spare paddle on extended trips, Jones says he had never considered the possibility of losing a paddle or kayak on a trip like this. Jones now realizes the value of carrying a spare paddle and using a paddle leash in windy conditions. Since this experience, whenever conditions are questionable, Jones and Smith discuss what could go wrong and remind each other "a kayak could blow away."

This incident illustrates some of the advantages of paddling with other skilled kayakers. Had Jones been paddling solo or with someone who lacked the skill and confidence to let him climb up on the rear deck of his or her kayak, this incident would probably have had a tragic ending. This is not the first time that a sea kayaker's life has been saved by a partner's ability to carry someone on

control. I wanted to surf in quickly with my passenger so I could get back out to help recover his kayak with my throwline before it reached the jetty.

Unfortunately, I couldn't get up enough speed to catch and surf the waves. I figured that my passenger's legs and feet, dragging in the water on each side, were slowing us down considerably. I asked him several times to lift his feet out of the water so we could catch a wave and go faster. Several waves passed us. Then he suddenly bent his knees and lifted his feet straight up just as we were hit by a breaker. The sudden change in center of gravity threw me precariously off balance; it took a very hard brace to prevent a capsize. He kept his feet low after that.

After dropping him on shore, I returned to find his kayak dangerously near the jetty. Soon it was swept out to sea by the beach rip along the jetty. The rear hatch failed in the big outside breakers, which ripped the now-vertical kayak in half. The bow, two foot pedals, and a float bag were the only things recovered. Oh, well. Better to lose the kayak than have the breakers bash a paddler against the rocks.

the rear deck; yet, few sea kayakers practice this. Next time you practice rescues or feel like going for a swim while paddling, take turns carrying one another on the rear deck. This practice is also good for building your bracing skills. If you have any difficulty with this, you need to work on your paddling technique before your next trip. For those who lack confidence in their bracing skills, a pair of sponsons will make it easier to manage the kayak with a person on deck.

It's discouraging that two paddlers as experienced as Jones and Smith would get into such a predicament. Equipment items as basic as a wetsuit, paddle tether, and a tow rope (which Smith could have used to tow Jones's kayak back to him) could have facilitated their recovery from the capsize. Even though they lacked such equipment, they decided they didn't have to avoid the rough crossing.

We often stress the importance of knowing the environment where you'll be kayaking. But in this case, familiarity with the area led these kayakers to lose respect for the dangers inherent in making a crossing. In spite of the windy conditions, cold weather, and cold water, they took no special precautions. They didn't check the marine weather forecast, bring any distress signals, or dress for the conditions or immersion. In spite of his extreme level of exertion, even Smith was moderately hypothermic upon reaching shore, and he wasn't the one who capsized. As you gain experience, don't let familiarity become complacency or overconfidence.

Any crossing that is farther than you can swim—whether it's between islands, points of a bay, or shores of a lake—puts you at increased risk of death if something goes wrong. And even an Olympic-caliber swimmer can't swim a mile in 50°F (10°C) water. If you choose to make such a crossing, you better know your limits, get the latest weather forecast, and be equipped and prepared to deal with an emergency.

Your judgment is largely dependent on your experience. If your experience is limited to rescue practice done in a swimming pool or calm water, then you may underestimate the difficulty you'll encounter when paddling in open water.

Practice wet exits and rescues in open water on a windy day, and you will very quickly learn the importance of not letting go of your kayak. It only takes about an eight- to ten-knot wind to make a kayak drift faster than most people can swim. It is essential, therefore, to practice wet exits until you can reliably get out of your kayak without letting go of either your boat or your paddle. This is not complicated—the hardest part is getting over the tendency to panic while upside down.

Since there is always the possibility of losing your kayak during a wet exit, the ability to swim efficiently with a paddle is another essential skill for sea kayakers. Unfortunately, this does not come naturally for most people; it takes practice.

Your rescue skills need to keep pace with the conditions that you choose to paddle in. Once you can wet exit without letting go of your kayak or paddle and can swim as fast with your paddle as without it, practice some rescues in light winds near shore (in wind waves but not in surf). As you start paddling in more challenging conditions, continue to test your rescue skills. If it is too rough for you to practice rescues, it is too rough for you to paddle farther from shore than you can swim.

accidents. *See* capsizes; drowning; hypothermia, death from; sudden drowning syndrome
Amato, Chris, 143, 186
Anchorage Daily News, 70
arches. *See* sea arches and caves
Armstrong, Alison, 94, 186

backups to critical systems, 35
bailing devices, 6, 9, 17, 41
use of, 43, 44, 49
beach rips, 10
boomers, 10, 46, 121, 123
booties. *See* footwear
braces, 13, 14, 72, 89, 182
types of, 4, 15, 16, 35, 45, 89, 120, 122, 149
use of, 32, 67, 72, 80, 109
bracing skills, 15–16, 17, 25, 34, 38, 79, 80, 153, 181, 182
broaching, 52, 53, 180
causes of, 64, 108, 115, 116
correction of, 108–109, 115
bulkheads, 6, 29, 41, 69, 93, 178
advantages *vs.* disadvantages, 63
for flotation, 52, 87–88, 130–131, 146, 150
vs. float bags, 29
buoyancy, 55
buoyancy compensators, 30, 89, 92

cameras, underwater, 65
capsizes, 2, 20, 28, 51, 62, 72, 120, 131, 149
in heavy seas and surf, 10, 17, 33, 43, 45, 68, 110–111, 121, 178
hypothermia and, 8, 26, 72, 111, 151
loss of gear in, 13, 53–54
prevention and recovery from, 30
self-rescue practice of, 4, 30, 69, 107, 122–123, 155
cardiopulmonary resuscitation. *See* CPR
Carlson, Eric, 22, 24, 25
caves. *See* sea arches and caves
charts, nautical, 10–11, 56, 88, 115, 116
clapotis, causes and effects, 44–45, 119
clothing, 6, 41, 52, 81, 94, 124, 125. *See also individual items*
hypothermia and, 16–17, 29, 121, 151, 155, 157, 166–167, 168, 171, 178, 180, 182
coamings, 158, 164
cockpits
covered, 71

entrapment in, 64
keyhole, 126
liners, 69, 140
pods, 69, 140
reentry of, 26
communication difficulties, on water, 19, 57
compasses, 8, 9, 10, 18, 41
use of, 20, 24, 49
The Complete Book of Sea Kayaking, 60
cords. *See* lines
core body temperature, 8, 14, 38, 47, 56, 83, 85, 112, 127, 137, 161
insulated garments and, 112
CPR, 84, 114, 126, 160, 176
cramps, 28, 36, 45, 124, 128, 159
Current Atlas, 57, 87
currents, 10–11, 47–48, 143, 150, 167
loss of control in, 13, 15, 17, 127, 175
terrain and, 15, 68, 157
types of, 47–48, 57, 129, 143, 150, 152, 155, 167, 169
currents, slack
vs. tide changes, 48, 57
current tables, 10–11, 18, 23, 88

Davis, Deborah, 22, 186
deck lines, 123. *See also* lines
dehydration, 175
Derek C. Hutchinson's Guide to Sea Kayaking, 60
Dowd, John, 16, 63
drowning. See also hypothermia; sudden drowning syndrome
death by, 4, 82, 106, 127
drybags, 94, 134, 164
drysuits. *See* wetsuits and drysuits
dye markers, 7, 82

eddies, 4, 10, 13, 15–16, 25, 47, 57, 68, 69
Emergency Locating Transmitter (ELT), 67
Emergency Position Indicating Radio Beacons. *See* EPIRBs (Emergency Position Indicating Radio Beacons)
environment
familiarity with, 79–80, 143–145
EPIRBs (Emergency Position Indicating Radio Beacons), 7, 38, 72–82
commercial tour guides and, 7–8
solo paddlers and, 7, 49, 112

equipment. *See* gear and equipment
Eskimo rolls, 38, 59, 88, 91, 178
need for proficiency with, 4, 16, 33, 34, 48, 56, 84
exits, wet. *See* wet exits
exposure suits, 71, 79, 81

Farthing, Bill, 22
fear, 2, 22–25
fire-making materials, 6, 9, 82, 170
firesticks, 73
first-aid kits, 4, 6, 9, 94, 170
flares, 7, 35, 49, 75, 56, 82, 89, 93, 94, 96, 115, 131, 150, 155, 157, 163, 168, 169, 170
types of, 31, 35, 37, 38, 72, 76, 82, 92
flashlights, 94, 137, 168
floats, paddle. *See* paddle floats
float bags, 5, 29, 58, 148, 170
floater coats, 72, 73, 79, 81
float plans, 53, 81, 89
flotation, 3, 5–6, 10, 63, 108
importance of, 2, 3, 9, 29, 46, 69, 164
lack of, 29, 60, 61, 69
self-rescue techniques and, 14, 36, 123
well-secured, 2, 56, 58
flotation devices, 5, 36, 62–63, 123
fog, 9, 24, 48–49
navigating in, 9, 19–20, 24, 48–49
Fons, Valerie, 139
food and water, 8, 9, 67, 94, 170, 175–176
footwear, 82, 89, 125, 128, 131
frostbite, 70, 78

gear and equipment, 58, 69. *See also individual items*
backup, 167, 181
checklist, 9
need for practice with, 57, 80
gear bags, waterproof, 5, 53, 55, 66
glaciers, 110, 172, 173, 174
gloves, insulated, 54, 71, 81
Gore-Tex, 54, 71, 85
group paddling, 2–3, 25, 115
communications, 19, 57, 111
mixed skills within group, 59, 115, 155
size of group, 24–25, 155
group rescues. *See* rescues, group
hatches, 5–6, 44, 52
failure of, 45, 52–53, 58, 62–63, 69, 137, 140

hazard avoidance, 24–26
head coverings, 81, 89, 90, 125, 131
heart failure, 8
Heathcote, Sheila, 103–104
heat loss, 28, 81
  body weight and, 85, 111, 118–119
  in turbulent vs. calm water, 85–86
  in water vs. air, 39, 112, 158
Helle, Robert, 52, 53
helmets, 45, 68, 126. See also head coverings
horns, 7, 108, 155
Hutchinson, Derek C., 60
hyperventilation, 112, 113
hypothermia, 7–8, 26, 34, 72, 84, 111
  alcohol and, 36–37, 67
  death from, 85, 113, 115, 126, 127
  prevention of, 8, 72
  research of, 81, 85, 112
  signs of, 47, 65, 136, 158, 159, 169–170, 171
  treatment of, 7–8, 29, 47, 55, 75–76, 77, 114, 160–161
hypothermic convulsions, 56

Ince, John, 31
injuries at sea, 8, 59, 149, 153, 174, 175
Inner Skiing, 24

jackets. See also clothing
  paddle. See paddle jackets
  pile, 126

Kayaking Puget Sound, the San Juans & Gulf Islands, 56, 87
kayak models
  Aquaterra Chinook, 142
  Beachcomber, 12, 15
  Eddyline, 88
    Wind Dancer, 65, 66, 67, 178
  Enetai, 65, 66, 67
  Escape, 66
  Icefloe, 88, 93
  Mariner II, 84, 85
  Nimbus Puffin, 133, 138, 140
  Nordkapp, 31, 34, 64
  Pacific Water Sports Sisiutl, 50, 70, 72, 79
  Polaris II, 60, 62, 65, 66, 67
  Prijon T-Slalom, 126
  San Juan double, 74
  Seafarer, 27, 36
  Seahawk, 41, 44
  Sea Horse, 59
  Sea Otter, 50, 58
kayaks
  assisted reentry of, 123
  control of, in surf zone, 103, 122, 180
  empty vs. loaded, control of, 4, 15, 16, 32, 34, 50, 58

handling skills and, 58, 80
  narrow vs. wide, 17
  pump out or bail out of, 28, 49, 88, 91, 93, 123
  separation from, 2, 36, 45, 96, 113, 117, 182
  stabilization during rescue, 20–21
  swamped, 21, 44, 54, 60, 150, 175
  towing of, 60, 92, 175, 176
kayaks, double, 153, 156, 164–165
kayaks, open-cockpit, 140
kayaks, river, 100–101, 117–118, 126
kayaks, sail-rigged, 94
kayaks, sit-on-top, 165
kayak surfing, 130
kayak trips, 36, 166–168
Keep It Moving, 139
Kelton, Ken, 100, 186
Köttner, Hedi, 31

life jackets. See PFDs (personal flotation devices)
life vests, inflatable, 30
lights, running, 94
limits, setting, 154
lines. See also deck lines; towlines
  types of, 18, 26, 32, 37, 44, 58
  uses of, 26, 31, 67, 69, 122
  locating devices, 7, 53, 81–82.
    See also dye markers; flares; flashlights; horns; mirrors; signaling; whistles
loop rescues. See rescues, loop

maps. See also current tables; tide tables
  in fog, 49
  topographical, 109, 115
matches, waterproof, 9, 17, 137
mirrors, signaling, 82, 94, 175

narrow passages, 59–69
night paddling, 11, 99, 167–168
novices vs. experienced kayakers, 27, 53
  safety checklist, 138

Oceanography of the British Columbia Coast, 124
ocean rock gardens, 61, 88
open coast paddling, 42–49
orcas, 141–145
outrigger self-rescue, 35, 86, 91, 131
overfalls, 10

paddle bracing, 20, 72, 153
paddle bridges, 20–21, 39
paddle-float self rescues, 36, 84, 91–92, 107, 178
  outrigger, 44, 84
paddle floats, 9, 16, 35, 36, 41, 85–86, 107, 119
  inflated, 85–86, 91

paddle jackets, 6, 31, 126, 131
paddle leashes, 17, 35, 73, 89, 119, 122
paddlers, solo, 38, 40–41, 166–168
  trip preparation and, 41, 89, 167–168
paddles, 15, 35, 39, 48, 91, 107
  broken, 128
  feathered vs. unfeathered, 35, 73, 127, 142
  loss of, vs. tethered, 34, 35, 45, 50, 53, 61, 73, 91, 111, 142, 149
  signaling with, 22
  spare, 9, 17–18, 35, 38, 39, 62, 107, 142
  swimming with, 73, 127, 131, 182
paddling. See also night paddling; paddlers, solo
  cold-water, 115–116, 125, 127, 171
  experience, value of, 59, 170
  in the lee, 151
  open-coast, 42–49, 59, 88–93
  solo vs. group, 2–3, 17, 49, 115
  techniques, practice of, 4, 15–16, 30, 80, 107, 121, 171
  with waves vs. into waves, 115–116
PFDs (personal flotation devices), 2, 9, 30, 124, 126, 157, 169, 174
  Coast Guard approval, requirements for, 5, 30, 58, 164
  loss of, 52
  pockets in, 82, 137, 140, 142, 164, 174
  swimming without, 28, 60, 69, 178
physical fitness, 54, 155
pogies, 41
points, paddling around, 25–26
preparedness, 14, 23, 24–26, 41, 49, 56, 69, 87, 89, 167–168
pumping out, 86, 158
pumps, 9, 17, 18, 26, 124
  bilge, 107, 119, 131
  deck-mounted, 6
  foot-operated, 88
  hand-held, 6, 41, 55, 146
  types (comparison), 88

radios, VHF and weather, 7, 18, 26, 38, 49, 56, 115, 118, 135, 140, 158–159, 163, 171, 174, 176, 177
rafting up, 39, 66, 138–139, 150, 153, 163
rafts, inflatable, 112–113
reentry. See rescues, reentry
repair kits, 4, 6–7
rescues, 60, 159–161. See also paddle-float self rescues; self rescues
  assisted, 178, 180

Index

deep-water, 26, 80
group, 20–21, 150–151, 157–158
loop, 36–37
practiced vs. unpracticed, 57
reentry, 139, 142
rescue skills, 2, 5, 121
rip channels, 129
rip currents, 10, 46–47, 129–131, 132
risk-taking, 30
rock formations, 61–69
Rogers, Joel, 59
ropes. See lines
rudders, 56, 58, 59, 63, 72, 107, 109, 149
lift lines for, 74
use of, 32–34, 33, 72
Ruuska, Dan, 62

safety checklists, 9, 138
safety gear access, 163–164
safety guidelines, 1–11, 56, 121, 153–154, 182
flotation devices and, 62–63
lines of defense and, 80–82
nighttime, 11, 167–168
weather conditions review and, 161–162, 182
safety principles, 29, 58, 177
saltwater
drinking, 77–78
inhalation, 29, 125
San Juan Current Guide, 87
SARSAT satellite, 76
sea anchors, 34, 112
sea arches and caves, 64–67
hazards of, 59–69
Sea Kayaker magazine, 16, 59, 63, 79, 124, 126
Sea Kayaking Canada's West Coast, 31
Search-and-Rescue (SAR)–trained surface vessels, 29
Sea Seats, 56, 112–113
seasickness, 133, 136, 139
medication for, 138
sea socks, 6, 56, 60, 61, 71, 79, 88, 90, 148
double kayaks and, 148–149, 153
as flotation aids, 45, 62, 63, 87, 123, 132, 149
self protection. See also
paddle-float self rescue;
preparedness; safety guidelines
lines of defense, 80–82
self rescues, 17, 72, 80. See also
paddle-float self rescues
devices and methods for, 9, 35, 44, 91–92, 167
failed attempts at, 84–88
practice of, 38, 142, 171
"Seven Steps to Survival," 173
sharks, great white, 100–104
shipping lanes, 11, 94–100

signaling devices, 9, 108, 155, 163, 168
carried on kayaker, 17
need for, 170, 182
skills improvement, 4, 69, 182
sleeping bags, 8, 79
small-craft warnings, 32, 41, 87, 135, 143
smoke signals, 76, 110
sneaker waves, 126
Soares, Eric, 129
Soggy Sneakers, 126–127
solo paddling. See paddlers, solo
spins and turns, 32–34
sponsons, 140, 153, 182
spray decks. See spray skirts
spray skirts, 5, 43, 67, 86, 107, 122, 125, 126, 128, 135, 137, 161
entrapment and, 34, 165
loss of, 53, 142
practice removal and replacement of, 3–4, 14, 91, 93, 155, 161
problems with, 6, 20, 150, 153
releasing 139, 162–163, 165
use of, while pumping, 21, 164
sudden drowning syndrome, 28–29, 145
heart failure and, 28, 29
prevention of, 28–29
sunglasses, 41
surf beaches, 129
surf zone, 21, 45–47
dangers of, 9–10, 45–47, 124–132
paddling in, 9–10, 88, 128
rescues in, 180–181
rip currents in, 129
survival for kayakers, 173–176
survival gear, 137
access to, 137, 158, 174
survival rafts, 112–113
sweep strokes, 32
swells, 41–43
difficulty paddling in, 19, 20, 41, 44–45, 121–122
swimming
against current, 77–78
in frigid waters, 72, 149, 182
with paddle, 73, 127, 130–131, 182
without life jacket, 60

temperature. See core body temperature
tethers, 17
Thomson, Richard, 124, 131
tidal basins, 10, 48
tidal hazards, 10–11
tide rips, 4–5, 10, 15, 47, 51, 109, 156, 161, 162–163, 164
capsizes in, 51–52, 87, 157
tides, 10–11, 48, 90, 175
vs. currents, 47–48, 87, 90
tides, ebb, 90
tide tables, 9, 18, 23, 24, 88

towlines, 6, 9, 21, 26, 31, 34, 35, 38–39, 75, 139
need for, 139–140, 150, 153, 162, 164, 182
rescues with, 117–119
turning problems, 72
turns and spins, 32–34

undertow. See rip current
underclothes, 89, 131, 157
University of Victoria
hypothermia research, 81, 112
U.S. Air Force survival rafts
CO_2 inflation system and, 112
U.S. Coast Guard, 52–53
PFD requirements, 5, 30, 58, 164
safety requirements, 5, 7
U.S. Navy
hypothermia research, 85, 112

Washburne, Randel, 56, 87
Watson, Tom, 173, 186
waves, 44–45, 51, 52, 57, 64, 108, 126
broaching and, 44, 51
dangers of, 8–9, 64, 132
vs. wind, 57
weather. See fog; surf zone; tidal hazards; tides; waves; wind
weathercocking, 32
weather forecasts, 18, 23, 49, 53, 170, 179
weather radios. See radios, VHF and weather
wet exits, 10, 61, 107, 111, 117, 120, 125, 131, 149, 169, 179
as escape device, 65, 67
panic during, 157, 165
practice of, 3, 107, 137, 142, 155, 182
surf and, 46
tethered paddles and, 35, 121
wetsuits and drysuits, 4, 6, 8, 9, 31, 56, 89, 107, 131, 133, 169
need for, stressed, 121, 124, 161
protection from hypothermia and, 28, 30, 38, 39, 88, 90, 93
wetsuits, farmer john, 38, 39, 125, 132
whirlpools, 10, 13, 17, 25, 47, 162
whistles, 9, 18, 41, 46, 94, 126, 155
wilderness ethic, 143–145
wind, 43–44, 57, 108, 143, 166
dangers of, 8, 17, 126–127
open-coast paddlers and, 43–44
in opposition to current, 143
terrain and, 15, 19, 43–44, 140
types of, 31, 43, 115, 151

About the Authors

In 1972, **Matt Broze** wrote *Freestyle Skiing*, the first book on the subject. Co-owners of Mariner Kayaks since 1980, he and his brother Cam have designed ten sea kayaks. Matt developed and promoted the now-common paddle-float rescues in 1981. His writing on sea kayak safety and rescues and experience in extreme conditions led to his becoming *Sea Kayaker* magazine's safety columnist in 1984. He's still a regular contributor on safety, paddling skills, recreational racing, and equipment. Matt has paddled over 400 sea kayak designs.

George Gronseth earned a Bachelor of Science degree in mechanical engineering and moved to the Northwest, where he took up kayaking and worked for the Boeing Company analyzing the strength and safety of airplanes. Before long he was teaching kayaking and leading trips for clubs and friends. He succeeded Matt Broze as safety columnist for *Sea Kayaker* magazine. George has published numerous articles on technique as well as safety and has given many presentations for kayak clubs and symposia. In 1991, he founded the Seattle-based Kayak Academy in order to devote all his time to teaching and writing about kayaking.

Christopher Cunningham is the editor of *Sea Kayaker* magazine. His travels in small sailing, rowing, and paddling craft have covered over 7,000 miles of North American waterways. His longest cruise was a 2,500-mile paddle from Quebec to Cedar Key, Florida. He has been building kayaks and other small craft since 1979. He has published accounts of his boat travels and articles on boatbuilding in *Sea Kayaker, Nor'westing,* and *Small Boat Journal* as well as two anthologies: *Oyo* and *Seekers of the Horizon.* Christopher occasionally teaches traditional kayak construction at The WoodenBoat School in Brooklin, Maine, and is a frequent lecturer at sea kayak symposia.

About the Contributors

Chris Amato (page 143) is a wildlife biologist who lives in New York City.

Alison Armstrong (page 94) lives in New York City and has kayaked extensively along the coast of Maine.

Deb Davis (page 22) is an author and former associate editor of *Sea Kayaker* magazine; she lives in Indianola, Washington.

Ken Kelton (page 100) is a building contractor living in San Francisco. He still goes surfing and kayaking on the California coast.

Tom Watson (page 173) is a kayak instructor in Kodiak, Alaska, and a member of Kodiak Island Search and Rescue.